IRELAND IN THE WORLD

First published in 2005 by Liberties Press
This paperback edition published in 2006 by Liberties Press
Guinness Enterprise Centre | Taylor's Lane | Dublin 8 | Ireland
www. LibertiesPress .com | info@libertiespress.com
Editorial: +353 (1) 402 0805 | sean@libertiespress.com
Sales and marketing: +353 (1) 415 1224 | peter@libertiespress.com

Trade enquiries to CMD Distribution
55A Spruce Avenue | Stillorgan Industrial Park | Blackrock | County Dublin
Tel: +353 (1) 294 2560
Fax: +353 (1) 294 2564

ISBN 10: 1–905483–12–0
ISBN 13: 978–1–905483–12–9

2 4 6 8 10 9 7 5 3 1

A CIP record for this title is available from the British Library

Cover design by Liam Furlong at space.ie
Index by Anna de Courcy
Set in Garamond

Printed in Ireland by Colour Books
Unit 105 | Baldoyle Industrial Estate | Dublin 13

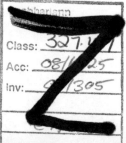

IRELAND IN THE WORLD

FURTHER REFLECTIONS

GARRET FITZGERALD

LIB
ERT
IES

CONTENTS

ACKNOWLEDGEMENTS

I should like to acknowledge particularly the assistance of my secretary, Sharon Kelly, in the preparation and presentation of this book, and also to express my gratitude to Seán O'Keeffe and Peter O'Connell of Liberties Press for the speed and efficiency with which they brought it to print. And I am grateful to my daughter Mary for permission to use her painting *Garret Reflecting with Friends* for the cover of the book.

*

The publishers would like to acknowledge the following, in whose publications earlier versions of some of the essays in this collection first appeared: Mercier Press for 'Eamon de Valera: The Price of His Achievement', from *De Valera's Irelands*, edited by Gabriel Doherty and Dermot Keogh (2003); the Royal Irish Academy for 'The Origins, Development and Present Status of Irish Neutrality', from *Irish Studies in International Affairs*, Vol. 9 (1998); Cambridge University Press for 'The Origins and Rationale of the Anglo-Irish Agreement of 1985', from *Northern Ireland and the Politics of Reconciliation* (1993), edited by Dermot Keogh and Michael H. Haltzel; the British Council for 'The Normalisation of the Irish–British Relationship', from *Britain and Ireland: Lives Entwined* (2004); and Columba Press for 'Church, Society and Family in Ireland', from *Between Poetry and Politics*, edited by Linda Hogan and Barbara FitzGerald (2004). The publishers have made every effort to trace holders of copyright material and would be happy to correct any oversights in this regard in future printings of the book. The maps that appear between pages 16 and 17 are reproduced courtesy of the Royal Irish Academy.

Introduction

Two years ago I published *Reflections on the Irish State,* comprising a dozen essays which sought either to fill a gap left by an absence of cross-fertilization between our political and economic historians or to deal with other aspects of the Irish State and Irish society that seemed to me to have been inadequately treated in works available to the general reader.

But during the last ten years I have also had occasion to write or speak about other aspects of recent Irish history, including Northern Ireland, and about issues involving aspects of social policy and global politics. A few of these contributions have appeared as chapters of books edited by others – and I am grateful for permission to include here revised versions of those contributions – but most of them originated as lectures delivered in some of the score of countries where during the last decade I have been asked to address various audiences. It has been suggested that, in anticipation of reaching the age of eighty in early 2006, I publish a number of these in a second volume of *Reflections.*

The first chapter in this volume summarises work I undertook between the late 1970s and the early years of this century on the geographical pattern of the decline of the Irish language in the eighteenth and nineteenth centuries, the results of which appeared in two papers published by the Royal Irish Academy, respectively in 1984, when I was Taoiseach, and in 2002. These papers drew on data in population censuses between 1851 and 1911 on language-speaking by age, which because of statistical problems with the data had not previously been used by historians or geographers. The presentation of these censuses derived data in the form of detailed maps – three of which are reproduced in this volume, challenged earlier theories about the timing of this language decline.

Other historical essays compare and contrast, for the first time, I believe, the reactions of Irish people to the two political and economic unions into which Ireland entered – in 1800, with Britain, and in 1972, with Europe – and discuss the roles of Lloyd George and de Valera in twentieth-century Irish history. Another essay deals with the manner in which, in the aftermath of the Civil War, the first government overcame great difficulties within as well as outside the government itself, to establish a stable Irish State. This historical section also includes essays on the circumstances in which the new Irish State sought to Catholicise and Gaelicize our society during the first half-century of independence, and on the evolution of Ireland's particular form of neutrality.

The second section contains essays describing, from my personal experience and from contemporary records, the origins, rationale and negotiating process that led to the 1985 Anglo-Irish Agreement and, second, reflections on the combination of factors – independence, EU membership, rapid economic growth, and the evolution of a common Irish–British approach to the ending of IRA violence – that had led by the end of the twentieth century to a normalisation of the historically troubled, centuries-old relationship between Ireland and Britain. Finally, I reflect on the possible future of Northern Ireland with the devolved power-sharing government that, after IRA decommissioning and an end to criminality by IRA members, will hopefully emerge in the near future.

The third section looks further afield. The first essay in this section traces the origins of recent trans-Atlantic differences and mutual misunderstandings back to the emergence in Europe in the second half of the twentieth century of a quite new and in many ways revolutionary set of moral values in respect of international relations, at a time when the United States was moving in an opposite direction, towards an enhanced belief in the use of power to achieve its objectives. Another essay in this section examines the complex interaction of Irish, British and American approaches to the Northern Ireland problem, and a third discusses Europe's role in a globalised world.

In the final section, the concept of civic republicanism as it has developed since the French Revolution is contrasted with what has come to be known as republicanism in Ireland. Other essays reflect on the Church, society and family in Ireland.

I hope that some at least of the issues addressed here will stimulate discussion and debate.

Garret FitzGerald
October 2005

1

THE DECLINE OF THE IRISH LANGUAGE

I am neither a historian, nor a geographer nor a linguistic expert. But all three disciplines interest me, and for much of my life I was puzzled about aspects of the process by which the Irish language was displaced by English throughout most of Ireland. I was quite unconvinced by what passed for conventional wisdom, viz. the suggestion that its displacement was due to the introduction of national primary education after 1831 or to the Famine. Both of these factors came much too late to have been more than contributory factors to the concluding stages of what had been a very prolonged process of anglicisation in Ireland.

Then, some time in the late 1960s, I heard it said that the nineteenth-century Irish Censuses of Population contained material on Irish-speaking *by ages of the population,* and I immediately realised that, by drawing on data on Irish-speaking amongst the oldest age groups in the earlier Censuses, it might be possible to deduce something of the geographical pattern of Irish-speaking back to the late eighteenth century. Here, I felt, was something that might be worth looking into further, when an opportunity arose to do so.

Then, when in 1977 I was elected leader of the Fine Gael Party and started to travel the country in a bid to reorganise the party into an effective political machine, I was casting around for some activity that would offer me relief and distraction from this fairly demanding political task – something that I could undertake during the many hours I would spend being driven at weekends around what were then forty-one parliamentary constituencies.

So I recalled my earlier interest, and a glance at the nineteenth-century Census volumes in the library of the Central Statistics Office confirmed that they contained the data I would need for such a study. Moreover, I found that the CSO was willing to lend me these volumes at weekends, when I would be undertaking my constituency tours.

Before presenting the outcome of the two studies I have undertaken on the subject of the geographical pattern of the decline of the Irish language in the eighteenth and nineteenth centuries, I should perhaps say something briefly about the Irish linguistic background – although on this subject I speak as a layman.

Nothing seems to be known about the language spoken by the people of Ireland during the first three-quarters of the period during which the island has been populated – first by a small number of hunter-gatherers and then, from about six thousand years ago, by an agricultural population that became numerous enough to spare from farming enough labour to build, well before the construction of the pyramids of Egypt, great monuments such as Newgrange, Knowth and Dowth near the Boyne. Each of these monuments, I believe, required up to two hundred thousand tons of rock, some of it brought from areas up to forty miles away.

These earlier, pre-Celtic inhabitants are the people who, according to current genetic research, seem to be responsible for some 80 percent of the genes of today's Irish population; thus the Celtic and all subsequent migrations appear to account for only a small minority of the ancestry of the present Irish population. This early Irish population may have been related to the only early European people whose language survives today – the Basques of northern Spain.

It is, of course, one of the great mysteries of Irish history how a small group of Celts – admittedly arriving with iron weapons, horses and chariots – came to dominate a far larger native population that had long mined gold and, with the aid of tin imports from Cornwall, had wrought bronze. How did the Celtic domination become so overwhelming that nothing whatever of the language or culture of our pre-Celtic ancestors seems to have survived? The contrast with the relative failure of eight centuries of English rule to displace our Celtic place-names or to wipe out our Celtic language is remarkable.

The Celts may have been almost the first Indo-European peoples to have entered Europe, coming from southern Russia. Only the Greeks, entering through Anatolia (now Turkey), seem to have preceded them, colonising that small corner of south-eastern Europe.

The Celts settled in the centre of the European continent, where they developed the production of iron. They failed to conquer Rome in 390 BC but eventually spread to places like Spain and the western Ukraine (both of which have their own 'Galicia', or 'land of the Gaels') and back to Anatolia, where St Paul had the task of addressing them in his Epistle to the Galatians. And it may have been from Galatia that Cleopatra secured her reportedly Celtic bodyguard.

The eventual disappearance of the Celts from central Europe seems to have been due to southward pressure from the Baltic Sea area by Germanic tribes, later Indo-European arrivals into Europe, while the Celts of northern Italy and modern France, the Gauls, were in turn conquered by the Romans.

Remarkably little seems to be known about how, or even when, the Celts came to Ireland, although it is clear that the version of their language that they brought to Ireland was an earlier form of that which later came to Britain, and which survives there as Welsh.

Thereafter, for some 1,500 years, Ireland was submerged in the culture and language of these immigrating Celts. But from the tenth century AD onwards, other languages came to be spoken in parts of the island – Old Norse in the Viking settlements in Dublin and the other ports that they developed around the coasts, and then Norman French, amongst the conquering ruling class after 1169.

The only non-Gaelic epic composed in Ireland, the Song of Dermot, composed in Waterford in the early fourteenth century, was, in fact, in Norman French. By the end of that century, however, this language had been largely displaced by some combination of an Irish cultural revival and the spread from Dublin of Middle English – which from the late twelfth century had displaced Norse at least in Dublin and other ports, and which survived in its medieval form in Fingal (north County Dublin) until the eighteenth century and in south-east Wexford until the late nineteenth century.

By the end of the fifteenth century, English had replaced Norman French even in the legislation and in the courts, and was also starting to displace Latin as a written language of record. But so long as the native

Irish rulers remained dominant throughout most of the country, Gaelic or Irish remained the language of the people outside the principal towns and certain limited areas of settlement, such as the east coast from Wexford northwards to Dublin, and parts of the midland counties of Laois and Offaly (re-named 'Queens County' and 'Kings County' from their settlement in the mid-sixteenth century), as well as parts of Ulster settled in the seventeenth century from Britain. As a good deal of Ulster was settled by people from Scotland, yet another language, Ulster Scots, was imported at that time. This language survives in parts of Northern Ireland and has recently been given official recognition by the Belfast Agreement.

The departure of the Irish rulers from north Ulster in 1603, and from elsewhere in 1691 (these latter included General de Gaulle's McCartan great-great-great-grandfather from County Down), created a new situation in which English became the language not just of the towns and of certain areas of settlement but also of administration, commerce and land ownership throughout the whole island. By 1775, only 5 percent of the land remained in the hands of the Catholic descendants of Gaelic and Norman families, although many members of these families had retained lands by joining the Established Anglican Church of Ireland.

Thus, after 1691, the native Irish-speaking population was left leaderless, save to the extent that, despite the Penal Laws, some Irish Catholic priests, educated and ordained in the Irish Colleges across Continental Europe, managed to infiltrate, and survive in, Ireland, either through secret action or by local tolerance. It was from that point onwards that the Irish language, now confined to a landless peasant population, began to decline rapidly – excluded as it was from any effective public role.

I have sought to trace the geographical pattern of this decline from a point in time less than a century after it began – using Census data on people of seventy to eighty years of age from 1851 onwards in order to trace the survival of Irish at the time of their childhood. For two distinct reasons, this task turned out to be more complex than I had expected.

First of all, I found that, in the Censuses of the second half of the nineteenth century (those from 1851 to 1901), the age-group data on Irish-speaking was published in respect only of baronies – the 320 medieval sub-county units, many of which may date back to the tuatha, or small sub-kingdoms, into which Gaelic Ireland had been divided before the arrival of the Normans in 1169.

In these nineteenth-century Censuses, however, the data on the *total* number of people in each age-group was classified quite differently – into almost eight hundred dispensary districts, within which there are almost four thousand district electoral divisions. The boundaries of these newer administrative areas were rarely co-terminous with those of the ancient baronies. In order to reconcile these two systems, a huge amount of calculation was needed and, at the micro level in many cases, some element of estimation also.

To give some examples of these geographical divisions, Mitchelstown, in the barony of Condons and Clangibbon in County Cork, is a dispensary district, for which an accurate figure of 49 percent is available for Irish-speaking amongst those aged over sixty in 1911. On the assumption that the proportion of the population who were over sixty years of age in all three district electoral divisions within the Mitchelstown dispensary district was similar to that in the Mitchelstown area as a whole, we get the following estimates for each of the district electoral divisions in this area:

Mitchelstown itself:	38 percent
Ballyarthur:	47 percent
Anglesborough:	70 percent

But because towns tend to have fewer older people than neighbouring rural areas, I suspect that the percentage for the town area was in fact more than 40 percent, with slightly lower figures for the other two district electoral divisions than those I have just given.

Across the border in County Limerick, in the barony of Coshlea, there is a second Mitchelstown dispensary district, where the Irish-speaking percentage amongst those aged over sixty in 1911 was a good deal higher, at 65 percent, with Kilbehenny and Kilglass slightly below this figure, and Knocknacrow very much higher, at 83 percent. In County Tipperary, in the nearby dispensary district of Clogheen, in the barony of Iffa and Offa West, the percentage of Irish-speaking amongst those aged over sixty in 1911 was much the same as in the neighbouring area of County Limerick, at 67 percent, but the district electoral division of

Ballyporeen showed an estimated figure of 77 percent.

(This means that there is something like a three-to-one chance that President Ronald Reagan's great-grandfather and my own grandfather, who both left Ballyporeen for London in the 1860s, and who must have known each other, were Irish-speaking. This might help to explain why my father, who was born and brought up in London, was an Irish-language enthusiast who learnt Irish in the Gaelic League in London, spent three weeks on the Great Blasket Island in 1910 and, when he came to live in Ireland with my equally enthusiastic Belfast mother, chose Ventry in Irish-speaking west Kerry as the place in which to take part in a hoped-for Irish revolution.)

The mismatch between the ancient barony boundaries and those of the nineteenth-century district electoral divisions may explain why this nineteenth-century Census data had not previously been used for the purpose of an analysis of past geographical patterns of Irish-speaking. But to me, this offered an arithmetical challenge that I simply could not resist – involving, as it did, several hundred thousand calculations!

I soon discovered, however, that there was also a second statistical problem. In the first three decennial Censuses in which the language issue was addressed – those of 1851 to 1871 – the language question was merely a sub-set of a question about literacy, and for that reason in very many cases it was not answered by a significant minority of people. The data on Irish-speaking in these Censuses was thus in varying degrees incomplete. Only in the Census of 1881 and its successors was the language issue made the subject of a distinct question that yielded reliable data.

As my study was to be based primarily on data in respect of those aged seventy to eighty, by itself the 1881 data would not bring me back to the eighteenth century. I filled this gap by using the 1881 Census data in respect of the older age groups in each barony as a check on the scale of understatement in respect of those particular age cohorts in each barony when they had been several decades younger, in 1851 and 1861. Using these methods, I derived estimates of a minimum level of Irish-speaking amongst those aged ten to nineteen for each decade from 1770 to 1870, in respect of each of 320 baronies and eight cities.

After refereeing and revision, this study was eventually published in 1984, whilst I was Taoiseach, in the form of Royal Irish Academy Paper Volume 4, C, No. 3. The tabular material in that paper was supplemented

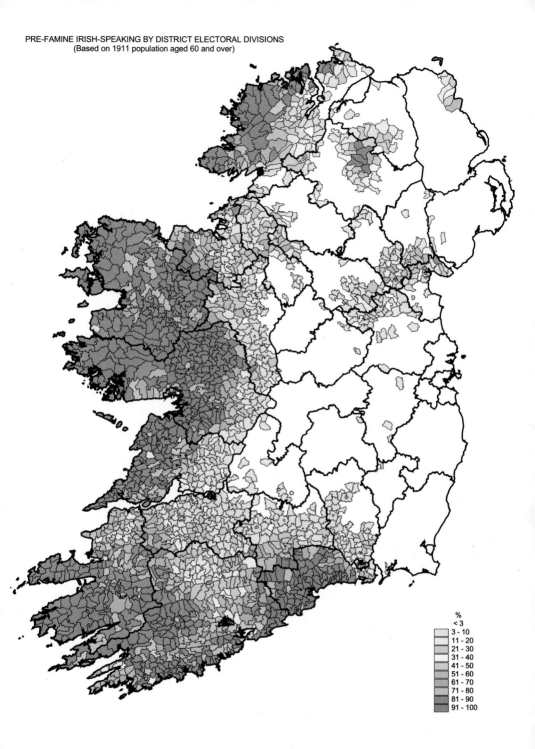

PRE-FAMINE IRISH-SPEAKING BY DISTRICT ELECTORAL DIVISIONS
(Based on 1911 population aged 60 and over)

%
< 3
3 - 10
11 - 20
21 - 30
31 - 40
41 - 50
51 - 60
61 - 70
71 - 80
81 - 90
91 - 100

MAP 1

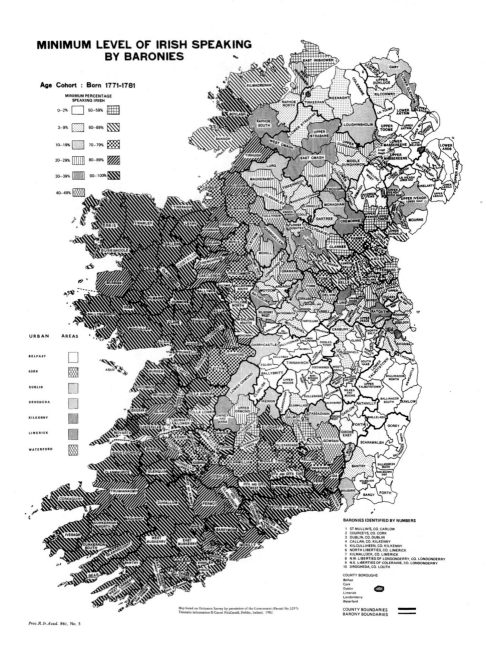

MINIMUM LEVEL OF IRISH SPEAKING BY BARONIES

Age Cohort : Born 1771-1781

MINIMUM PERCENTAGE
SPEAKING IRISH

0–2%		50–59%	
3–9%		60–69%	
10–19%		70–79%	
20–29%		80–89%	
30–39%		90–100%	
40–49%			

URBAN AREAS

BELFAST

CORK

DUBLIN

DROGHEDA

KILKENNY

LIMERICK

WATERFORD

BARONIES IDENTIFIED BY NUMBERS

1 ST MULLIN'S, CO. CARLOW
2 COURCEYS, CO. CORK
3 DUBLIN, CO. DUBLIN
4 CALLAN, CO. KILKENNY
5 KILCULLIHEEN, CO. KILKENNY
6 NORTH LIBERTIES, CO. LIMERICK
7 KILMALLOCK, CO. LIMERICK
8 N.W. LIBERTIES OF LONDONDERRY, CO. LONDONDERRY
9 N.E. LIBERTIES OF COLERAINE, CO. LONDONDERRY
10 DROGHEDA, CO. LOUTH

COUNTY BOROUGHS

Belfast
Cork
Dublin
Limerick
Londonderry
Waterford

Map based on Ordnance Survey by permission of the Government (Permit No 3297)
Thematic information © Garret FitzGerald, Dublin, Ireland, 1982.

COUNTY BOUNDARIES
BARONY BOUNDARIES

MAP 2

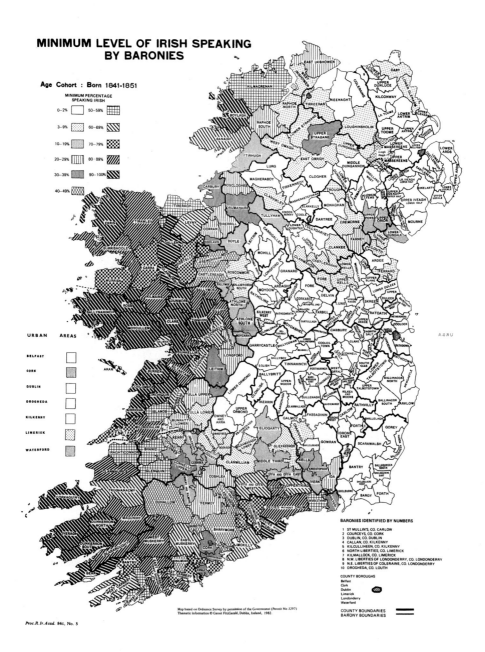

MINIMUM LEVEL OF IRISH SPEAKING
BY BARONIES

Age Cohort : Born 1841-1851

MINIMUM PERCENTAGE
SPEAKING IRISH

0-2%   50-59%

3-9%   60-69%

10-19%   70-79%

20-29%   80-89%

30-39%   90-100%

40-49%

URBAN   AREAS

BELFAST

CORK

DUBLIN

DROGHEDA

KILKENNY

LIMERICK

WATERFORD

BARONIES IDENTIFIED BY NUMBERS

1 ST MULLIN'S, CO. CARLOW
2 COURCEYS, CO. CORK
3 DUBLIN, CO. DUBLIN
4 CALLAN, CO. KILKENNY
5 KILCULLIHEEN, CO. KILKENNY
6 NORTH LIBERTIES, CO. LIMERICK
7 KILMALLOCK, CO. LIMERICK
8 N.W. LIBERTIES OF LONDONDERRY, CO. LONDONDERRY
9 N.E. LIBERTIES OF COLERAINE, CO. LONDONDERRY
10 DROGHEDA, CO. LOUTH

COUNTY BOROUGHS
Belfast
Cork
Dublin
Limerick
Londonderry
Waterford

COUNTY BOUNDARIES
BARONY BOUNDARIES

Map based on Ordnance Survey by permission of the Government (Permit No 3297)
Thematic Information © Garret FitzGerald, Dublin, Ireland, 1982.

MAP 3

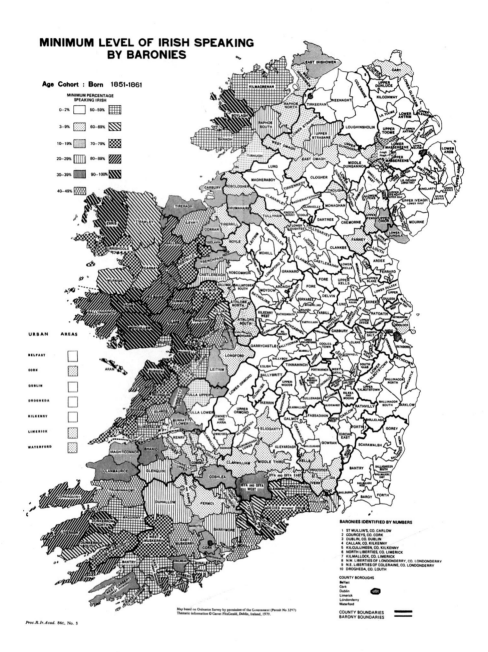

MINIMUM LEVEL OF IRISH SPEAKING BY BARONIES

Age Cohort : Born 1851-1861

MINIMUM PERCENTAGE
SPEAKING IRISH

0–2%	50–59%
3–9%	60–69%
10–19%	70–79%
20–29%	80–89%
30–39%	90–100%
40–49%	

URBAN AREAS

- BELFAST
- CORK
- DUBLIN
- DROGHEDA
- KILKENNY
- LIMERICK
- WATERFORD

BARONIES IDENTIFIED BY NUMBERS

1 ST MULLIN'S, CO. CARLOW
2 COURCEYS, CO. CORK
3 DUBLIN, CO. DUBLIN
4 CALLAN, CO. KILKENNY
5 KILCULLIHEEN, CO. KILKENNY
6 NORTH LIBERTIES, CO. LIMERICK
7 KILMALLOCK, CO. LIMERICK
8 N.W. LIBERTIES OF LONDONDERRY, CO. LONDONDERRY
9 N.E. LIBERTIES OF COLERAINE, CO. LONDONDERRY
10 DROGHEDA, CO. LOUTH

COUNTY BOROUGHS
Belfast
Cork
Dublin
Limerick
Londonderry
Waterford

COUNTY BOUNDARIES
BARONY BOUNDARIES

Map based on Ordnance Survey by permission of the Government (Permit No 3297)
Thematic information © Garret FitzGerald, Dublin, Ireland, 1979.

Proc.R.Ir.Acad. 84C, No. 5

MAP 4

by maps drawn by my retired elder brother Fergus. His maps, by the use of different shading, showed for each of the decades from 1770 to 1870 the estimated minimum level of Irish-speaking in just under 330 areas.

I say 'minimum level' because people living in areas where, during their lifetime, the language was weakening may, of course, have forgotten Irish by the time they reached their seventies, while on the other hand, during the late eighteenth and nineteenth centuries, virtually no one acquired a knowledge of Irish after childhood.

I must explain at this stage that, while this baronial data was adequate for areas where either everyone or no one spoke Irish, it could be misleading for what might be described as transitional areas – especially where the baronies were large. In such cases, the baronial percentages could represent an average of very different Irish-speaking levels – ranging, conceivably, from 0 percent to 100 percent in different parts of the same barony. For that reason, during the summer of 2002 I set about preparing an analysis of data based on the 1911 Census in respect of those aged sixty or more at that time, viz. people who had been born before 1851 – most of them between 1831 and 1851.

Once again I faced a statistical problem. In the 1911 Census, age-group language data was available in respect of almost eight hundred dispensary districts, devised in the mid-nineteenth century, and this had been used in the 1970s by G. B. Adams of Belfast to plot levels of Irish-language speaking in Ulster and several neighbouring counties in the nineteenth century. But that Census contained no overall age-group data for the almost four thousand smaller district electoral divisions, in respect of which the 1911 Census published data on Irish-speaking by age.

However, by applying to each of these district electoral divisions the proportion of the population of age sixty or more for the dispensary district to which each of them belongs, it is possible to get reasonably disaggregated data for these small units, and this makes possible a more precise contour of Irish-speaking in transitional areas where the language was already in decline in the immediate pre-Famine period.

It has to be stressed, however, that, unlike the dispensary district data, this more detailed district electoral divisions data is subject to a margin of error which in certain areas could involve a displacement by one decile. In other words, a figure of 75 percent Irish-speaking shown on the third map might in fact have been somewhat over 80 percent – or perhaps 69 percent or somewhat less.

So much for the methodology of these two studies.

MINIMUM IRISH-SPEAKING PERCENTAGES FOR COUNTIES, 1770–1870

Decades of birth

	1771–81*	1801–11	1831–41	1861–71
LEINSTER				
Carlow	5	2	0	0
Dublin	7	4	2	2
Kildare	2	2	1	0
Kilkenny	57	45	14	1
Laois	6	1	0	0
Longford	22	8	1	0
Louth	57	42	9	1
Meath	41	28	3	0
Offaly	4	2	1	0
Westmeath	17	7	2	0
Wexford	3	1	0	0
Wicklow	1	1	0	0
TOTAL	17	11	3	0
MUNSTER				
Clare	92	90	72	33
Cork	84	82	66	21
Kerry	93	93	86	45
Limerick	76	73	34	3
Tipperary	51	45	16	2
Waterford	86	81	67	35
TOTAL	80	77	57	21
CONNACHT				
Galway	91	89	78	56
Leitrim	52	43	19	1
Mayo	95	94	89	60
Roscommon	74	65	26	3
Sligo	84	82	59	8
TOTAL	84	80	63	40

Decades of birth

	1771–81*	1801–11	1831–41	1861–71
ULSTER				
Antrim	3	2	1	0
Armagh	18	15	8	1
Cavan	39	29	8	0
Donegal	56	53	40	29
Down	3	1	0	0
Fermanagh	16	9	2	0
Derry	10	7	4	1
Monaghan	33	28	11	1
Tyrone	19	14	7	3
TOTAL	19	15	8	4
IRELAND	45	41	28	13

* The figures in the first column are an estimate of what the level of Irish-speaking would have been in this cohort if measured in the same manner as in the 1881 Census. Their reliability is accordingly lower than that of the figures in the other three columns.

The totals at the bottom of this table, derived from nineteenth-century Censuses, show that, in the island as a whole, at least 45 percent of older people in the 1770s were still Irish-speaking. Allowing for some loss of the language during their lifetime by people living in areas where English had already made inroads, this means that, in the 1770s, probably more than half of the younger generation must still have been Irish-speaking.

The table also shows that this percentage did not decline by much during the following three decades – in fact, by barely 1 percent per decade – so that, allowing for the quite substantial number who, during a long life spent in areas where the language was in decline, may have lost the capacity to speak Irish, even in 1800 the proportion of the younger generation speaking Irish in the island as a whole must still have been close to 50 percent.

It was after 1800 that the language began to decline more rapidly. In the following sixty years, the national percentage of Irish-speaking dropped three to four times faster than in the late eighteenth century, viz. by 4 to 5 percent per decade.

It can be seen from this table that, during the thirty-year period from the 1830s to the 1860s, which included both the Famine and most of the early stages of the establishment of the national schools, the rate of disappearance of Irish-speaking nationally was only fractionally faster than in the immediately preceding thirty-year period – a drop of 15 percent as against one of 13 percent. This offers no support to the theory that those two events – the Famine and the establishment of the national schools – were of crucial significance in the decline of Irish-speaking.

The baronial percentage figures in respect of Ulster might on the face of them suggest that, in the late eighteenth century, there was some measure of Irish-speaking almost everywhere in the province outside of four areas – the Coleraine hinterland, south Antrim, north Down and north Armagh. But the data from my more recent study, which shows much more detailed geographical data in respect of the immediate pre-Famine period, demonstrates that this is misleading. (See Map 1.) Within parts of the Ulster baronies where Irish is shown by this map as having survived, there were in fact many settlement areas where Irish had, in fact, virtually disappeared – as well, of course, as others where it survived in strong measure. The baronial averages, especially for large baronies, hid these wide variations.

All that said, the 1770s map makes it clear that, by that time, English had displaced Irish in many parts of mid and south-east Leinster outside the areas of earlier settlement. It survived in considerable strength – at least 50 to 80 percent Irish speaking – both in parts of south-east Ulster and in contiguous parts of north Leinster, however – even in some areas that had always been part of the medieval English-controlled Pale. However, throughout virtually all of Munster except most of north Tipperary, and also throughout Connacht, in the 1770s Irish remained the language of the vast majority of the population – as was also the case in the southern part of County Kilkenny.

Within the first three decades of the nineteenth century, English had replaced Irish to a substantial degree throughout the eastern part of north Munster, along the eastern edges of Connacht, and in much of Donegal and other parts of the north-west, and the language had virtually disappeared from most of north Leinster and neighbouring south-east Ulster.

During this period, there was also a weakening of Irish-speaking in and around a number of ports on the south and west coasts – the start of a process which, in conjunction with the spread of English along the main trade routes from Dublin to these port cities, was eventually to fragment the Irish-speaking areas around the south and west coasts, leading to their eventual decline into the small Gaeltacht, or Irish-speaking, areas of the present day, viz. the tiny Ring Gaeltacht of west Waterford, that of Ballyvourney in west Cork, those of Iveragh and Dingle in Kerry, of Connemara in Galway, of north-west Mayo, and of west Donegal.

By the 1860s, the railways radiating from Dublin along the main trade routes, together with the further growth of English-speaking in and around the southern and western ports, had effectively completed this process of isolating today's Gaeltacht areas geographically from each other – an isolating process that has to some degree been culturally reversed in recent times by radio and television: Raidió na Gaeltachta and TG4.

One additional point may be worth making. Almost all the areas where Irish has survived today coincide with those in which, 150 years ago, half or more of Irish speakers were monoglots – speaking Irish only. Only in one area with such a high proportion of monoglot Irish speakers in 1851 has the language since effectively disappeared, viz. the barony of Kilmaine in east Mayo.

I turn now to the results of my more recent study of the state of the Irish language in much smaller areas – dispensary districts and district electoral divisions – in the period shortly before the Famine. The data in this study is presented in the 2004 paper in the form of a seventy-page table setting out the results for each of the 2,400 district electoral divisions (60 percent of the total) where there is evidence that, at the time of the Famine, the language survived.

Map 1 shows the pattern of Irish-speaking around the time of the Famine in these 2,400 district electoral divisions. In preparing this map, I came up against an unexpected further problem. While, in our State, there have not been significant changes since 1911 in the district electoral divisions used for Census purposes in the Republic – apart from a radical re-numbering of them with which I have been able to cope – in Northern Ireland the older counties and district electoral divisions have all been abolished and been replaced by twenty-six districts and some ten thousand postal codes. Even with the aid of a very cooperative Central Statistics Office – to whose computer mapping service I am indebted for the preparation of this and other maps – I was not able to find any computer mapping of Northern Ireland using the old units and boundaries; this gap was generously filled by a private firm in Dublin, GAMMA.

This study shows that, at the time of the Famine, there was a quite large Irish-speaking area in County Tyrone. For fifteen miles northwards from a point just north of Omagh, Irish was then still the sole language of the population, and throughout a surrounding area thirty miles long by thirty miles wide, some Irish was still spoken. But in the Foyle Valley to the west of this area, which had been heavily settled in the seventeenth century, no Irish at all was spoken – although the language survived, of course, in the Donegal hills to the west of that valley and on beyond that to the west coast.

The data for these small district electoral divisions that is thrown up by this much more detailed study is particularly useful in respect of parts of the country where many of the baronies are large, e.g. in north and central Cork and in Donegal – the latter being an area where, moreover, there are small patches of settlement to be found in valleys that lie between the intervening hills, up in which the indigenous population survived.

Of course, in areas which remained solidly Irish-speaking, or where Irish had already disappeared by the time of the Famine, this detailed district electoral division map and accompanying data add little or nothing to our knowledge, but throughout the many transitional areas where the language survived at the time of the Famine but was already in decline, this map offers a far more accurate picture of what might be called the 'language contours'.

An example of how this throws up quite new data is to be found in north Connacht. The baronial language map for the 1840s shows a slightly higher level of Irish-speaking in north-west Cavan and a contiguous part of north Leitrim than in immediately surrounding areas, but the district electoral division map reveals that, behind this misleading appearance, there lay something quite different, viz. a relatively high measure of Irish-speaking surviving at that time within a forty-mile-long salient running north-west from Ballaghadereen to the border of Fermanagh.

2

IRELAND'S TWO UNIONS: 1800 AND 1972

However paradoxical it may at first sight appear, the ultimate justification for Irish independence will, I believe, eventually be seen to lie in Ireland's accession in 1972 to the European Union. For it was through accession in 1972 to what was then the European Community that the Irish State finally completed the process of separating itself economically as well as politically from Great Britain. Until then, it had remained almost totally economically dependent on its neighbour, even for a full half-century after securing political independence. It was by freeing itself from extreme economic dependence upon that near neighbour, and securing access to a much wider European market, that the Irish State was, for the first time in history, empowered to take its place as an equal partner in economic terms, and not just politically, with the rest of the states of western Europe. This is the main theme of what follows.

I should like to start with a personal experience of thirty-three years ago, recalling a day, in September 1972, when, as chairman of the Irish Council of the European Movement, I had the task of giving a preliminary briefing to a group of European journalists whom Taoiseach Seán Lemass had asked the Movement to invite to Ireland with a view to persuading them and their readers that Ireland was ready for Europe – which we certainly were not at that time!

After my address and subsequent questions, an elderly British journalist from the Times, A. P. Ryan, approached me and introduced himself. 'Mr FitzGerald,' he said, 'forty-two years ago I came to Dublin and met in the Shelbourne Hotel your father, Desmond FitzGerald, the Dáil Government's Director of Publicity, who was then 'on the run', and he explained to me why Ireland had to be a sovereign independent state.

Now I return, to be told by his son why Ireland should give up that sovereignty. Can you explain this to me?' I shall at the end of my remarks reflect briefly on how my father might himself have responded to Ryan's question.

(Going back a little further in history, I recall that this was the same A. P. Ryan who used to tell a story of the time when, as a young Times journalist before the First World War, he used to see an aged bearded figure slipping into the Times editor's office each month. Ryan believed that this was Pigott the forger, who, he thought, had *not*, as had been generally believed, committed suicide in Madrid a quarter of a century earlier, but was coming in regularly to get his pension for having assisted the Times in its attempt to destroy Parnell!)

Why did the first of these two Unions – one in which Ireland was given one-sixth of the seats within the new Union Parliament – prove so controversial at the time when it was effected, and so enduringly unpopular with the great majority of Irish people thereafter, when, in sharp contrast, the much more recent sharing of sovereignty with many other European states, on a basis that has given Ireland, proportionately, a very much smaller voice within the councils of this second Union, has proved so widely acceptable to the people of the Irish State?

Before trying to answer this question, I should perhaps say something about the origin of the Union of 1800 – for this was the seminal event that was to determine, directly or indirectly, the course of Irish history for two centuries thereafter. For me, this task has been immensely eased by the publication in 1999 of Dr Patrick Geoghegan's work *The Irish Act of Union* and by the series of bicentennial essays edited by him in conjunction with Dr Michael Brown and Dr James Kelly.

First of all, it needs to be said that frustrated Irish Protestant enthusiasm for a Union with Great Britain at the time of the Union of England and Scotland in 1707 – an idea then rejected by the English government as not being in their country's interest – evaporated during the course of the eighteenth century. So much was this the case that, when William Molyneux's 1698 pamphlet *The Case of Ireland Stated* was re-published in the 1770s and 1780s, his statement that such a Union was 'a happiness that we can scarcely hope for' was carefully omitted from the reprints.

Dr Geoghegan opens his book on the Union with this statement:

The Union was an act of arrogance. It was arrogantly conceived, and executed with the ruthless inefficiency that characterised much of government activity in the period. The outbreak of rebellion on the night of 23 May 1798 forced William Pitt, somewhat reluctantly, to direct his attentions to Ireland.

A union between the two kingdoms was something long desired in high political circles in Britain [at least since the 1770s]. In particular, Pitt saw in union the only practicable solution to the difficult problems posed by the neighbouring island.

The author goes on to summarise how the situation in the aftermath of the 1798 Rebellion appeared to the British prime minister:

Legislative independence in 1782 had clouded the Anglo-Irish relationship . . . [Subsequent] events . . . convinced Pitt that an independent Irish legislature could never guarantee security for Britain or tranquillity for Ireland.

Only union offered a framework within which these related aspirations could be addressed. Joining the Irish and British legislatures made possible the eventual inclusion of the Roman Catholics in parliament, and thereby offered a mechanism for gaining their support.

More importantly, union offered the means for Pitt to restructure the relationship between Britain and Ireland in a way that would enhance the security and strength of the empire.

From the outset, Pitt's plan depended upon combining Catholic emancipation with parliamentary union – for he recognised that a union without emancipation would do little or nothing for Britain's security. Unrest would remain endemic so long as the vast Catholic majority of the population was excluded, by the 10 percent governing minority who adhered to the established Anglican Church of Ireland, from any participation in the government of their own country.

In the midst of what looked like being – and in the event turned out to be – a long war with France, a country that in the preceding few years had mounted two separate invasion attempts on Ireland, such a situation clearly posed a huge risk to the security of Britain. Unfortunately, it soon became clear to Pitt that if, as part of this plan, the emancipation issue was to be broached publicly in the Irish parliament, the Anglican Ascendancy in Ireland would be likely to reject the Union, which thus had to be pushed through on a thoroughly ambiguous basis.

So far as the Catholic population was concerned, during the first half of the year 1800, in Dr Geoghegan's words, 'the influence of the Roman Catholics was mobilised without any explicit promises being made, but with just enough hinted at to persuade them to remain aloof from any attempts against the Union.' This followed Cabinet meetings in November 1799 attended by Castlereagh, after which Castlereagh felt able to reassure the Lieutenant, Lord Cornwallis, that 'as far as the sentiments of the Cabinet are concerned, His Excellency need not hesitate in calling forth the Catholic support in whatever degree he found it practicable to obtain it.'

However, the British Cabinet's intention to proceed to emancipation shortly after the enactment of the Union was kept secret not just from the Irish parliament and its Speaker, John Foster, who opposed the Union, but also from FitzGibbon (Lord Clare, the Irish Lord Chancellor), who was the minister given the task of presenting and advocating the proposal for Union to the Irish House of Lords.

Even more serious was the decision to keep word of the Cabinet's intention from King George III for as long as possible. The king (who, following the 1798 Rebellion, had told Pitt that he should not lose the opportunity thus afforded to carry hitherto anti-Union Irish Protestants into supporting a legislative union) knew, of course, that Pitt and several of his colleagues personally favoured Catholic emancipation. Pitt's personal commitment to the issue had in fact been demonstrated in his speech on the Union in Parliament on 31 January 1799, when he had argued that it was only in a United Kingdom Parliament that the Catholic question could be solved in such a way as to gratify the political ambitions of Catholics without endangering the position of Irish Protestants. But the king was never told that the Cabinet had decided to enact such a measure after the Union was safely through.

Pitt's own determination to persist with the matter immediately after the Union had been effected is evident from the fact that he persisted with the proposal even after a Cabinet meeting on Sunday 25 January 1801 had shown that, with three absent ministers opposed, there was now a majority of only one in favour of such action.

Given that the king was known to be strongly opposed to such a measure, which, he believed, ran counter to his Coronation Oath, this was a very risky approach for Pitt to have adopted. It might nevertheless conceivably have had some chance of success, had not several treacherous Cabinet colleagues sought, with short-term success, to oust their prime minister by apparently tipping off the king just before Pitt was about to initiate the very difficult process of persuading his monarch to change his mind on the issue.

Furious at having been kept in the dark, at a well-attended levee the king – who was already showing signs of a recurrence of the mental instability that had disabled him years earlier – publicly attacked one of Pitt's loyal Cabinet colleagues, Henry Dundas, on this issue 'in a loud voice and agitated manner'.

That public row sounded the death knell for post-Union emancipation. Twenty-eight years were to pass before this measure could be enacted, with the support of the king's eldest son and successor, George IV. (On the occasion of his 1821 visit to Ireland, that monarch is reported to have told 'leading Irish figures' that, in his view, if they had taken a tougher line at the time, they 'could have got any terms' – including 'their national religion' – as, he pointed out, the Scots had done in 1707.)

Several points need to be made about the process that brought about the legislative union of the two islands. First of all, Irish nationalist historians have traditionally believed that the support of the Irish parliament for its own abolition was bought by bribery. Forty years ago, however, this thesis was challenged, with some apparent success, by the historian G. C. Bolton. Bolton demonstrated that the payments that were known to have been made had mainly consisted of compensation to owners of eighty-one rotten boroughs for the loss of what in the eighteenth century was accepted as being owners' private property rights in these constituencies – although the fact that the payments were not conceded or made until after an early 'snap' defeat of the Union proposal in the Irish House of Commons in January 1799 had led to contemporary accusations of bribery in relation to the legislation.

What Bolton was not aware of forty years ago, however, was that, in addition to this publicly known compensation, further payments were made out of a Secret Service Fund, details of which did not emerge until 1997. Moreover, peerages and judicial office were also offered to persuade members to vote for the Union. The reversal of the Irish parliament's initial vote against the Union in January 1799 must be regarded as having been at least partly due to what, even in eighteenth century terms, would be described as corruption.

Secondly, it should in fairness be said that Castlereagh, the principal architect of the Union – who ever since has been the subject of universal Irish revulsion – was genuinely committed to, and fought vigorously for, emancipation, suffering a nervous breakdown following the collapse of this scheme. It has to be added, however, that a major factor in this illness was the fear that his abuse of the Secret Service Fund would be exposed. This danger was not averted until 1804, when, in a remarkable act of venality, former Speaker Foster, the leading opponent of the Union and during this period a most vocal critic of suspected bribery, appears to have agreed to remain silent on this matter in the hope of thus making himself, with the support of the British government, 'the most powerful man in Ireland'.

So much for the circumstances in which the Union was enacted. Could the Union have proved more enduring if, as had been the plan, it had in fact been accompanied, or immediately followed, by emancipation, thus making Daniel O'Connell's great campaign of the 1820s redundant? This is but one of many hypothetical questions that the Union of 1800 raises.

Of course, most historians frown on hypothetical history. But there is a case for occasionally reflecting on what might have been, for this can help to dispel the false sense that what actually happened was inevitable. For the truth is that all history is in some measure contingent: it is at least partly a product of a series of accidental events which of course occur within a broad framework of evolutionary change occasioned by such underlying factors as the flux of ideas about society and the state, technological change, and the interplay of economic forces.

There was nothing inevitable about the course of Irish history in the nineteenth century. For, instead of succeeding, the attempt to achieve parliamentary Union in 1800 might well have failed. Had that happened, a fundamental problem for the Anglican Ascendancy thereafter would have been the fact that a polity in which this 10 percent minority of the Irish people held an absolute monopoly of political power – something unique in the post-Reformation Europe of *cujus rex, ejus religio* ('the religion of the king is the religion of the people') – would in the nineteenth century have become inherently unstable. Given that fact, it is impossible to assess with any certainty how, without the Union, such a situation would eventually have been resolved.

Of course, if the Protestant Irish parliament had survived, it would at some point in the nineteenth century have had to face the issue of Catholic emancipation. If it had indefinitely resisted such a measure, eventually, given the combined growth of democracy and of nationalism in Europe throughout the nineteenth century, it would have faced a revolution.

If, on the other hand, the Ascendancy in a surviving Irish parliament had at some stage conceded emancipation (which, it has to be said, was in 1800 already favoured by a not-insignificant minority of the members of that Protestant Irish parliament), the very restrictive property-based franchise of that period in a country where most of the Catholic majority lived in extreme poverty, owning no property whatever, could nevertheless have preserved the Anglican power structure for the time being. The crisis would then have centred on the franchise issue.

A Protestant majority in a post-emancipation, restricted-franchise Irish parliament would almost certainly have sought to resist, or at any rate to slow, a widening of the franchise along the lines of what actually happened in Ireland under UK law. For with the secret ballot, introduced in 1872, and all adult males being enfranchised by 1884 – as, of course, were women over the age of thirty in 1918, and younger women a decade later – the Anglican voting majority would have disappeared.

Just how determined such a Protestant majority might have been in resisting a widening of the franchise in a nineteenth-century Irish parliament may be judged from the fact that, as recently as the 1970s, a two-to-one Protestant majority in Northern Ireland's parliament remained determinedly resisting a reform of the restricted property franchise that was then still employed for local government elections. In the light of that reality, it is difficult to envisage, within a separate Irish polity, a peaceful and orderly nineteenth-century transition from minority Protestant rule to a fully democratic system.

With or without emancipation, in an Ireland governed throughout the nineteenth and perhaps into the twentieth century by an Irish parliament, a critical point would at some stage have been reached when the democratisation of political systems elsewhere in Europe, including in Britain, would have faced a restricted-franchise Protestant majority in an Irish parliament with pressures that could have been resisted only with force. In the absence of Union, violence might thus have come sooner and perhaps on a larger scale than proved to be the case within that structure.

One can only speculate as to how Britain would have reacted to such a violent conflict in Ireland in the late nineteenth or early twentieth century. Such a conflict would, by creating a strong temptation for a Continental power to intervene in Irish affairs, have posed a potential risk to Britain's security.

Needless to say, these reflections are not intended to make a case for the Union. What I draw from all of this is rather the conclusion that the unique Irish situation – a country governed by a group drawn from a mere 10 percent of its population – was so inherently unstable that things were almost bound to end with violence – and, ultimately, with Irish independence, either with or without a political division of the island.

Let me turn now from these reflections on what might have been to the question of why the two Unions of 1800 and 1972 are today seen in such different lights. There seem to me to be at least eight factors involved:

1   The first Union was designed primarily with regard to the strategic interest of Britain rather than for the benefit of Ireland. In the second Union, the reason for initiating and continuing it was uniquely the perception of the vast majority of the people of the part of the island involved that this lay in their interest.

2   Both religions in Ireland had in fact been divided on the Union question. On the Protestant side, anti-Union Orangemen feared that a Union would threaten their power to dominate the island in their own interest, whilst other Protestants favoured it as providing them with security against the kind of threat that had

been posed to them by the 1798 Rebellion in areas like Wexford.

The Catholics were divided between those who, like the Hierarchy, had been encouraged to see a Union as offering them an early prospect of emancipation, and a probably less coherent proto-nationalist group that was influenced rather by dislike and fear of the prospect of closer involvement with England. But although the Union of 1800 was not designed to favour the interests of either of these divided religious groups, it came in time to be seen as having been directed in favour of the Protestant minority, Presbyterian as well as Anglican. This made it deeply controversial. No such divisive factors operated in the case of the second Union.

3   In the short run, the first Union disappointed expectations in relation to both Catholic emancipation and economic growth. The continuation of the Napoleonic Wars until 1815, together with the post-war depression, adversely affected the economy, as did the fact that many landlords moved to London and spent their rents there rather than in Ireland. Although the second Union was followed by two global oil crises and by the self-imposed Irish financial crisis of the late 1970s – from which the country's economy did not recover until the end of the following decade – the economic impact of the second Union itself was seen to be positive, especially from the early 1990s onwards.

4   In the first Union, the trade effects for Ireland were uncertain, or seen as negative. In the second, they were, and were seen to be, hugely positive. Associated with these trade effects, the first Union eventually intensified Ireland's economic dependence upon the British market, which persisted even through the first half-century of political independence. Throughout that period, the only market to which Irish products had free access was that of Britain, the economy of which in all sub-periods between the 1890s and the 1980s grew much more slowly than that of the rest of western Europe. Moreover, since the 1840s, when the Corn Laws protecting British cereal production were abolished, Britain had pursued a 'cheap food' policy, designed to keep down wages

in order to enhance Britain's external competitiveness. This policy bore particularly hard on small-scale Irish agriculture, especially after 1949, when the cheap-food policy was intensified by the introduction of direct payments to UK farmers.

Accession to the EU by the UK and Denmark at the same time as Ireland rescued Ireland from this debilitating neo-colonial situation. Not alone did the Union give free access to what were then the much more dynamic markets of Continental western Europe – enabling Ireland for the first time to exploit its potential attractions for extra-European industrial investors, especially US high-tech investors – but it also forced Britain to abandon overnight its cheap-food policy and thus gave Irish farmers for the first time access to markets in Britain and on the Continent at much more attractive, and for some years after accession also rising, prices. Thus the second Union reversed the surviving negative trade features of the first Union.

5   The first Union involved negative financial transfers throughout the nineteenth century, because, arising from the absence at that time of welfare transfers from richer to poorer regions of states, taxation raised nationally was almost all spent centrally on government and defence. This entailed perverse net transfers from poorer to richer areas. In the Irish case, these transfers were identified objectively by a British Royal Commission in 1896, and may have amounted at different periods of the century to between 2 and 5 percent of Irish GNP. By contrast, in the second Union, financial transfers through the EU Budget from richer member states to Ireland during most of the first three decades of Irish membership added 4 percent to Irish GNP each year.

On average, during the first decade of the twentieth century, these perverse intra-UK financial transfers had, however, been reversed, through a combination of capital transfers initiated by Irish Chief Secretary Arthur Balfour during the Conservative government of his uncle, Lord Salisbury, and social transfers arising from the introduction of old-age pensions and unemployment payments by Lloyd George in the subsequent Liberal government. Had the Union survived into the period of welfare government,

an opposite problem would have been created – a scale of positive transfers that would have made it very difficult indeed for
Ireland ever to have become independent because of the size of
the financial penalty to be paid. The greater part of Ireland got
out of the UK just in time to enable it, without too great a shock,
to secure the independence without which it would later have
been unable to pursue the policies needed to secure eventual economic parity with the rest of Europe.

6   The first of these Unions was marked by huge divergences of
religious and cultural values between the majorities of the population in each of the two partners. In the second Union, there was
a large, although not total, intra-EU convergence of values in relation to such issues as respect for international law, supranational
supervision of human rights, the creation of a European zone of
peace, peacemaking and peace enforcement, the abolition of capital punishment, and global ecological issues.

7   The first Union imposed – and in Northern Ireland still
imposes – uniformity in matters in respect of which the interests
of its component parts ultimately diverged, e.g. taxation. The second Union involved only harmonisation of policies by agreement;
this was designed to eliminate actual or potential barriers to trade
that might have inhibited Irish exports.

8   Finally, at the time of the first Union and throughout its dura-
tion, the majorities in both islands held very negative views of
each other, arising from a combination of memories of conquest
and respective complexes of superiority and inferiority – as well
as sharp and persistent divergences in their living standards. By
contrast – although this was little realised at the time – with the
second Union, these features of the Irish–British relationship
diminished rapidly as the Irish economy caught up with the EU
economy as a whole, and as Ireland proved an effective, and
increasingly self-confident, member of the European Union – as
well as a creative and constructive partner to Britain in relation to
the Northern Ireland problem.

All that having been said, it should of course be stressed that

Ireland also gained some often undervalued social and economic advantages from the first Union. For example, it inherited from it a non-corrupt civil administration and an independent judicial system, the universal use of the English language (albeit, of course, at the cultural cost of substantially losing its own Irish language), and avoidance of over-regulation on the Continental model, as well as of high-cost social welfare and a high burden of taxation. All of these have proved to be economically very beneficial to the Irish State since it joined the second Union.

Looking back over Irish history, I believe that, once the Reformation had failed to 'take' amongst the indigenous Irish population, Ireland could never in the longer term be accommodated comfortably within a British context. A common religious culture had made it possible for many of the Norman lords to adapt to Gaelic culture in the medieval period and had opened the way to an admittedly uneasy alliance between the 'Old English' Catholics and the surviving Gaelic lords in the 1640s. But that route was simply not open to Protestant settlers of the seventeenth and eighteenth centuries.

The very rapid decline of the Irish language between 1700 and the mid-nineteenth century may eventually have eliminated one cultural division between settlers and the indigenous population. As was seen in Yugoslavia in the 1990s, however, even when no significant language barrier exists, religious differences have the potential to create deeper and more bitter cultural, and thus political, divisions.

The problem of the relationship between Scotland and England was always less acute than in the case of Ireland – especially once the Act of Union of 1707 (enacted when a queen of a century-old Scottish dynasty still ruled England, thus providing some kind of personal link between the two parts of Britain) had given recognition to Presbyterianism as the established religion of the Scottish realm. Such recognition of the religion of the country's majority proved impossible in the Irish case, and Ireland was also virtually unique in western Europe in never having provided England with a dynasty. At one time or another, a bewildering number of other countries had done this – not just Scotland and Wales, but also Denmark, Normandy, France, the Netherlands and Germany – and even

Spain, briefly, in the form of King Philip as consort to Queen Mary.

There were, of course, several routes through which a post-Union Ireland could have moved towards independence. One would have been through an initial period of Home Rule, peacefully conceded on the basis of appropriate guarantees for the Protestant minority. But that was consistently blocked by the British Conservative Party, partly in solidarity with Protestant co-religionists in Ireland, but also for the same strategic reasons that had originally impelled Pitt to effect a union of the two islands in 1800.

Unhappily for Ireland, throughout the century following initiation of the campaign for Home Rule, the world, and Europe in particular, remained a very dangerous place. This, together with a concentration of post-Reformation settlers in a corner of an island in the rest of which their co-religionists were a small minority, made some British politicians very reluctant to concede Home Rule, let alone independence.

The remaining, and more direct, route to independence involved violence. Today, our island is still suffering from the consequences of Britain's decision to block the gradualist route through Home Rule.

Finally, I would like to add a personal view that, for more than one reason, Irish independence could not have been postponed beyond the first quarter of the twentieth century without seriously prejudicing the long-term interests of the Irish people. First of all, the emergence and growth of the welfare state, involving significant transfers from the centre to the periphery, which would have ceased with independence, would have made a postponement of independence increasingly costly and traumatic. Moreover, in retrospect we can see that any such postponement would have uncomfortably foreshortened the new Irish State's period of finding its feet within a Europe of sovereign states, and would thus have made the transition to shared sovereignty within the European Union much more uncertain and difficult.

Within the new framework of the European Union, the interests of the majority of the Irish people, distinct from and in many ways very different from those of the inhabitants of the neighbouring island, have clearly required that they be represented in that Union in their own right, rather than as a subordinate part of a United Kingdom – the policy stances of which within the Union must necessarily be dominated by the interests (and at times also the prejudices) of its English majority.

Moreover, in order to be able to enter the European Union with self-confidence and a capacity to make itself at home in this novel political structure, the new Irish State needed, I believe, at least forty years of untrammelled political independence during which it could make its own mistakes and learn how to accommodate itself to the outside world.

We in Ireland have not merely benefited materially from closer involvement with the countries of the European land mass, but within this wider multilateral relationship we have also been able to develop a new, much healthier and relaxed, and genuinely warmer, relationship with the neighbouring island, to which we have been so closely tied by geography – but from whose unsought attentions we suffered greatly throughout much the greater part of the second Christian millennium.

*

Finally, reverting to the challenge posed to me by A. P. Ryan of the *Times* forty-three years ago, I believe that, if my father had survived to age seventy-five to answer for himself on that occasion, he would have had little hesitation in responding in much the same terms as I have done here.

The son of Irish parents who emigrated to London in the 1860s, as a young man he learnt Irish in that city and was one of the earliest visitors, in 1910, to the Great Blasket Island (although, for some reason, he is ignored in the excellent Visitors Centre at Dun Chaoin, which lists other visitors who went there later). Having spent the first two years of their married life in Brittany, he and my mother chose to come to live near Dingle in the spring of 1913 in the hope of taking part through the medium of the Irish language in a hoped-for movement for national independence – but as the local organizer of the Volunteers in west Kerry, he was expelled from the county by the British authorities two years later.

With that background, he could scarcely be accused of being 'anti-Irish'. He was a realist, however, and after both he and my mother had participated in the Rising in the GPO, on his emergence from his third period in prison he is recorded as having said, in May 1919, that Irish would never replace English as the language of the Irish people: English was, he added sadly, even more the language of Ireland than French was of France. (Remember that he had lived two years in Brittany and knew, of course, that Flemish and German, as well as Provençal and Basque, were also spoken in different parts of France.)

He concluded that this reality made the separation of Ireland from England even more urgent in cultural terms than in political ones. So, logically, what Ireland needed above all were outside influences – to be sought on the Continent of Europe.

Throughout his life, he remained a dedicated European, deeply engaged with French literature and philosophy. And his sons were all sent away for periods not only to Coláiste na Rinne before secondary school, but also, between Irish secondary and university education, to schools in Switzerland – although, because of the war, I missed out on this latter experience.

So I have no hesitation in asserting that my father, whose skills as director of publicity of the underground Dáil government helped to secure Ireland's independence, would have told his friend A. P. Ryan in 1962 that EU membership was the ultimate vindication of that independence.

But, had he been alive today, as a realist my father would also, I believe, have had to recognise regretfully, as I too have to do, that we in Ireland have failed to make as much use of our access to our European heritage as both he in 1919 and I in the 1960s had hoped we would. In the event, neither Gaelicisation nor Europeanisation has proved capable of saving us from many of the consequences of Anglicisation.

3

Lloyd George and Ireland

How Ireland Came to Be Divided

David Lloyd George's name is not one that immediately evokes a favourable response from the average Irish nationalist. Very many people in Ireland remember him simplistically as a British politician who, having first sent the Black and Tans to intimidate the Irish into submission by means of a policy of reprisals, then, using what many in Ireland see as machiavellian tactics, persuaded the Irish delegation to the 1921 London peace talks to sign a Treaty that confirmed the partition of Ireland and kept that country in the British Empire against its instincts – thus precipitating the disastrous Irish Civil War of 1922–23 and, ultimately, the violence of the years since 1968.

This does not seem to be the way Lloyd George is remembered in England – or in his native Wales. Of course, he is not the only British politician to be seen quite differently in the two islands: this is also true, for example, of Cromwell, and also of Lloyd George's colleague, Winston Churchill.

In this essay I seek – hopefully with some measure of objectivity – to explain why the Irish view of Lloyd George has been so negative, and to consider to what extent this view has or has not been vindicated by historical research.

First of all: where did Lloyd George stand on Home Rule for Ireland? It is clear that for much of his career, Lloyd George favoured Home Rule for Wales, for Ireland, and indeed for all parts of these islands. His first known involvement with Irish affairs came when, in 1886 – the year of the first Irish Home Rule Bill – at a meeting in Wales he proposed a vote of thanks to Michael Davitt, the leader of the land-reform movement in Ireland to whom we owe the fact that, by early in the twentieth century, Ireland had become a land of peasant proprietors rather than insecure tenants, liable to eviction at the whim of largely absentee landlords.

Lloyd George's vote of thanks to Davitt on that occasion proclaimed that Ireland, through its land-reform and Home Rule agitation, had shown Wales how to secure justice and redress. Indeed, eight years later, in October 1894, he told the Cymru Fydd League that Ireland was the only Celtic nationality that organised and drilled the whole of her forces – with the result that it had moved ahead of Wales in the drastic and comprehensive measures it had succeeded in forcing from the imperial power. There was a note not just of envy but even perhaps of jealousy in these comments.

Although he included a reference to Irish Home Rule in an early election address, Lloyd George's support for Irish Home Rule always, understandably, came second to his commitment to home rule for Wales. Accordingly, William Gladstone's enthusiasm for the cause of Irish Home Rule irritated him: in 1892, on the eve of the Second Home Rule Bill, he reminded Gladstone that, although his minority government had the support of many fewer Welsh than Irish votes in the Commons, he was nevertheless politically dependent on Wales as well as Ireland. He had no inhibition, however, about recognising the formidable character of the Grand Old Man's talents deployed in the Irish cause – as when, a year later, he wrote enthusiastically to his wife Margaret of Gladstone's 'magnificent performance' in opening the debate on the new Irish Home Rule Bill in the Commons.

Another, negative, factor affected Lloyd George's attitude towards Ireland, however. Whilst in religious terms he could not be described as an active non-conformist, that was his cultural background: his secularism had a strong non-conformist tinge to it. And although on a visit to Rome he had been at least momentarily impressed when he attended a Mass celebrated by Pope Leo XIII, like many nineteenth-century English Protestants he was strongly prejudiced against Roman Catholicism, which, at least privately, he was prone to describe as 'Popery'.

His attack on the Irish Catholic University proposal of 1898 temporarily estranged him from the Irish Party in Parliament, the members of which for a period stopped speaking to him. But a few years later, he was loudly cheered – at least by the Parnellite section of the Irish Party – when he described the 1902 Education Bill as benefiting Ireland's enemies – the Catholic Hierarchy – at the expense of the non-conformists, who, he said, had been more true to Home Rule than had the Irish Bishops.

Four years later Lloyd George was in office, launching into the most radical series of reforms that Britain had – one might even say has ever – seen. Through one of these reforms, he indirectly had a major impact on Irish affairs even before Home Rule became for the third time a controversial issue in British politics following the loss by the Liberals of their overall parliamentary majority in the 1910 election. In order to explain how this came about, I must briefly explain the financial relationship that existed between Britain and Ireland during the period of the parliamentary Union of the two islands that had begun in 1800.

Within any state, there are bound to be regional disparities of income and wealth, with the peripheral areas being usually poorer than those closer to the centre. Also, within any state the raising of revenue and the spending of public funds will involve some measure of net transfers between regions. Nowadays such net transfers generally operate to reduce underlying disparities in living standards. First of all, principally through the operation of a progressive income tax, richer areas pay a higher proportion of their income into the Exchequer. And, in the second place, mainly through the operation of social-welfare schemes, the poorer areas – which generally have more unemployed people, higher illness rates and, because of the effects of migration, higher proportions of retired people in receipt of state pensions – benefit from a higher rate of state spending per head.

We are all accustomed to this concept of public resource transfers from the better-off to the less-well-off – both geographically and as between different income groups in society. And we know that these exist today not merely within states but also, to some degree, between states – most notably within the European Community and, more generally, albeit still minimally, through the operation of development aid programmes.

What we tend to forget is that transfers from rich to poor are a relatively recent innovation. For most of recorded history, resources were transferred from poor to rich. Within states, this was the case most strikingly in pre-nineteenth-century *anciens régimes* – and, between states, through conquest and colonial exploitation. Even in the more economically benevolent conditions of the nineteenth century, this pattern largely survived, both socially and geographically. So long as government operated on a minimal scale, confining itself largely to securing peace abroad and order at home, most spending took place centrally – but was financed by funds raised locally Throughout the nineteenth century, therefore, poorer Ireland subsidised richer Britain; this fact became a major grievance of Irish nationalists, especially in the later years of the century.

In the 1890s, Irish protests on this score were finally taken on board by the British government of the day, to the extent that a Commission on Financial Relations was set up to establish the facts. The evidence of the Treasury to that Commission showed that net contributions by Ireland to what were then described as 'Imperial Services' had ranged between £2.5 million and £5.5 million at different periods during the nineteenth century – sums which probably represented a not-inconsiderable 2 to 5 percent of Irish GDP.

According to the Treasury evidence, this had involved Ireland paying in taxes on average three to four times more than had actually been spent there by the British government – although by 1889, the situation had improved to the point where the outflow of revenue was said to exceed by only 50 percent the amount remitted back for local spending purposes. However, because, both Robert Peel and later Chancellor of the Exchequer G. J. Goschen had accepted, given its political role, that the cost of the armed Royal Irish Constabulary should have been regarded as an imperial charge, this calculation underestimated the true ratio of income outflow to local expenditure.

The report of this Commission contributed to a major policy change by the Conservative government of Lord Salisbury. The new policy became known as 'killing Home Rule by kindness' – accompanied, of course, by coercion. So, by the time the Liberals came to power in 1906, increased local spending in Ireland had effectively eliminated the net outflow. Moreover, Lloyd George's social reforms – in particular the five shillings a week old-age pension for those over seventy years of age – had the effect of reversing the flow of resources between the two islands. The result was that, for the first time, Ireland became something of a drain on the British Exchequer.

Although they were slow to admit it publicly, Irish nationalists thereby lost what had been until then a powerful economic argument for independence, viz. that separation from Britain would enable taxes to be reduced, thus releasing a dynamic of growth. Irish unionists, on the other hand, were not slow to exploit this weakening of the nationalist case for ending the Union. There is clear evidence of an awareness of this in the contemporary writings of the Irish nationalist economist Tom Kettle, who was killed on the Western Front shortly after the 1916 Rising.

It would be surprising if this was not at least a subconscious factor in the radicalisation of Irish nationalism around this time. Historians have tended to attribute the re-emergence of militant separatism among Irish nationalists to disillusionment with the postponement of Home Rule after the outbreak of the Great War. But that process was greatly intensified – as my father, Desmond FitzGerald, recorded in his memoirs of the 1913–16 period – by a fear that the huge numbers of Irish nationalists, as well as unionists, joining the British army at the outset of the war might portend the imminent extinction of Irish national feeling. It was believed – by my father, among others – that this feeling could be re-aroused only by a dramatic rebellion.

But it may well be that the ground for the re-emergence of militant Irish nationalism had in fact been to some degree prepared by the fear that Irish financial dependence on Britain would eventually undermine Irish separatist feeling. Because nationalists were naturally unwilling to admit that the economic case for nationalism had been weakened, however, by the nature of things there is little historical evidence as to how significant this factor may have been.

Whether or not Lloyd George's social reforms contributed to the hardening of Irish nationalist sentiment that culminated in the 1916 Rising, it is clear that Ireland was not one of his major priorities. Although, in the view of John Grigg, Lloyd George was more committed to Home Rule than was Herbert Asquith, because he was sympathetic to Celtic autonomy and was also, as I mentioned earlier, an advocate of 'Home Rule all round', he was nevertheless 'repelled' by Irish-separatist ambitions to create a separate state outside the United Kingdom.

In office, Lloyd George's relations with the Irish Party were not always smooth. At the time of the controversial 1909 Budget, concessions which the Irish leaders believed they had secured on liquor taxation in Ireland – their party depended heavily on support from publicans – failed to appear in the text of the Budget. Asquith, as prime minister, explained that there had been a misunderstanding, but a resentful Irish Party, feeling that they had been deceived, voted against the second reading of the Budget – but abstained on the crucial third reading rather than be seen to vote with the Conservative and Unionist Party.

The loss by the Liberals of their overall majority in the January 1910 election left them thenceforward dependent on the support of the Irish Party – thus bringing the Home Rule issue back to the forefront of British politics for the third time. Home Rule had not been promised by the Liberals in 1906, nor had there been any real expectation that the issue would be addressed in that Parliament. In the 1910 election campaign, however, in his Albert Hall speech Asquith nailed his colours to the mast of Home Rule for Ireland – even though Home Rule had not been included as a commitment in the Liberals' election manifesto.

To Lloyd George, an Irish veto was scarcely preferable to one by the House of Lords. For one thing, while remaining committed to Home Rule, he shared some of the northern unionists' feelings about Roman Catholicism. As events were to show, in different moods he swung between, on the one hand, an instinctive sympathy for the reluctance of unionists to be placed from the outset under an all-Ireland, overwhelmingly Roman Catholic, Home Rule government in Dublin and, on the other, frustration with the Ulster Unionists' determination to block Irish Home Rule.

The first signs of this ambivalence – an ambivalence that was perhaps unsurprising in a nineteenth-century Welsh politician from a nonconformist background – came in February 1912, when, in conjunction with Winston Churchill, Lloyd George proposed to the Cabinet that areas of Ulster where Protestants were in a clear majority should be allowed to opt out of an all-Ireland Home Rule parliament. The Cabinet eventually decided not to include this in the Bill as introduced, however, but to hold back this possibility for a later stage, instead simply warning the Irish Party leaders that the government held itself free to make changes later should it become clear that some special treatment must be provided for the Ulster counties.

In his opening speech in the debate, Asquith's firm commitment to all-Ireland Home Rule gave no hint that any such compromise might be considered, however. This stance has been much criticised by some historians, and it certainly displeased Lloyd George and Churchill at the time. But when, in June, a backbench Liberal amendment to the Bill proposed a four-county opt-out, Lloyd George opposed the amendment on the grounds that the rationale for such an opt-out was not clear: the area where a majority opposed Home Rule was, in his words, 'variable and indeterminate'.

Lloyd George's efforts at compromise on this issue seem, in fact, to have made him more rather than less determined to face down the unconstitutional opposition of the Ulster Unionists, backed by the Conservative Party in Britain. As he put it, 'when we have exhausted conciliation, we shall have a perfectly free conscience', and the government would then confront unionist defiance. Ulster had always, he said, been an integral part of Ireland, and he approved the foundation at the end of 1913 of the Irish Volunteers as a counterpoise to the Ulster Volunteers.

It was, nevertheless, Lloyd George who, following three secret meetings between Asquith and Bonar Law, during which the idea of a six-county opt-out first took shape, proposed to the Cabinet on 13 November 1913 a temporary exclusion of unionist areas from government by an all-Ireland administration. His calculation was that it would be difficult for the unionists to resist with violence a proposal that left them for the time being in the United Kingdom. He and Churchill went so far as to threaten to resign on this issue.

As the end of 1913 approached, Lloyd George took on the task of persuading John Redmond to consider something of this kind – telling him of the king's deep concern at the prospect of civil war. What eventually influenced Redmond to consider some kind of concession on Ulster, however, was Asquith's revelation to him in February 1914 that Bonar Law had told King George V that, if Parliament was not dissolved and a further general election held, a civil war would follow. This threat had persuaded the king actively to consider reviving a monarchical prerogative that had not been used since the days of William IV and was long thought to be dead: dismissal of the Liberal government, despite their command of a majority in the Commons, and the installation a minority Conservative government which would then call a general election. Even if the Liberals won that election, Asquith pointed out to Redmond, this would involve restarting the whole process of bypassing the Lords by getting the Home Rule Bill through three further sessions of the Commons. (Curiously, this suggestion from the monarch that he might overturn a government with a Commons majority because of a threat of civil war by the minority Opposition does not seem to feature in received British history, even though it has for many years past been well documented.)

Thus reinforced, Lloyd George returned to the attack in a private approach to Redmond, repeating his November proposal. Redmond, recognising *force majeure,* responded that, while he would have preferred an opt-out for the Ulster counties after ten years – an opt-out which, he believed, would not be exercised – he could accept an initial three-year opt-out for these counties if he could be assured that this would be the government's last word on the issue. But Asquith went back to him with a proposal for a six-year opt-out that would leave time for two British general elections to be held – and Redmond agreed. This proposal was rejected, as expected, by the northern unionist leader Edward Carson, who described it as a 'sentence with a stay of execution for six years'.

When, after the failure of this proposal to secure Ulster Unionist acceptance, and after the Curragh 'Mutiny', the Buckingham Palace Conference was called in July 1914, it was at the suggestion of the Irish Party that Lloyd George rather than Lord Crewe was nominated as the second Liberal-government representative with Asquith – 'perhaps', Asquith surmised, 'partly from their experience as victims, that his peculiar gifts and blandishments in negotiation would prove invaluable!' At one point in the discussions about how much of Ulster might be allowed an opt-out, Lloyd George proposed the division of County Tyrone. But eventually the solution found, and acquiesced in by the Irish Party, was one of county opt-outs – without automatic re-inclusion in Home Rule Ireland after a period of years.

With hindsight, we can see that when, on the outbreak of war a week later, even this partitionist version of Home Rule with an indefinite opt-out for Ulster counties was postponed until the war had ended, the option of a peaceful solution to the Irish problem was effectively closed off.

Lloyd George's next controversial involvement in Irish affairs came in the immediate aftermath of the 1916 Rising, in which both my parents participated. He had been shocked by the severity of the post-Rising measures taken by the military authorities, which had involved executing not just the leaders of the Rising but also Patrick Pearse's brother, Willie, simply because he was Patrick's brother. Even before the executions — but following publication of the news of the murder by a British officer of the pacifist Francis Sheehy-Skeffington – he had already expressed his fears to the War Committee that the whole of Ireland might be set ablaze by the unconsidered action of some subordinate officer.

Some weeks later, Asquith, after his post-Rising visit to Ireland, asked Lloyd George to take up the Irish issue, at any rate for a short time. This, he said, was a unique opportunity – and no one could do as much as Lloyd George to bring about peace in Ireland. Just how important the issue had become in Lloyd George's eyes – and how great he judged the potential effect of the Rising to be – may be seen from his remark to Carson, recorded by Tom Jones, that 'if some solution were not found, within six months the Irish-American vote will go over to the German side. They will break our blockade and force an ignominious peace on us unless something is done, even provisionally, to satisfy the Americans.' Such was the first significant appearance, just eighty years ago, of American involvement in Anglo-Irish relations.

Lloyd George must, of course, have suspected that Asquith expected him to fail, thus damaging his prospects of displacing his boss, who by then was feeling threatened by him – and with some reason. But Lloyd George was not one to play safe: he took on the challenge without hesitation and indeed with enthusiasm, believing that he might succeed where everyone else had failed. And, in truth, he very nearly did!

Within a few weeks, Lloyd George had sounded out the unionist and nationalist leaders on the issue of Home Rule. And – partly because Carson and Redmond had both misunderstood a reference of Asquith's to the whole machinery of government in Ireland having broken down, which Redmond had taken as meaning that Home Rule was the only alternative – by mid-June he had apparently, miraculously, secured the agreement of both Irish leaders to a plan to extend Home Rule to most of Ireland at once – a proposal that was in fact quite outside the brief he had been given.

Immediate Home Rule for the greater part of Ireland was, however, to be accompanied by the exclusion of the six Ulster counties until twelve months after the end of the war. Then, if there were no decision by Parliament at that stage, the opt-out would continue as long as necessary, ultimately becoming a matter for an Imperial Conference. Another feature of this tentative agreement was that, whereas the 1914 Act had reduced the number of Irish members at Westminster to forty-two – to the satisfaction of the unionists, who did not relish a continued presence of eighty nationalists at Westminster – the entire 103 Irish members at Westminster were to be retained.

The whole deal depended, however, upon what might charitably be described as a constructive ambiguity. Lloyd George had given Carson a written assurance, saying that 'we must make it clear that Ulster (defined for this purpose as six counties) does not, whether she wills it or not, merge in the rest of Ireland'. With that assurance in his pocket, Carson had, with great difficulty, secured the consent of the standing committee of the Ulster Unionist Council.

But Lloyd George had simultaneously persuaded Redmond and his colleagues that the arrangement in respect of the Ulster counties was temporary. As recorded by Redmond in his notes of his meeting with Lloyd George (Redmond was a meticulous record-taker), in response to a question from him Lloyd George had confirmed that the Irish Party could rely on him and the prime minister not to tolerate any further concessions being thrust upon them. He had, he said, placed his life upon the table and would stand or fall by the agreement arrived at.

This might have worked – but for the fact that he had failed to clear his proposals with the Cabinet before publishing them. Outraged by this fact, the right-wing Conservatives in the Cabinet revolted. The Cabinet dispute continued for five weeks – blowing Lloyd George's cover and arousing the hostility of both camps. Lloyd George told John Dillon, Redmond's lieutenant, that all the Unionist (i.e. Conservative) members were in a state of mutiny. When, a month later, the Cabinet agreed to the definitive exclusion of six counties and withdrew the offer to retain the

103 Irish seats, Redmond had no choice but to back off. As a result, on 27 July Asquith told the king that it had been decided to abandon the whole project.

The historian A. J. P. Taylor has contended that the failure of this initiative was not in fact due to Lloyd George's conflicting assurances about the future status of the northern counties. He argues that the objections from two Conservative members of the Cabinet related rather to the proposals for immediate Home Rule in the rest of the country. This had, indeed, been their initial objection, but they later concentrated on the issue of the permanent exclusion of the northern counties. That this was in fact the key issue is clear from Asquith's letter of 28 July to Redmond, quoted by Nicholas Mansergh in his final and very important book, *The Unresolved Question,* published in 1991.

This records that Asquith said to Redmond: 'I say nothing as to the responsibility of this person or that,' (a palpable dig at Lloyd George) 'but I am sure that you agree with me . . . that the real point is the future of the excluded area. Carson naturally wants safeguards against the possibility of 'automatic inclusion'. You, with equal reason, desire to keep open, and effectively open, the possibility of revision and review – at an early date.' 'The important thing,' Asquith added, 'is to keep the negotiating spirit alive.'

The truth is that Lloyd George had gambled on a long shot and it had not come off. Many observers at the time thought that he should have resigned following the ignominious public collapse of his settlement proposals. When the storm had first broken, he had drafted a letter of resignation, saying that 'without a united government, a settlement is impossible' – but, like a number of other such missives written during his ministerial career, this letter was not sent.

Even Frances Stevenson, Lloyd George's secretary, felt that he would have done himself less harm if he had resigned at that moment: failure to do so, she thought, was 'not quite playing the game'. But Stevenson changed her mind a couple of days later, and his failure to resign then did not prevent him from becoming prime minister six months later. He was right in judging that the desperate need for a change of war leadership would eventually transcend any other consideration.

The first inkling we have of Lloyd George's attitude to Ireland and Ulster as prime minister comes in a comment he made to Bonar Law on

12 January 1918. 'This is the opportunity for Ulster to show that it places Empire above everything. If the little Protestant community in the South, isolated in a turbulent sea of Sinn Féinism and Popery' – the non-con-formist background showing through! – 'can trust their lives and their property to the majority there, surely the powerful community of the North might take that risk for the sake of the Empire in danger.' And he hinted at what might follow if Ulster declined.

But that approach yielded no result, and when Lloyd George met Redmond a fortnight later, the nationalist leader formed the impression that although, as prime minister Lloyd George 'had [Ireland] on his mind, he had not given it any serious attention and in any event still seemed to be thinking of some kind of partition as the only possible solution.' Six weeks later, Lloyd George told the Commons that the unionist inhabi-tants of the North 'are as alien in blood, in religious faith, in tradition, in outlook, as alien to the rest of Ireland in this respect as the inhabitants of Fife or Aberdeen.' Despite this statement, however, he told his Cabinet later that a settlement during wartime was possible only on the basis of one parliament for the whole of Ireland, with Customs and the police force retained under the control of Westminster. To say the least, at this stage Lloyd George's views on Ireland were far from fixed!

In May 1917, Lloyd George initiated a further attempt at a settlement, proposing to Redmond Home Rule with six counties excluded, subject to reconsideration by Parliament after five years, and a Council of Ireland with equal North/South membership, and with the power to extend, or to initiate the ending of, the area of exclusion. When this proposal failed to evoke a positive response from Redmond, Lloyd George set about establishing an Irish Convention – the first meeting of which took place in Trinity College, Dublin, on 25 July 1917. The chairman of the Convention was Sir Horace Plunkett, a southern Protestant who had pio-neered the agricultural cooperative movement in Ireland and who was himself an anti-partition Home Ruler who favoured a united Ireland – but one that would play an active role in the Empire.

The Convention had little chance of succeeding. Sinn Féin, which by that time had already defeated the Irish Party in three crucial by-elections and was well on its way to becoming the party representing the vast majority of Irish nationalists, was excluded from the Convention and was hostile to it. The Ulster Unionists attended the Convention but were determined to wreck it by demanding the permanent exclusion of all nine Ulster counties. Had the southern unionists known that this would be the position of the northern unionists, they would not have taken part in the Convention.

The outcome, as eventually reported to Lloyd George by Plunkett in April 1918, was that agreement had been reached between the Irish Party and the southern unionists on all-Ireland Home Rule – with disagreement, and therefore postponement, of the issue of control of Customs. But this was accompanied by a flat rejection from the northern unionists – and, of course, by the equally flat opposition of Sinn Féin from outside the Convention.

The failure of the Convention did not worry Lloyd George too much. It had helped to calm opinion in the United States and the Dominions, which was probably as much as he ever hoped would come from it.

John Redmond died five weeks before the close of Convention. Four days after the report of the Convention was presented, his Irish Party left Westminster in protest against an Act, concerning the wisdom of which Lloyd George himself was doubtful, which empowered the government to extend conscription to Ireland. He accompanied this action with an invitation to Parliament to frame a measure of Irish self-government. Lloyd George told a newspaper proprietor privately that he would resign if Home Rule was not put through as a prelude to conscription. Nevertheless, in October, despite the fact that no action had been taken on Home Rule, Lloyd George seriously contemplated imposing conscription on Ireland; the war ended a month later, before he had had time to give effect to this change of heart.

Lloyd George had been right to doubt the wisdom of raising the conscription issue in the first place. From a British point of view, in Churchill's words, the government was left with 'all the resentment against compulsion and in the end no law and no men.' And resentment there certainly was in Ireland – deep and universal resentment – for the Irish Party, the Catholic Hierarchy and Sinn Féin came together on anti-conscription platforms throughout the country. So far as the Irish Party was concerned, this was a hopeless gesture: their electoral support had already largely drained away. Upon Sinn Féin, however, these anti-conscription platforms conferred respectability – making this emerging separatist party acceptable to a much wider section of the population than had previously been the case.

I might add that my father, who at that time was serving his third jail sentence, and who shortly after his release a year later was appointed director of publicity of the Dáil Government, always believed that it was the threat of conscription rather than the 1916 executions that finally swung opinion decisively towards Sinn Féin. It should be noted, however, that Sinn Féin had already won the North Roscommon seat from the Irish Party before the conscription issue had been raised in April 1918.

In December 1918, through the working of the first-past-the-post electoral system, Sinn Féin won 70 percent of the Irish seats with only 47 percent of the vote cast. However, if allowance is made for the party's almost certainly greater strength in constituencies where its candidates were not opposed by the Irish Party, this latter figure would have marginally exceeded 50 percent.

The Irish Party, despite securing 23 percent of the popular vote, won only five seats in Ulster and just one in the rest of the country. After that outcome, it is little wonder that the British government substituted proportional representation for the first-past-the-post system in advance of the 1921 elections to the northern and southern Home Rule parliaments – a system that was retained in Northern Ireland until 1929 and reintroduced there in 1973, and which since 1921 has operated in the Irish State.

The establishment of a separate Irish parliament by 70 percent of the representatives democratically elected in the island was in accordance with Sinn Féin's election manifesto – from which the Censor had, incidentally, deleted a commitment to stand by the 1916 Proclamation of Irish Independence! And, of course, this changed the political situation fundamentally – although many politicians in Britain were slow to come to terms with the new reality.

So, in a very different way, did the election result in Britain make a major change in the British political situation: the Liberals lost 110 of their 275 seats, and only 136 of the 165 survivors supported Lloyd George's coalition government. The Conservatives – or 'Unionists', as they were then generally known – correspondingly gained 114 seats, and

339 of the 387 Conservatives elected supported the coalition. As these 339 represented a majority, Lloyd George thereafter remained on as Coalition leader only on sufferance.

Since he had become prime minister three years earlier, Lloyd George had been extremely conscious of the importance of retaining Conservative support. While he had centralised the process of government in an almost presidential manner, he had been careful to exercise the power that this step gave him very sensitively vis-à-vis his Conservative coalition partners. But now he had to tread even more carefully, for he remained prime minister solely because of the stature he had gained in turning what had at times seemed likely defeat in the war into eventual victory. At any moment in the life of the new parliament, the Conservatives could replace the coalition with an all-Conservative government – which they in fact did four years later. Given the deeply held unionist views of most – though not all – Conservatives, he had to be careful above all about how he handled the Irish question. How much this affected his subsequent behaviour, for example in relation to repression in Ireland, is difficult to say. Perhaps he himself was not always conscious of how far he was being pushed by his dependence on Conservative support in a direction that he might not otherwise have gone. However that may be, in all that he did thenceforth in relation to Ireland, he was extremely careful to bring with him leading Conservatives in his Cabinet.

His own preference at that time was for a federal system in these islands – for which there was, however, little support in Parliament – and, as he told the historian H. A. L. Fisher in April 1919, he favoured an all-Ireland parliament with an Ulster Committee given power to protect the interests of Ulster unionists. This was an arrangement that had not been ruled out by Carson at that time. But under no circumstances was Lloyd George prepared to coerce the northern unionists into an arrangement that was unacceptable to them.

The coalition position, as distinct from his own personal one, had been set out in an election manifesto: an openness to any solution that involved neither 'a complete severance of Ireland from the British Empire' nor 'forcible submission of the six counties of Ulster to a Home Rule Parliament against their will.' The use of the words 'six counties' in the manifesto ruled out, by implication, the county option – the concept of individual counties exercising an option either way.

There was a time constraint on the resolution of the problem. Unless some other settlement was agreed, the Home Rule Act of 1914, with its provision for a county option, would come into effect twelve months after the signature of the peace treaties, and by October 1919 only the Turkish treaty was outstanding. No one could then have known that this would not be finally signed until 1923, so the 'Irish problem' appeared to be a matter of considerable urgency. And, as Austen Chamberlain, the leader of the English Unionist (i.e. Conservative) Party and Chancellor of the Exchequer, told the Commons: 'You cannot safely repeal the Act of 1914. You cannot safely allow it to come into force' – for either of these could have brought down the coalition.

It was against this background that the Irish Situation Committee of the Cabinet started work in October 1919, under the chairmanship of Walter Long. It faced the major problem that its members were unwilling to address the reality of Sinn Féin's election victory in December 1918. The committee's approach was based on the extraordinary belief that a Home Rule party could re-emerge in Ireland, replacing Sinn Féin. Edmond Montagu, who submitted proposals to the committee, was typical: he found it 'impossible to believe that the Irish really wanted separation.'

The committee's solution was the establishment of two Home Rule parliaments, together with a Council which, as well as discharging certain functions straightaway, would be primarily concerned to promote the union of the whole of Ireland under one parliament.

There were doubts about how northern unionists would react to the offer of a Home Rule parliament for Ulster, or part of it. The Lord Chancellor, Lord Birkenhead, in particular was dubious: although he supported the proposal on the grounds that it would strengthen Britain's tactical position in relation to the rest of the world, at the same time he believed that Sinn Féin was sure to turn it down.

In order to get an Ulster Unionist view, the government turned to Sir James Craig, who was then an Ulster Unionist junior minister in the government but who, little more than a year later, replaced Carson as that party's leader. (Sir James Craig's family were whiskey distillers; my northern grandfather was managing director of their Royal Irish Distillery.)

Craig said that the proposal for a Home Rule parliament for Ulster would be acceptable on condition that only six rather than nine Ulster counties were included, because, in his view, that would make it 'easier to govern'. He added later, however, that he favoured a Boundary Commission to define the precise area to be excluded. He also stated that he would prefer an all-Ireland House of Lords to the proposed Council of Ireland, as the former would be a more effective way of arresting inappropriate legislation.

The southern unionists were effectively ignored: no attention was paid to their prescient warnings against any form of partition as 'politically impossible, impracticable in operation' and bound to create 'continuous agitation by a considerable nationalist and Catholic minority.' In their own words, they suffered 'base desertion' by both the northern unionists and the Unionist Party in England.

In the event, the Bill introduced by Lloyd George on 22 December 1919 followed the lines of the committee's proposals – without, however, the addition of the Boundary Commission suggested by Craig. To the Commons he defended on strategic grounds the proposition that Ireland should not be separated from Britain: 'A hostile republic, or even an unfriendly one, might very well have been fatal to the cause of the Allies,' he said, and accordingly, 'any attempt at secession will be fought with the same determination . . . with the same resolve, as the Northern States of America put into the fight against the Southern States' – a shrewd bid for American support and sympathy. In the debate that followed, Asquith said that to use the term 'Home Rule' of this Bill was 'manifestly an almost aggressive use of language', but Wedgwood Benn, later Lord Stansgate, described it simply as 'a Bill for partition'.

In nationalist Ireland, where the government established by Dáil Éireann was engaged in setting up an underground administration to which all the county councils outside a few Ulster counties soon gave allegiance, all this seemed simply irrelevant. Sinn Féin and the Dáil had been proscribed in September – a move which six months later Lloyd George privately agreed had been a mistake. That, and the fact that even Dominion status was ruled out by the British government (Lloyd George himself being strongly opposed to it, and Walter Long describing it as late as September 1920 as something that 'could never be conceded'), left no room for political manoeuvre and ensured that a bitter conflict would precede any solution.

Whether from conviction at that stage or to impress his Conservative ministers, Lloyd George was indubitably a hardliner in relation to the War of Independence. At a July 1920 policy conference, he sought definite and final proposals for the restoration of law and order – which led to the introduction of court-martials. And at an October conference he said that it would be a mistake to make any concessions – for example in relation to fiscal autonomy or the contribution to the cost of imperial services. He further stated that a concession on Customs should be considered only as a last resort if it were the sole thing standing in the way of peace. He even suggested that, in an amending Bill, provision should be made for Britain to retain control of parts of southern Ireland – although this suggestion was quickly dropped. On the military side, he described his Irish opponents in November 1920 as 'a small nest of assassins', 'a murder gang' to be rounded up – for, he told the Guildhall Banquet, 'We have murder by the throat.'

Two months earlier, Lloyd George had resisted taking responsibility for the reprisals policy being pursued by the military. When told by the chief of the Imperial General Staff, Sir Henry Wilson, that 'if these people ought to be murdered, then the government ought to murder them', Lloyd George 'danced with rage', according to Wilson – who was, to be sure, a prejudiced witness – and said that no government could take responsibility for such an approach. But he later agreed to do so once the 'cursed election' in the United States was over.

The issue, it may be noted, was not whether people should, in Sir Henry Wilson's words, be 'murdered' in reprisals, but who should take responsibility for the murders, such as that of the Lord Mayor of Cork, Thomas Mac Curtain. The result of all this was that Britain lost the propaganda war by a mile. Having to explain, and often cover up, atrocities, the British authorities soon lost the confidence of both the world press and public opinion. My father, as director of publicity for the Dáil Government, had a correspondingly easy task. By simply refusing to publish in his daily underground newspaper, the *Bulletin,* any atrocity story not backed by sworn affidavits, he soon won the confidence of the world press – even if at times he infuriated many of his own side by this cautious approach.

Inevitably, in this situation, some way out eventually had to be sought. From late 1920 onwards, many feelers, authorised and unauthorised, were put out. When, on 12 May 1921, the Cabinet had a serious discussion about a truce, there was considerable support for the idea, but Lloyd George opposed it resolutely. What guarantee, he asked, was there that such a gesture would produce any response? A truce would raise the price of concessions in subsequent negotiations to too high a level, he argued. And if the Irish demands were impossible to concede, as was likely, there would then be resistance by public opinion to a resumption of the war. What he still feared, and implacably opposed, even at that stage, was a settlement that would make Ireland a Dominion of the British Commonwealth, similar to Canada and Australia.

Twelve days later, Sinn Féin were unopposed in the elections for the Southern Home Rule Parliament – from the first, and only, session of which they then stayed away. In the guerrilla war being carried on by Irish Volunteers, the British army was by that time reputed to be in a 'precarious, near-desperate situation' and was, in fact, 'besieged'. The army authorities believed that an additional one hundred thousand men would be needed to carry through repression, with the trial and possible execution of the Sinn Féin leaders. (Arthur Balfour proposed transportation as an alternative!)

At that crucial point, the South African premier General Smuts, on a visit to London, lunched with King George V, who was at that moment anxiously awaiting receipt from the government of a draft of his speech for the opening of the northern parliament. He told Smuts he had reason to believe the draft that had been prepared was a 'bloodthirsty document'. Smuts prepared a counter-draft for the king and sent it to Lloyd George. This document contained a proposal for Dominion Home Rule. Lloyd George vetoed that proposal – but he allowed the conciliatory language in the rest of the speech stand.

The speech made a profound impression on Irish opinion, and on his return from Belfast, the king urged an immediate follow-up. The Cabinet met the next day and agreed on a letter to Éamon de Valera proposing a conference. Smuts went to Dublin to meet the Sinn Féin leaders de Valera, Arthur Griffith, Eamon Duggan and Robert Barton. (The latter three were later that year to be signatories of the Treaty.) Smuts persuaded the Irish not to refuse this proposal – despite the fact that the Northern Ireland government had also been invited, whereas the Irish were concerned that the discussion should be purely bilateral. (In the event, the northern government declined the invitation.)

Smuts also made a persuasive case to de Valera and his colleagues in favour of Dominion status. Although he failed to convince de Valera, the latter went so far as to say that, if the British insisted on Dominion status, this should not contain irksome limitations. The British should, he believed, make a great gesture: the settlement must be an everlasting peace. This certainly did not amount to a flat rejection of Dominion status.

When Smuts reported back, the Cabinet agreed on a truce, to operate from 11 July. The die having being cast, Lloyd George settled down to the task of persuading the Irish to accept what he himself had until the last moment implacably opposed, viz. Dominion status, albeit with some important subtractions. For when he met de Valera on 14 July, his Dominion-status proposal was qualified by requirements that Britain retain naval and air bases in the Irish Dominion and that Ireland, unlike the other Dominions, would have no right to impose duties on British goods. Moreover, the Northern Ireland government must be formally recognised by the new Irish government.

De Valera's response in August was a rejection of Dominion status because, he said, what had been proposed lacked the explicit guarantees which, in view of Ireland's close geographical proximity, would be needed to put it on a par with the status of the other Dominions. Once again, it was far from a flat rejection of such status. Instead, de Valera proposed a Treaty Association with the Commonwealth group – if accompanied by an assurance that this would secure the allegiance of the northern unionists to the Irish State. Lloyd George's response made it clear that, in the British view, no right of Ireland to secede from her allegiance to the king could ever be acknowledged by Britain.

At this point, Lloyd George was holidaying in Scotland; he called a Cabinet meeting to be held in Inverness Town Hall – the only such meeting ever held outside London. At that meeting, he argued in favour of persisting with the demand for an Irish commitment to Crown and Empire as a precondition of negotiations. The Cabinet was at first evenly divided but then came down against making that a precondition. The reply sent to de Valera invited him simply 'to enter a conference to ascertain how the association of Ireland with the community of nations known as the British Empire could best be reconciled with Irish national aspirations.' And that, despite a further fortnight of confused communications between the two sides, became the agreed basis on which the conference leading to the Anglo-Irish Treaty of 1921 took place.

If Lloyd George had been a late convert to Dominion status for Ireland, and a reluctant assenter to a negotiation that was not preceded by a declaration of acceptance of Crown and Empire, he nevertheless threw himself into the subsequent negotiations with a clear determination to find a basis for agreement. All his skills were fully deployed. He had no illusions, however, about the tightrope he would have to walk between the the Irish and the Tory diehards – upon whose support his fragile position as prime minister depended.

De Valera had decided not to participate in the negotiations personally – a fateful decision. His reason, as recorded by my father, who was a witness to all these discussions and who had a private discussion with de Valera in which he sought a reversal of de Valera's decision to remain in Ireland, was that whoever went to London must compromise. But even with compromise, there might be no settlement, and the Irish might have to return to the old fighting methods. But you could not ask people to fight for a compromise. Rightly or wrongly, the people looked upon de Valera as a living symbol of the maximum Irish claim to the Republic, and he wanted to be in a position to rally the people if no settlement was reached by compromise.

He insisted to the Dáil, however, that the members of the delegation should be plenipotentiaries – that is, having full powers to reach an agreement. After that decision had been taken, my father spent some time trying to convince de Valera to withdraw this provision – as did one of the members of the proposed delegation. De Valera refused to be swayed, however. He probably felt that, unless they were denominated as plenipotentiaries, a serious negotiation with the British would not ensue.

De Valera named as head of the delegation Arthur Griffith, the founder of Sinn Féin in the early years of the century and someone who had always been a monarchist and had no time for an Irish republic. Privately, de Valera asked Griffith to get him out of the straitjacket of the republic and told him that it might be necessary to have a scapegoat, to which Griffith answered: 'I am ready.'

In those preparatory events lay the roots of the bitterness of the political division that followed the signature of the Treaty and the subsequent Civil War. Arthur Griffith, Michael Collins and those who supported them found it difficult to forgive de Valera's radical change of position, as they saw it, between the time the delegation was despatched in early October and the immediate aftermath of the signature of the Treaty.

I do not propose to give a blow-by-blow account of the negotiations that followed. I shall rather concentrate on one key issue: the relationship between Northern Ireland and the new Irish State. On 30 October, three weeks after the start of negotiations, Lloyd George saw Griffith alone for the first time, at Churchill's house. Both leaders accepted that, through the first weeks of the negotiations, they had been fencing with each other. Lloyd George told Griffith that there were three essentials: the Crown, free partnership with the Commonwealth, and naval facilities. Given an unequivocal personal assurance on these three items, he would go down next night to the House of Commons to smite the Conservative diehards and would fight on the Ulster matter to secure essential unity for Ireland.

Griffith replied that the Irish delegates would recommend to the Dáil recognition of the Crown if they were satisfied on other points of issue – the formula for such recognition to be discussed later. An association of Ireland with the Empire could be agreed in principle, the formula defining it also to be left over till later. They got nowhere, however, on the issue of defence, or on the trade issue: the right of Ireland to apply its own Customs duties to British goods.

In response to Griffith's statement, Lloyd George said that he could carry in the government a six-county parliament subordinate to an Irish national parliament. Alternatively, he would try to carry a plan for a new boundary, or a vote by Ulster as a single unit on inclusion or exclusion from the new Irish State. A vote by the inhabitants of the whole of nine-county Ulster might conceivably have produced a majority for an all-Ireland parliament.

A Tory-diehard motion was heavily defeated in Parliament on 1 December. Shortly afterwards, Griffith showed his delegation a letter that Lloyd George had asked him to write to present to a crucial Conservative Party conference in Liverpool on 17 November. After a row among members of the delegation, Griffith agreed that the letter should go from them all rather than from him personally, as he had originally proposed, and that the phrase 'a recognition of the Crown' be qualified with the words 'as head of the proposed association of free states'. At a meeting with the British attended by Griffith and Collins on 2 November, that phrase was changed to 'free partnership with other states associated within the British Commonwealth' – which was arguably open to an interpretation that neither Collins nor Griffith at that stage intended, i.e. accepting Irish membership of the Commonwealth rather than external association with it.

Next morning, Birkenhead told Griffith and Collins that this letter had provided them with a document upon which they could deal with Sir James Craig – who earlier that year had replaced Carson as leader of the Ulster Unionists – and that, if Ulster proved unamenable, they – presumably himself, Lloyd George and Churchill, but possibly also others – would resign rather than use force against Sinn Féin. Writing to de Valera, Griffith made the point that, after such a resignation, 'no English government is capable of formation on a war policy against Ireland'.

Lloyd George, for his part, was also happy, telling Lord Riddell that it looked as if the Irish would accept the sovereignty of the king: 'They will agree to remain part of the British Empire and will also agree to give us the facilities we want for our navy.' But he also told Riddell that the quid quo pro for this was an all-Ireland parliament. He went on to tell Riddell that 'I have made up my mind that I will not coerce Southern Ireland. I may lose everything but I shall know I have saved my soul anyway.' He said much the same to C. P. Scott, the editor of the *Guardian* and a close friend of his, and to others. To Tom Jones, assistant secretary to the Cabinet and a man who was very close to Lloyd George, he said that, following his resignation, there would be five or six years of reaction – time for progressive forces to be organised. But, he went on, 'there is just one more possible way out, and I want to find out from Griffith and Collins if they would support me on it. Would they agree to a Boundary Commission? We could then refuse Ulster additional powers.' (Craig had been seeking Dominion status, much to the fury of Lloyd George and other members of the Cabinet.)

The next day, Jones called on Griffith and Collins. He told them that Craig had rejected the all-Ireland parliament and that, if this was confirmed by his government in Northern Ireland, Lloyd George would go down to the Commons, resign and leave public life. Birkenhead and Chamberlain would also resign, he thought. There would be no dissolution of Parliament: Bonar Law would form a militarist government against Ireland.

There might, however, be a way out to avoid this, Jones suggested. Suppose the South got all the new powers proposed, and Ulster was restricted to its present powers, and also submitted to a Boundary Commission set up to delimit her area?

Griffith reserved his position in the discussion, but he wrote to de Valera that 'the arrangement would give us most of Tyrone and Fermanagh and a part of Armagh and Londonderry, Down etc . . . [The possibility of a militarist Conservative government replacing Lloyd George] is partly bluff, but not wholly.' In response, de Valera sent his congratulations to the delegation, warning, however, that 'as far as the Crown–Empire connection is concerned, we should not budge a single inch.'

On 10 November, Jones returned. Craig was maintaining his hard line, and Lloyd George wanted to play a second card if he persisted in refusing an all-Ireland Parliament – namely a Boundary Commission to delimit Ulster 'so as to give us the districts in which we are now in a majority' (Griffith's words writing to de Valera). Did Griffith think that Ulster would accept this, together with restrictions on the powers that they now have, de Valera asked? 'No,' said Griffith.

If Ulster refused the Boundary Commission, Jones went on, Lloyd George could nevertheless present it as a possibility, and, instead of resigning and letting in a militarist government, he could remain on as the only man who could solve the problem. Would the Irish stand behind such a proposal? It would be a British proposal not an Irish proposal, Griffith replied, and 'we will not be bound by it, but we realise its value as a tactical manoeuvre, and if Lloyd George makes it, we would not queer the pitch.'

Two days later, Griffith met Lloyd George privately. In correspondence over the previous two days, Craig had shocked the British by demanding Dominion status and rejecting anything except a 'voluntary' contribution to the British Exchequer. The British were going to reject these disloyal proposals, as they saw them, and would reply to Craig that he could be offered the right to opt out of an all-Ireland parliament within six months – but that, if this occurred, a Boundary Commission would be set up to delimit the area of opt-out, and the rest would be subject to equal financial burdens with England. This would be the government's last word, and if the Unionists rejected it, he, Lloyd George would summon Parliament, appeal to it against Ulster and either dissolve or pass an Act establishing an all-Ireland parliament. Griffith's response was again that this was Lloyd George's proposal, not his. He could not guarantee acceptance, but he would guarantee that, while Lloyd George was fighting the 'Ulster crowd', the Irish would not help them by repudiating him.

Committed to paper the next day and shown to Griffith, the informal agreement provided that 'If Ulster did not see her way to accept immediately the principle of a parliament for all-Ireland . . . in this case it would be necessary to revise the boundary of Northern Ireland. This might be done by a Boundary Commission which would be directed to adjust the line both by inclusion and exclusion, so as to make the boundary conform as closely as possible to the wishes of the people.'

Griffith accepted this proposed letter to Craig; it was in fact expressed in precisely the same terms as what had previously been verbally discussed. Because of that, he did not think to tell either the other members of the delegation or de Valera that he had been shown the letter – an oversight that was later to cause a problem for the Irish in the closing stages of the negotiations.

Much was to happen in the following three weeks – and it was of course over the quite different issues of Dominion status and an oath of faithfulness to the king in virtue of common citizenship and membership of the Commonwealth that the Treaty was to founder, and a Civil War was to be fought.

The issue of the Ulster opt-out was scarcely mentioned in the Dáil debates that preceded the ratification issue. And at no stage was Griffith ever attacked or criticised because of his handling of the Boundary

Commission, although this Commission ultimately consolidated, instead of undermining, the division of Ireland.

When, on the evening of 4 December, the Irish delegation, which was already deeply divided over the issues of the oath and Dominion status, met their British counterparts, Griffith attempted to centre the debate upon Ulster, so to ensure that, if a break came, it would come on this issue. But at this point, his pledge not to let the British down against the Ulster unionists was recalled. The British pointed out that they were presenting the northern unionists with a proposal for an all-Ireland parliament – which the unionists would of course refuse, thus bringing the Boundary Commission, to which Griffith had agreed, into play. Faced with this, Griffith felt unable to press the Ulster issue further at that point. The debate moved on to other issues.

When, next day, Collins saw Lloyd George, he told the prime minister that he was perfectly dissatisfied with the situation relating to Ulster. Lloyd George replied, pointing out that Collins had himself said that a Northern Ireland limited to the predominantly unionist areas would be forced economically to come in the new Irish State. Collins said that, if the northern unionist leadership rejected an all-Ireland parliament, 'we would save Tyrone and Fermanagh, parts of Derry, Armagh and Down by the Boundary Commission'. Collins left the meeting apparently content, although in fact, nothing seems to have been said by Lloyd George that would have given him grounds for ceasing to be 'perfectly dissatisfied', as he had been at the outset of the meeting.

At the final session, the Griffith commitment was played up again. This time, the issue centred on whether the Irish should agree to the proposed Boundary Commission solution before or after Craig had replied to the proposal relating to the all-Ireland parliament. The British contended that his reply was irrelevant either way: either Craig accepted an all-Ireland parliament or, if he did not, the alternative of the Boundary Commission would come into play.

Eventually, Lloyd George produced the letter that Griffith had approved – but which, as we have seen, Griffith had never thought to mention to anyone because its terms were identical with what he had already fully reported to his colleagues in London and to de Valera in Dublin. Neither de Valera nor the hardliners in Dublin had seemed in any way perturbed about these terms in relation to Northern Ireland, because all the debates within the delegation and at home in Ireland had centred on the issues of Dominion status and the Oath.

But in London, in the fevered atmosphere of the final session, the fact that his colleagues were clearly disconcerted when the letter that Griffith had seen and approved was produced must have given the British a crucial moral advantage. And Griffith, unwilling, as an honourable man, to quibble over the fact that he had promised not to let the British down only 'while they were fighting the Ulster crowd', replied simply: 'I have never let a man down in my life and I never will.'

All of this raises several questions to which the answers are not clear. First, why did the Irish think that a truncated Ulster of one county and the majority of three others would not be economically viable, and that it would have to be forced into the Irish Free State? In fact, it could be argued that such an area would be more viable than a six-county area, as the parts to be transferred to the Irish State were – and still are – the poorer parts of the six-county area. In economic terms, there was no case for the belief that the Boundary Commission would leave Northern Ireland economically non-viable. And if the Irish leaders at home and in London felt that the area would be too small to be politically viable, were there not many European examples – such as Luxembourg, Monaco, Liechtenstein, San Marino and Andorra – to demonstrate that size was irrelevant to survival as a polity.

Second, why were they so certain of what the Boundary Commission would award them on the basis of 'the wishes of the people'? Even in Tyrone and Fermanagh, there were predominantly unionist enclaves, and in the absence of agreement on the unit to be used in determining how the popular will should be applied on the map – by county, by barony or by some other geographic entity – the clear-cut result which they pre-sumed would be secured was far from self-evident. All of the Irish side seem to have been mesmerised by their own propaganda on this aspect of the Ulster issue.

I have not been able to satisfy myself as to how and when what had been agreed in November and included in the controversial letter, viz. a Commission directed to adjust the line to make the boundary conform 'as closely as possible to the wishes of people', was in the Treaty heavily qualified by the addition of an overriding sub-clause 'so far as may be compatible with economic and geographic conditions'. It was on a not-completely-unreasonable view that, syntactically, this sub-clause overrode the main clause that, in 1925, the literal-minded South African chairman of the Boundary Commission, Mr Justice Feethan, made his minimalist proposals for boundary changes. These proposals were limited to some transfers of rural hinterlands of towns on either side close to the border, and ignored some hundreds of thousands of nationalists living in several thousands of square miles of territory a little further inside Northern Ireland, most of them in districts linked to the border by areas of clear nationalist allegiance. Whoever on the British side inserted that qualifying phrase was very clever. The failure on the Irish side to spot and contest it was not.

It seems to me that, at the end of the day, one can reach only one conclusion. In many respects, the Treaty represented an extraordinary victory for the Irish: they won Dominion status, which Lloyd George had dismissed earlier that year as 'never open to concession', and, moreover, Dominion status on terms that, as they emerged in later discussion about the Irish Constitution, eliminated the Crown from any effective role in Irish domestic affairs, in a manner that had never been either sought or conceded in respect of any other colony in the process of becoming a Dominion. The possibility of a different solution to the Northern Ireland problem was lost, however, because of the gross over-concentration of the Irish side on the peripheral issue of the Oath and because of de Valera's preoccupation with his concept of external association with the Commonwealth – which at that point in history had no hope of acceptance.

Lloyd George's problems were in fact greatly eased by this deep-seated weakness in the Irish negotiating position. He secured a Treaty that both Commons and Lords endorsed, thus preserving his coalition – for a further twelve months. (The Treaty was, however, an element in the circumstances that led to Lloyd George's fall at the end of that year; and after that fall, he never returned to office. Indeed, only one other signatory survived the fall of that government to return to office later: Winston Churchill.)

On the Irish side, Griffith and Collins were dead within nine months, in the middle of a bitter Civil War: Griffith, whose heart failed because of the strain of subsequent events, and Collins, at the hands of those who had rejected the Treaty, thus fulfilling his own prophecy that, in signing this document, he had signed his own death warrant. De Valera, for his part, in rejecting a treaty the terms of which were close to what he himself had seemed to expect and to have been prepared to settle for, incurred the undying resentment of those of his former colleagues who had signed the Treaty or who supported its signature.

In the Second World War, de Valera defended a neutrality that he believed essential to prevent a recurrence of that civil war in respect of which he always seemed to carry a suppressed feeling of guilt – a neutrality that Churchill, for his part, saw as treachery. The two of them met once more, amicably, at a dinner in Downing Street in 1955. By then, Lloyd George had been dead for ten years; the two surviving leaders were to live on, for a further decade in Churchill's case, and for two decades in the case of de Valera.

I shall not attempt a verdict on Lloyd George or on his Treaty negotiation. It was certainly the ultimate triumph of his formidable negotiating skills, and it won for Britain fifty years of freedom from the 'Irish question'. That freedom might, moreover, have lasted even longer if Britain had honourably enforced the provisions of the Government of Ireland Act 1920 in respect of discrimination in Northern Ireland.

But for Ireland, the Treaty proved deeply divisive. Perhaps it could not have been otherwise. An important minority of those who had carried on the War of Independence against Britain had become completely committed to the concept of a Republic and were not prepared to settle for anything less. Yet, when the Civil War was over and the internment camps had been emptied a year later, the process began of establishing a stable, democratic state, which in time became a positive and constructive building block of the European Community.

But Lloyd George's ultimate failure to negotiate with the Ulster unionists a better solution to the problem of Northern Ireland, and the failure of the entire Irish side to give to this matter the priority is deserved, left our two states with the unresolved issue of a potentially explosive character. Due, however, to the consequent danger to the peace and order of these islands, the governments of our two states have long since moved from being disputants to being partners in seeking a peaceful solution of the Northern Ireland problem, which had eluded even such a skilled

66

negotiator as Lloyd George. The catalyst to the emergence of this unity of approach to the Northern Ireland problem has, of course, been the Provisional IRA. That is only one of very many paradoxes that have flown from the efforts of David Lloyd George to resolve the Irish problem.

4

ÉAMON DE VALERA

THE PRICE OF HIS ACHIEVEMENT

With O'Connell and Parnell, de Valera was one of three Irish political leaders of the nineteenth and twentieth centuries who had not alone the capacity and the ability to play a major political role over an extended period of time, but also the opportunity to do so. There are others who, if they had lived and had had the opportunity to exercise their remarkable talents in the political sphere under conditions of peace, might have rivalled or even outshone some or all of these three – most notably, in the twentieth century, Michael Collins. But those whom the gods love die young, and the nature of Ireland's almost always tragic, but at times heroic, history has been such that many people of exceptional talent have died or, more frequently, been killed before they reached the age of thirty-five – and therefore no more than a third of the way through their potential working life.

All three of the men I have mentioned – O'Connell, Parnell and de Valera – excited controversy and division amongst Irish nationalists at some point in their lives. This is perhaps especially true of O'Connell towards the end of his life, when he and the new generation of Young Irelanders found themselves at odds, and also of Parnell at the end of his career and life because of his involvement with Kitty O'Shea, the wife of one of his supporters. De Valera, by contrast, became a controversial figure amongst Irish nationalists before he was forty and, living as he did well into this nineties – longer than any other major political figure in modern Irish history, continued to divide Irish politics thereafter. This has made particularly difficult an objective assessment of his achievements

and defects within his own lifetime, or even during the generation following his death in 1975.

The political system of the Irish State remains today largely based
upon a party system, the origins of which are to be found substantially in
the polarisation that occurred around de Valera. The issues that led to this
polarisation ceased many decades ago to have any current relevance in
domestic politics, and the two major political parties moved on to seek,
and find, new roles as they addressed the complex and difficult problems
of Ireland in the last third of the twentieth century. Nevertheless, the
memory of the circumstances that brought these two parties into existence lingered on, and whilst none of the members of these parties today
have any direct recollections of these events, even the youngest voters
continue to associate the two parties vaguely with their historical origins.
Because of this, many Irish people still have difficulty in seeing the two
parties in question as they actually are today, with their current policies
and different styles of leadership and organization. To many Irish people,
and especially to those who support other parties or none, they remain
the two 'civil war' parties.

In twenty-seven years in active politics, I can recall only a single disagreement or argument with an active politician of the Fianna Fáil Party
founded by de Valera that related to that distant past – the Anglo-Irish
Treaty of 1921 or the Civil War of 1922–23 – or indeed to the other
events of the 1920s and early 1930s that provided the basis for the main
divide in the party system that we know today. Consequently, I – and I
believe most other active Irish politicians of these two parties – are often
frustrated, and indeed irritated, to hear people outside politics referring to
'the perpetuation of civil-war politics' in our party system. Yet, insofar as
this is the external perception of so many outside politics, it is, like all
myths that are still believed, a reality that must be faced.

I have made this point at the outset for several reasons. First, in so far
as our existing political party system owes its origins to divisions eighty
years ago in which de Valera played a crucial role, this represents a significant part of his influence on contemporary Ireland.

Second, because however anachronistic – in the eyes of active politicians at least – may be the common public perception that what divides
the parties and their political representatives in parliament today is still
'civil war politics', this belief is a reality of modern Ireland that is equally

a product of the controversial events eighty years ago.

And, third, because having made these two points I do not feel that it is necessary, or indeed relevant, to contemporary Ireland to discuss the controversial role played by de Valera in those historical events, except where, in very specific but relatively limited ways, that role impinged indirectly upon subsequent events. What is, I think, more relevant is to consider how the actions and policies of de Valera in the period after the Civil War that ended in May 1923 have left their mark upon the institutions, and possibly in some respects upon the character, of contemporary Ireland.

In attempting even a provisional assessment of this influence, one must have regard, first, to the problems that faced the new Irish State in the aftermath of the Civil War and, second, to the condition of Ireland today, more than eighty years later. What has been achieved, what has been left undone, and what has been made worse over this period? And, in relation to each of these questions, what was de Valera's role?

The most fundamental problem facing the Irish State after the Civil War, in which those who wished to continue the struggle with Britain for an independent republic rejected Dominion status within the British Commonwealth, was the stability of the State itself. A substantial proportion of its people – at least one-third, on the evidence of the general election of August 1923 – withheld their consent from the new State in its early years and, by so doing, challenged its legitimacy. The resolution of this fundamental problem of the legitimacy of the State required a development of its initial status. For, like the other Dominions of the Commonwealth at that time, the Irish State when established was an autonomous, self-governing, political unit – but one with a question mark hanging over its absolute sovereignty vis-à-vis Britain.

Another different but related problem was that created by the partition of the island, which had been brought about by the decision of the provincial parliament in Northern Ireland to opt out of the new State on the day after its foundation as an internationally recognised political unit through the enactment of its Constitution, viz. 6 December 1922. This right for Northern Ireland to opt out had been agreed as part of the Treaty terms and, contrary to popular mythology, had not been the subject of much discussion in the debate on the Treaty in Dáil Éireann which had preceded the outbreak of the Civil War. That debate had centred instead on the issue of the symbols of monarchy that the Treaty had imposed upon the independent Irish State. Would this division of the island – a division that had no historical precedent – endure, or could it be reversed, and the parts brought together again?

Next, there was the fundamental question of what would be the political ethos of this new State. Would it be pluralist, giving full recognition to the cultural and religious tradition of many centuries of settlers, as well as to the native cultural and religious tradition, or would it attempt to become mono-cultural, elevating to a position of primacy the native Gaelic and Catholic tradition of the great majority of its people whose leaders had sought and secured its independence – with all the problems that this might create for an eventual coming together of the predominantly Protestant North with the overwhelmingly Roman Catholic State comprising the remainder of the island?

There was also the problem of the economics of a country that had suffered colonial exploitation in the eighteenth century and earlier, as well as considerable neglect at the hands of laissez-faire Britain during much of the nineteenth century. This unhappy economic history, together with the State's peripheral geographical location, particularly in relation to the rest of Europe, had deprived Ireland of the possibility of industrial development. That had in turn left it a predominantly agricultural country, endowed with exceptionally high fertility and birth rates.

In the absence of opportunities for employment in its weak agricultural sector, the State continued to suffer massive demographic erosion by way of the emigration of a high proportion of those born within its territory during the first quarter-century of political independence. Of that generation, one-third had emigrated and one-sixth had died by the age of thirty-five, principally due to infant mortality and TB, thus halving the initial size of each age cohort.

Finally, there was the question of the social organisation of the new State: would it develop into a property-owning democracy or into a socialist State? And, if the former, would it be a socially conscious democracy, caring for the underprivileged in Irish society?

These were the five main challenges that faced the new State – although, of course, there were many others, including the immense task of physical reconstruction in the immediate aftermath of a civil war that had involved much more damage to its infrastructure than had the struggle against Britain that had immediately preceded independence.

In the midst of the Civil War, in which the very foundations of the new State were challenged in arms, albeit unsuccessfully, the legitimacy of the State was judicially established and internationally recognised. In 1923, the Irish Free State became a member of the League of Nations. Moreover, by mid-1923, with the defeat of those who opposed the Treaty, domestically, the authority of the State had been established.

But there remained the problem of securing free acceptance of this legitimacy and authority by those who had rejected it at the outset. This posed a problem both for victor and vanquished in the Civil War. The victors were, of course, the government led by W. T. Cosgrave, the supporters of which had, during the latter stages of the Civil War, formed themselves into a political party, Cumann na nGaedheal. Later, in the aftermath of their loss of power in 1932, and following a merger with several other groups, this party developed into the present Fine Gael Party.

Cumann na nGaedheal's contribution to securing acceptance of the authority of the new State lay partly in a sustained external diplomatic campaign to transform the Dominions of what was then commonly known as the British Empire into sovereign independent states within a Commonwealth in which Britain would no longer claim or exercise any authority over the countries enjoying Dominion status. In this diplomatic battle, Canada, for much of the period, played an active part, although the primary impetus in the crucial period from 1926 to 1931 has been attributed – with, I believe, some justice – to the Irish government. Indeed, the extent of the Irish contribution has been well reflected in the title, as well as in the contents, of the authoritative work on the subject by David Harkness: *The Restless Dominion.*

By 1931, British resistance to the sovereignty of the Dominions had been overcome: through the Statute of Westminster of that year, Ireland and Canada, as well as the other Dominions, including a rather reluctant Australia and New Zealand, had secured unfettered sovereignty. But this achievement did not itself satisfy the aspirations of the many Irish people who remained hostile to the monarchical forms of Dominion status, under which the Crown remained the nominal fount of authority in each of the several Dominions. Given the importance of symbols – which in Ireland, as in many other countries, sometimes count for more than reality – this was an important qualification. In these early years of the new State, there were in fact few indications that political independence and sovereignty achieved within a theoretical monarchical structure would induce those who had been defeated in the Civil War to go beyond a mere cessation of hostilities and to accept and join in the political institutions that had been established.

Moreover, even if such a degree of popular acceptance of this status could have been achieved, there was the further potential problem of securing that, if and when the political representatives of the anti-Treaty tradition, having entered parliament, came to secure a popular mandate to govern, the resulting handover of power could be accomplished smoothly and without any attempt to inhibit it on the part of the Irish army. For that army had established the authority of the State during the Civil War and might perhaps be expected not to relish serving within a few years under a government drawn from among those whom they had defeated in that struggle.

In the immediate post–Civil War era, de Valera found himself the leader of a dispirited group, many members of which at that point did not hold him in high regard: they felt that, as a politician, he had not been explicitly republican. In any event, those whom de Valera now led had rejected the constitutional foundations of the new State and were little disposed, as they emerged from internment in 1924, to sit down to work a system they had fought to destroy.

To many people in that situation, the way ahead must have seemed hopeless – and many did indeed give up hope and emigrated to the United States. For what chance was there that, if a political U-turn were to be attempted involving the recognition and acceptance of that which they had just sought to reject in arms, the Irish people would accord respect or support to those who had undertaken this humiliating policy reversal?

And, even if de Valera were to attempt to lead the republicans of the post–Civil War era along such a constitutional path, how many would be willing to follow him? Would that number be sufficient to ensure stability and peace under the new dispensation, or would too many remain outside the system, continuing to challenge its legitimacy and to claim the right, if a suitable opportunity arose, of using arms against it?

It is for the historians to give their verdicts in due course on the manner in which de Valera tackled this problem. In particular, it will be interesting to see to what extent historians eventually judge the events of the period 1926 to 1937 – from the decision to found a constitutional party, Fianna Fáil and to bring it into the Dáil in 1927, to the enactment of the new constitution of 1937 – to have been the result of a plan thought out from the outset, or to have been the product merely of a process of groping towards a goal perhaps only imperfectly defined, even in de Valera's own mind. For the observer of contemporary Ireland, it is sufficient to remark that the outcome of the process started by him in 1926 included a very substantial achievement, in the form of the largely successful conversion of the 1922 Constitution – the verbal formulation of which, although not its real content, had necessarily been determined in a number of key respects by the outside force of the Anglo-Irish Treaty provisions – into a document expressed in the language of nationalism to a degree that would render it acceptable to the vast majority of those who had rejected the Treaty.

Although the resultant reconciliation with republicanism was necessarily incomplete – witness the amount of blood spilt in Ireland, north and south, especially in the past thirty-five years – it would be wrong to underestimate the seminal importance of the process of establishing within the new State a new national consensus.

It is to that achievement that we owe the preservation of peace within this State both during the last war, when the IRA as a result lacked the support needed to create conditions of unrest that might have attracted a German invasion, and again in the early 1970s, when the cohesion of our political system was strong enough to resist the efforts of a handful of misguided politicians to embroil our State in the violence that engulfed Northern Ireland.

The fact that, even today, the extent of the potential dangers we faced on those two occasions remains largely unappreciated by the general public is itself a tribute to the success of de Valera's 'stabilisation' policy. His unexpected decision to oppose the Treaty had severely destabilised the State at the moment of its foundation, greatly increasing the difficulty of mastering the inevitable resistance by extremists to a compromise settlement with Britain. But he spent an important part of his life successfully putting together again the Humpty-Dumpty he had helped push off a wall in December 1921.

The peaceful accession to power of Fianna Fáil under de Valera in 1932, only nine years after the defeat of the republicans in the Civil War, was a seismic event for all those who were politically active at the time. It involved what appeared to contemporaries to be a sharp discontinuity in public policy, especially in the State's relations with Britain – relations that immediately deteriorated into an economic war centring on both constitutional and financial issues.

But from a historic perspective, this discontinuity can be seen to be an illusion. The events between 1932 and 1937, when the new Constitution was enacted, can now be seen to have been rather a continuation under different leadership of the policy of seeking a separation of the new Irish State from Britain that Cumann na nGaedheal had initiated in the 1920s through successful diplomatic action. The difference lay in the fact that the new Fianna Fáil government was not committed to the terms of the 1921 Treaty and felt free to disregard some of its elements.

It was in this light, indeed, that the officials of the Department of External Affairs, as it was then called, seem to have viewed the change of government in 1932, despite the personal ties they had naturally formed with members of the Cumann na nGaedheal government that had appointed them and had built up that department. Certainly, within days of taking over the reins of government in February 1932, de Valera's initial suspicion of that department – which he chose to head himself in addition to leading the government – had dissolved, encouraged by what today reads as a cloyingly sycophantic letter from its permanent head, Joe Walshe. Suspicion was replaced by a conviction that the external-affairs officials saw their role as helping de Valera to pursue the nationalist aim beyond the limits that had been imposed on the former government by their moral obligation to honour the Treaty.

The extent to which members of that first government had felt that this sense of moral obligation tied their hands in moving outside the Treaty obligations cannot be over-estimated, nor should the extent to which this sense of moral obligation was felt by them as a burden inhibiting the realisation of an aspiration which they largely shared with their anti-Treaty opponents. But, unhappily, having achieved sovereign independence within the Commonwealth through the Statute of Westminster, their judgement of de Valera's effort to go further became seriously distorted. This reflected their continuing bitterness at what they saw as his role in the initiation of the Civil War – a role, in their view, motivated by personal vanity and pique rather than by principle.

The fact that complete continuity of public administration was provided after 1932 by the civil service, the army and the police force that had served the Cumann na nGaedheal government during and since the Civil War was an achievement the credit for which must be widely shared: by the public service itself, which thus established its political neutrality in the most difficult circumstances possible; by the outgoing government, which had consciously prepared the way for the changeover, including in particular W. T. Cosgrave and my own father, Desmond FitzGerald, whom Cosgrave appointed as minister of defence with the task of taking tough steps to ensure that the army would be loyal to a future Fianna Fáil government; and, of course, by de Valera himself, who effectively resisted great pressure to purge the army, the police and the public administration that he had inherited. In this respect Ireland differed from many other states that emerged from colonial rule. Apart from removing two police officers, he resisted this pressure – which paralleled very closely the pressures, documented in minutes of party meetings, which the Cumann na nGaedheal government had faced from its supporters in 1923 to purge its new administration of those who had served under the British government.

The Constitution of 1937 came to provide the basis for a consensus on which the modern Irish State has been built. It represented an assertion of sovereignty in terms more acceptable to nationalists than those of the Statute of Westminster six years earlier. That statute had secured sovereign independence for the Dominions, including the Irish State. In international law, this independence clearly included the right to leave the Commonwealth as well as the right to remain neutral in a conflict involving Great Britain. But many British politicians cherished the illusion that the member states of the Commonwealth, whilst independent, must necessarily join with Britain in any major war in which she was engaged – relying in some cases upon the abstract concept of the indivisibility of the Crown.

For many Irish people, and particularly for de Valera himself, however, the right to remain neutral, and the assertion of that right, was an ultimate test of sovereignty and independence. A practical obstacle to the exercise of this right was the continued occupation and use of certain port facilities in the Irish State by British forces under the terms of the Treaty. In 1938, as part of the settlement that ended the Economic War, de Valera negotiated the return of these facilities and the departure of British forces. Despite discussion during these negotiations of a possible defence pact between the Irish Free State and Great Britain, this evacuation was eventually secured without any commitment to make these bases available again in time of war.

That obstacle to neutrality having been removed, de Valera – who was by that time disillusioned by the collapse of collective security under the League of Nations, first in the case of Manchuria and later in the case of Italy's invasion of Abyssinia – declared Irish neutrality, and maintained formal neutrality throughout the war – while at the same time secretly working closely with the British authorities. This policy commanded the full support of the political opposition, with the single outstanding exception of James Dillon, who, after US entry into the war in 1942, retired as deputy leader of the principal opposition party, Fine Gael, and became an independent member of the Dáil on the issue of Ireland not declaring war on Nazi Germany.

While the assertion of Irish sovereignty may have been the primary motivation of neutrality, it would be wrong to suggest that it was the sole consideration for de Valera, or indeed that it played any part in the ready acceptance of this policy by his political opponents. Amongst all political parties, there was, I believe, the further, powerful – albeit for obvious reasons unspoken – consideration that to have entered voluntarily into the conflict on the Allied side within sixteen years of the end of a Civil War would have created the danger of a revival of that bitter conflict. This perceived danger had been increased by the IRA's decision, announced shortly before the outbreak of war, to 'declare war' on Britain and to set off bombs in British cities. As was very clear in Spain during the last quarter of a century of Franco's rule, a people who have experienced a Civil War will go to immense lengths to avoid a recurrence of it.

The significance of this factor in securing all-party support for neutrality has, I believe, been underestimated by historians because, during the Second World War, it was never explicitly stated by any politician of any party – for obvious reasons. But it was, I believe, subsequently

mentioned in retrospective interviews by two senior Fianna Fáil politicians, Seán Lemass and Sean McEntee – and, I believe, it explains my own
father's support for neutrality, despite his deep personal commitment to
the Allied cause.

Of course, de Valera also used another argument for neutrality, viz.
that, so long as Ireland remained politically divided, with part of the
island under British sovereignty, the Irish State should not engage in hostilities as an ally of Britain. The employment of this argument – largely,
perhaps, for tactical political reasons at the time – laid the ground for the
decision by a later Irish government, led by de Valera's opponents, with
Seán MacBride as minister for external affairs, not to join NATO in 1949
– a decision that subsequently hardened into a commitment to neutrality
that has survived to the present day.

This commitment has in more recent years been strongly held by
many who have forgotten the fact that partition had been presented as the
initial rationale of this policy, and who know nothing of the pragmatic
basis for wartime neutrality – the fear of a renewal of civil war. There are
indeed many today who would wish Irish neutrality to be maintained even
if the North and South of the island were to be brought together
politically.

What is more generally recognised by historians, however, is the
extent to which the consensus on neutrality, as well as the entry into the
army in 1940 of many children of the leading members of both political
parties, healed the divisions of the Civil War, uniting all in a common
cause.

To return to de Valera's concern to legitimise the Irish State in the eyes of
republicans, there was a price to be paid for this, for it was inevitable that
the single-mindedness with which de Valera felt it necessary to pursue this
goal would impinge unfavourably on the attainment of certain other
objectives. First, by pressing ahead to remove the Crown from the
Constitution – while avoiding at that stage declaring the State to be a
Republic – and by the insertion in the new Constitution of certain provisions designed to secure the assent of as many republicans as possible,
and of other provisions designed to head off any potential opposition
from the Roman Catholic Church, de Valera certainly made the resolution

of the problem of Northern Ireland more difficult – to a greater extent than he himself perhaps recognised.

From the outset, the Northern Ireland entity had been based on shaky foundations. First of all, its boundaries were, of course, arbitrary – chosen to maximise the territory involved, subject to a concern to limit the Catholic nationalist minority to one-third of the population.

And second, whatever may have been said publicly at that time, I believe that the most that many unionists then hoped to secure from this arrangement was a temporary postponement of the united Ireland that had been clearly envisaged as an eventual outcome in the British Act establishing a Northern Ireland parliament in 1920.

The survival of Northern Ireland for eighty-five years, and the determination of the majority of its unionist population today to resist unification, obscures the possibility, that if the Irish State had evolved in a different way, the North–South relationship might also have turned out differently during this period. Even in 1937, when de Valera presented his new Constitution to the people, a sense of the temporary character of the arrangement under which Northern Ireland remained part of the United Kingdom was, I believe, still an underlying feature of northern unionist opinion – despite the rhetoric of 'no surrender'. This is an under-researched element of the history of this island – partly, of course, because it is not documented, belonging as it does more to the minds rather than to the words and actions of those involved.

The Constitution of 1937 helped to harden northern unionist attitudes in three respects. First, the elimination of the Crown from the Constitution offended the monarchist sentiments of most northern unionists. Second, the unionists were upset at the inclusion in this Constitution of provisions which had found no place in the 1922 Constitution and which seemed to involve a claim to sovereignty over Northern Ireland on behalf of the government and parliament elected in the truncated Irish State (albeit a claim that was accompanied by an abrogation in practice of this claim to sovereignty).

Third, the inclusion of a provision recognising 'the special position of the Catholic, Apostolic and Holy Roman Church as the guardian of the faith of the great majority of the people' (a provision which, however, also recognised a list of named Protestant Churches and the Jewish community, and which was eliminated from the Constitution in 1972 by an overwhelming majority in a popular referendum) served to confirm northern unionist prejudices about the predominantly Roman Catholic character of the new Irish State. This view, incidentally, found further confirmation in unionists' eyes in another new provision banning legislation for the dissolution of marriage. While most Protestants in Ireland at that time did not personally favour divorce for religious reasons, they saw this new constitutional provision as evidence that the Catholic Church wielded influence over the government of the Irish State.

Finally, the policy of neutrality in the Second World War, designed both to proclaim Irish sovereignty and to maintain the consensus painfully brought about over the preceding years regarding the legitimacy of the Irish State, had the effect of further alienating unionist opinion in Northern Ireland and of greatly increasing British sympathy for the unionist position. This was a further inevitable but unintended consequence of the policy to which de Valera had in practice given priority since the immediate post–Civil War period, viz. the achievement of a more complete separation of the Irish State from Britain.

Thus, in pursuing the unspoken objective of establishing the Irish State on a solid domestic foundation that would command the loyalty of all but a handful of its people, de Valera had found it necessary to pursue a course that divided this State more deeply from Northern Ireland and made re-unification more difficult, more distant, and more problematic. This was paradoxical, because he himself frequently publicly proclaimed the reunification of Ireland as one of the two major national aims – the other, and prior, aim being the revival of the Irish language.

De Valera's real order of priorities was, however, disclosed in a speech in reply to a debate in the Senate on 7 of February 1939. There, in his customary, rather tortured style, he said:

> Although freedom for a part of this island is not the freedom we want – the freedom we would like to have – this freedom for a portion of it, freedom to develop and to keep the kernel of the Irish nation, is something, and something that I would not sacrifice, if by sacrificing it we were to get a united Ireland and that united Ireland was not free to determine its own form of government, to determine its relations with other countries and, amongst

other things, to determine, for example, whether it would or would not be involved in war.

The relationship he saw between neutrality and sovereignty is there suggested, as well as the priority he always in practice accorded to the achievement and maintenance of the sovereignty of the partitioned Irish State, as against the political reunification of the island. In the same speech, he even made it clear that reunification was not just second, but actually third in order of priority in his mind: for he emphasised that the object of restoring Irish as the spoken language of the majority of the people also took priority over reunification:

> For instance, speaking for myself – I am not talking about gov-
> ernment policy in the matter, which has been largely embodied in
> the Constitution – I would not tomorrow, for the sake of a unit-
> ed Ireland, give up the policy of trying to make this a really Irish
> Ireland – not by any means. If I were told tomorrow: 'You can
> have a united Ireland if you give up your idea of the national lan-
> guage to be the spoken language of the majority of the people, I
> would for myself say, No. I do not know how many would agree
> with me. I would say No, and I would say it for this reason, that I
> believe that as long as the language remains, you have a distin-
> guishing characteristic of nationality which will enable the nation
> to persist. If you lose the language, the danger is that there would
> be absorption.

On the issue of partition itself, as distinct from the priority that he accorded to it, it is evident from the many oscillations in the position he took up in relation to Northern Ireland that de Valera himself shared to a great degree the ambivalence and confusion of thought about the nature of Irish nationhood which was a feature of Irish nationalism throughout the twentieth century. Even in the brief period between 1917 and 1921, his ideas on this subject seem to have gone through several phases. As John Bowman has pointed out in *De Valera and the Ulster Question*, in 1917–18 de Valera advocated the expulsion or coercion of northern unionists. In 1919–20, when in the United States, he modified this position to one of proposing that northern unionists should be assimilated into the new Irish Ireland. And in 1921, when the issue of partition had to be faced in a practical way in preparing for the Treaty negotiations, he shifted his position to one of accommodating the unionists within a federal Ireland which would be externally associated with the British Commonwealth. Indeed, at that time he even went so far as to propose that individual Ulster counties should have the right to opt out of the new Irish State.

There were further changes of approach on de Valera's part later, and it is not easy to detect any consistent pattern through these changes. It is possible, however, that the view to which he ultimately came – and one which is in fact strikingly relevant to the problem as it is now seen by many people in both parts of Ireland after decades of continuous violence – was expressed in a speech made towards the end of his first sixteen-year term of office as head of the Irish government. On 24 June 1947, he rejected, as he had done so often before, the use of force as a solution:

> I believe that [partition] cannot be solved, in any circumstances that we can now see, by force, and that if it were solved by force, it would leave a situation behind it which would mean that this State would be in an unstable position.

And he went on to observe that the problem was one primarily between North and South, and that Britain was not the ultimate obstacle to a solution – something that is now very generally understood in Ireland, although still not grasped by some Irish-Americans:

> In order to end [partition] you will have to get concurrence of wills between three parties – we here, who represent the people of this part of Ireland; those who represent the majority in the separated part of Ireland; and the will of those who are the majority for the time being in the British Parliament. It is true, I think, that if there were agreement between the peoples of the two parts of Ireland, British consent to do the things that they would have to do could be secured.

In an earlier period, Britain's emotional and strategic commitment to Northern Ireland was, of course, a major additional obstacle to a united Ireland, but the disappearance of these factors in the later decades of the twentieth century has revealed, in stark relief, the fact that, as de Valera implicitly recognised in that 1947 speech, the fundamental obstacle to the political unity of Ireland is the attitude of the northern unionist population. And this is a problem that the irredentist policies pursued by de Valera long after he made that speech – policies that from 1949 until at least 1969 came to be pursued also by other parties in the Irish State – served to intensify, rather than to moderate.

From the outset, the new State had a clear choice between two approaches to the definition of its identity. The State could have founded itself on the tradition of the leaders of the Rebellions of 1798 and 1848, who, influenced by the French and American Revolutions, had proclaimed that the national objective must be to unite Catholic, Protestant and Dissenter in the common name of 'Irishman'. This would have entailed adopting an overtly pluralist approach, in both religious and cultural matters, placing the different religious on a genuinely equal footing and recognising the Irish and English languages as equally valid alternative means of expressing the Irish identity.

The path that was actually chosen by the new State in these matters was a very different one, however. In relation to the language, a clear policy had already begun to emerge during the period of Cumann na nGaedheal government, when de Valera was still in unconstitutional opposition. The language policy that was then adopted was determined by the sense of indebtedness felt by the leaders of the national political movement which was to emerge in the late nineteenth and early twentieth centuries towards the language movement, within which so many of them had found their initial national inspiration – and had, in many cases (including that of my own parents), also found each other.

The pursuit of the objective of the revival of the Irish language had led, even before the First World War, to the introduction of an Irish-language requirement for entry to the colleges of the new National University of Ireland – to which, until the 1970s, the Catholic majority in the greater part of the island almost exclusively went in search of university education. This had a profound influence on the teaching of the language at secondary level. But in the early years of the new State, Cosgrave's Cumann na nGaedheal government also decided to make the

Irish language a required subject both at primary level and in the national Intermediate-level School Certificate Examinations, which students took at the age of fifteen or sixteen.

When he came to power, de Valera went on to extend this policy by making the Irish language an essential element in the school Leaving Certificate itself, which was taken at the age of seventeen or eighteen and was the qualification that was used by most employers as an educational test for recruitment purposes, especially for clerical employment. Moreover, as mentioned earlier, in his speeches de Valera elevated the revival of the Irish language to the status of the first national aim, taking precedence even over national reunification.

By making Irish an essential requirement for so many purposes, and by requiring a knowledge of Irish for entry to and promotion within the public service, in the hope of reviving a language which had been moving towards extinction for several centuries before the State was founded, successive governments were effectively making a choice *against* a culturally pluralist society. For this process involved *de facto* – though unintended – discrimination against people of the Protestant tradition, north or south, whose culture had effectively always been exclusively English-speaking. And this was of course also true of other subcultures that had developed amongst the many Roman Catholics who, in the cities and towns, and throughout most of Leinster and parts of other provinces, had been English-speaking for several centuries.

By the 1950s, the retention of the Irish-language requirement for the purposes of school-examination certificates and entry and promotion within the public service had started to become a controversial political issue. Nonetheless, during the long continuous period in office of the Fianna Fáil Party from 1957 to 1973, no change was made to this policy.

Seán Lemass and Jack Lynch, de Valera's successors as Taoiseach after his elevation to the constitutional presidency in 1959, were unwilling to tackle this problem – at least in de Valera's lifetime. It was left to the National Coalition government of 1973–77, led by Liam Cosgrave, the son of W. T. Cosgrave, whose government had initiated this policy in all good faith in the 1920s, to make the changes that eliminated discrimination in examinations and in public employment against Irish people whose cultural tradition is non-Gaelic. Nevertheless, the Irish language remains one of the three core subjects in all primary schools and is still taught throughout the second-level cycle to all pupils. It also still remains a requirement for matriculation to the four NUI universities.

Religious pluralism is a somewhat different issue. Just as he intensified the divisive impact of the language policy formulated by his predecessors, so also did de Valera's religious policy drive a second wedge between north and south. The 1922 Constitution had at least proclaimed a form of separation between Church and State, forbidding the endowment of religion by the State, although this did not inhibit state support for an educational system that had always divided along religious lines – at all levels, including the State's own primary-school system. Nor did it prevent some of the State's leaders from addressing the Holy See in terms of 'filial piety'.

But in relation to religious pluralism, de Valera had to dispel lingering suspicions amongst the Catholic Church authorities about his party – suspicions that derived from pronouncements by the Catholic hierarchy of the early 1920s against those who had opposed the Treaty in arms during the Civil War. And he also had reason to fear that the triumphalist attitudes that were prevalent in the Catholic Church in the 1930s might lead the institutional Church to oppose his new Constitution unless he gave some kind of formal recognition to that Church.

This led de Valera to include in that Constitution the provisions already referred to in relation to the specific position of the Catholic Church as the guardian of the faith of the great majority of the people, as well as a constitutional ban on legislation for divorce, and other provisions in relation to education and private property – to all of which he then added non-judiciable provisions on social policy which derived directly from Catholic social teaching of that period.

All this must, of course, be seen in the context of a situation where de Valera was under considerable pressure from Rome to declare Ireland to be a Catholic State (a constitutional proposal which he firmly resisted), although, oddly enough, in speeches in relation to the State, he often used this phrase loosely himself. It must also be said that the Protestant Churches did not object to these constitutional provisions at the time they were enacted, and that de Valera, like his predecessor W. T. Cosgrave a fervent Catholic, subsequently gained the respect of the leaders of the

Protestant community in the Irish State and also at various stages in his career showed a measure of independence vis-à-vis the Catholic Church authorities. Although de Valera can be criticised in the light of hindsight for not having sustained religious pluralism in its fullest sense, like most of his supporters, and also his opponents, he was inevitably influenced in this by the climate of opinion of his time.

De Valera's protectionist economic policies, designed to make Ireland economically self-sufficient, also proved divisive vis-à-vis Northern Ireland, because they involved imposing restrictions on imports from that part of the island. In fairness, it must be said that almost none of those who emerged from the struggle for independence and survived the Civil War, on either side, had any deep interest in or understanding of economic or social questions: de Valera himself certainly did not have such an interest. But when he came to power in 1932, the Cabinet that he led initiated significant economic changes that profoundly influenced the future economic development of the Irish State.

There are several ironies here. First, the policy of industrial protection which de Valera implemented in the autarkic climate of the early 1930s had in fact been proclaimed as a nationalist dogma by Arthur Griffith, the leader of the pro-Treaty government who died during the Civil War. But Griffith's successors in the Cumann na nGaedheal government of 1922 to 1932 had not felt able to pursue to any significant degree a policy that would have been in sharp conflict with the free-trade spirit of the 1920s. Such a policy might, they feared, have provoked from other states retaliatory measures which could have been very damaging to a small, export-dependent economy, such as Ireland's was.

In hesitating to initiate such a radical policy, that government had also been influenced by a more general consideration, viz. its concern with the establishment of the new State's credibility and credit vis-à-vis the outside world, a consideration to which the government attached an overriding importance.

Although de Valera almost certainly did not realise the impact that a protectionist economic policy would have on Irish politics, by implementing in the quite different conditions of the 1930s the protectionist policy formulated by Griffith, he laid the foundations of two new classes –

protected industrialists and industrial workers – whose consequent support for Fianna Fáil across the class barrier came to supplement the support of most small farmers, which this party had held from the outset. From this combination of sectoral groups that party thereafter derived its remarkable strength, both financial and electoral, which enabled it to secure between 44 and 51 percent of the popular vote at a score of general elections during the first half-century of the party's existence.

De Valera envisaged protection as a means of making Ireland more self-sufficient and less dependent on trade and on exchanges with an outside world, which he regarded as ultimately dangerous to the Irish sense of identity. Yet, ironically, the consequences of his protectionist policy were in fact to reduce Ireland's self-sufficiency sharply, as materials for industrial processing flowed in and as the new class of industrial workers spent much of their wages on imported goods. By the time protection was firmly in place, around 1950, the share of external trade in Ireland's economy had consequently risen by almost a third, leaving the State much *less* self-sufficient than it had been when de Valera came to power!

The protectionist policy secured the establishment of many small and generally unspecialised industries. The efficiency of these industries was relatively low because of the very high level of protection afforded to them, but they eventually provided an industrial base much of which was capable of being converted – albeit painfully and at great cost – to an industrial structure of which more than half survived the freeing of trade with Britain after 1965, and with other EC countries after 1973.

But despite such moves as the establishment by the Inter-Party Government in 1949 of the Industrial Development Authority (which had a little-exercised tariff-review function), this process of reorientation of industry towards export markets was continued long after the time when it should have been phased out in the early 1950s. This delay, for which de Valera's continued leadership of Fianna Fáil well beyond the age of seventy was almost certainly largely responsible, contributed substantially to the economic stagnation of the Irish State during the 1950s, a time when in most other countries national output expanded rapidly,

If de Valera had contested the constitutional presidency in 1952, his elevation to that position might have left the way clear for his eventual energetic successor, Seán Lemass, to tackle this problem when Fianna Fáil were in office later in that decade. In the event, action was delayed until

October 1956, when a subsequent coalition government started to challenge the traditional economic policies of protection and hostility to foreign investment – a policy reversal that was then vigorously expanded and developed by Seán Lemass when he became Taoiseach following de Valera's belated election as president at the age of seventy-six.

De Valera was a natural conservative: he venerated the past and wished to keep 'the old way'. Frugal in his own ways of life, like many of his generation who had entered politics via an idealistic national movement, he was unambiguously anti-materialistic. In his conservatism, he did not differ much from most of his political opponents. They had all become engaged before or during the First World War in a nationalist movement that, despite James Connolly's participation in the 1916 Rising, had for the most part little about it that was radical.

De Valera's social philosophy was expressed in a St Patrick's Day broadcast in 1943. This broadcast, with its reference to maidens dancing at the crossroads, has often been made the subject of humorous comment, and its language certainly sounds strange to modern ears. Nonetheless, it should be seen as the simple but sincere aspiration of a romantic conservative, talking in the kind of terms that may have been common enough during his childhood more than a century ago. However, in the mid-twentieth century, and in the course of the most destructive war in history, these aspirations were so far removed from reality that they served only to highlight the difficulty of posing any alternative to the growth of materialism in an increasingly urbanised society.

In this respect, de Valera outlasted his own era and became irrelevant as an ideologue for the new generations that were growing up in the middle decades of the twentieth century. Ireland was moving on beyond him, to become an industrialised society with increasingly materialistic values.

De Valera's most enduring achievement lies, I believe, in the manner in which he made the assertion of sovereignty not just an end in itself but also the means of securing assent by the vast majority of those who, with him, had challenged in arms the legitimacy of the State that had been established under the leadership of his predecessor, W. T. Cosgrave. De

Valera himself does not seem himself to have articulated this objective clearly, however. Perhaps he recognised that he could not do so without endangering the achievement of this objective and that it could best be secured by subtlety and stealth. In any event, he dedicated an important part of his political career to this process.

The dissonances of party politics have perhaps hidden from supporters of either of the main political traditions of the Irish State the extent to which its first two governments, and their leaders, Cosgrave and de Valera, were successively responsible in different ways for establishing that State on a rock-like and enduring foundation. The aims to which de Valera himself gave priority in his utterance were, of course, quite different: maximising Irish sovereignty, reviving the Irish language and unifying Ireland politically. But he – and others – failed to halt the long-term decline of the Irish language as a national means of communication, and he may even have contributed to some degree to the rate of this decline by endorsing and extending increasingly unpopular measures taken by his predecessors in office to make the language an essential element in the educational system and in public employment.

At the same time, the methods that he found it necessary to employ in order to secure his objectives of sovereignty and legitimisation of the State in the eyes of all but a dissident handful of its citizens helped to undermine seriously, perhaps fatally, the prospect of making progress on the second national aim, of political unification. And his intensification of the language-revival policy, together with the concessions he felt it necessary to make to the institutional Catholic Church when drafting his Constitution, raised formidable additional obstacles to Irish unification – to which, by his own admission, he never gave a high priority.

The price we have had to pay for de Valera's successful post–Civil War stabilisation of our State has been substantial and enduring. In the economic sphere, he sought self-sufficiency through industrialisation but in fact achieved industrialisation with a reduction in self-sufficiency. In the social sphere, his influence was extremely limited because his conservatism – to which in today's more materialistic Irish society, only a small minority still looks back with nostalgia – was too much a product of the nineteenth century to make an effective impact on the Ireland of the mid-twentieth century.

In the world outside Ireland, however, he added to his country's stature. A controversial figure at home, and for much of the time in his relations with Britain, he became known worldwide as an apostle of nationalism, but was also an exponent in the 1930s of other values, such as the concept of collective security, which he sought, in vain, to have established through the League of Nations.

Many facets of his character and career will for a long time remain a puzzle to historians, for he was an enigmatic man. Deeply concerned about the historical judgements that would be made about him, he sought to influence these consciously both through an 'authorised biography' and by calling together a group of historians to hear his answers to pre-pared questions relating to his career. Even today, judgements about de Valera are bound to be no more than provisional, both because we are still too close to the man himself – he died only three decades ago – and because much research remains to be undertaken, and many veils remain to be lifted, before the achievements and failures of this remarkable Irishman can be definitively evaluated.

5

The First Government

Establishing a Stable State

The subject of the foundation of the Irish State is a vast one. I have already written at some length in my previous book Reflections on the Irish State on what seems to me to have been the reasons why it was necessary, in the interests of a majority of the Irish people, for such a State to come into existence.

Our State found its origins in what might be described as an anti-colonial war fought within part of a well-established but culturally diverse parliamentary democratic structure. Perhaps because of this, the State's founders included very different kinds of people. I shall try to disentangle the tensions that divided the leadership of the first government of the State during its early years – a subject about which we have known very little until quite recently. These tensions and divisions led, within two years of the foundation of the State, to a grave crisis among the leadership, but the intense patriotism and commitment to the common good of these political leaders, and their sublimation of personal ambition, led them ultimately to overcome these tensions. As a result, our State was built on foundations that proved capable of surviving many severe tests in the remaining decades of the twentieth century.

There were also separate, but in some respects similar, tensions between the Cumann na nGaedheal Party, founded in April 1923, and the government that it had been established to support. An understanding of this is necessary in order to explain why, for much of the twentieth century, the circumstances of that party's origins condemned it, and its successor party, Fine Gael, to a less successful political role than Fianna Fáil.

Third, I shall mention some of the achievements of that first government but, because these are fairly well known – even if they are not universally recognised or adequately appreciated – I shall treat them more briefly than they deserve. Finally, I shall reflect briefly on some of the problems that this early period of the history of the State left for subsequent generations to overcome – in some respects very successfully – in the second half of the twentieth century.

In all of this I have to acknowledge a major debt to John Regan's *The Irish Counter-Revolution*, a book which, although it is in my view marred by interpretative defects and some linguistic excesses (including an attempt to prove a somewhat strained thesis about counter-revolution), revealed for the first time the full details of the dramatic events of those early years. As someone whose father was deeply involved in those events – of which, however, he never spoke to me – and as someone who subsequently led Fine Gael, the successor party to Cumann na nGaedheal, this book relieved much of the frustration I felt when, in that position, I remained largely ignorant of the early history of the party, and thus of our State.

Let me start at the beginning. At the end of the Treaty Debate in early January 1922, de Valera resigned as president of the Dáil Cabinet and Arthur Griffith was elected in his place by the Second Dáil, which comprised the Sinn Féin majority of those who had been elected in June 1921 to the Southern Parliament established under the the Government of Ireland Act 1920.

Five days later, the Southern Parliament itself (comprising the pro-Treaty southern Ireland Dáil members and the Dublin University members) met and elected a parallel Provisional Government under Michael Collins's chairmanship, as provided by the Treaty. Thenceforward, until 6 December 1922, these two governments ran in parallel. That Dáil Government, and subsequent ones until 1927, had only seven members, as in the pre-Treaty Government, but there were a number of non-Cabinet ministers or directors of various subsidiary bodies. Ernest Blythe and my father, Desmond FitzGerald, had held office in this form since 1919. As it happens, Blythe and my father, together with Cosgrave, were the longest-serving members of the 1919–32 governments.

Let me now jump ahead from January to the death of Michael Collins on 22 August 1922. News of Collins's death reached Dublin at 3 AM on 23 August, and Cosgrave was chosen as president of the Executive Council by consensus at a meeting of the Cabinet, law officers, army leaders and Dick Hayes TD that lasted from four until seven thirty that morning.

Kevin O'Higgins was unhappy at this choice, he told Minister for Defence and Chief of Staff Richard Mulcahy. O'Higgins had worked under Cosgrave in the very successful 'underground' department of local government, and thus knew Cosgrave well; he had, for whatever reason, formed a negative view of him. Whether, if there had been a vote, O'Higgins would actually have supported Mulcahy instead of Cosgrave, as Mulcahy believed, is less certain.

It was recognised at the time that Cosgrave would make an uncharismatic leader, but he was seen as being preferable to the two alternatives – Mulcahy and O'Higgins. Mulcahy was seen as indecisive and pedantic – and too close to the army; O'Higgins was viewed then as something of a 'wild card', and not sufficiently republican. Cosgrave, by contrast, offered continuity and stability, and had an excellent administrative record and longer political experience than anyone else. Moreover, he had already been chairing the government since Collins had become commander-in-chief in July – although Collins had continued to exercise authority from a distance.

Collins himself had opposed a meeting of the Dáil whilst the fighting continued, but after his death Cosgrave, having been chosen informally as president, immediately called the Third Dáil into session for the first time. The Labour Party had been threatening to withdraw from the Dáil if such a meeting was not held. The IRB was also dissolved immediately: with Collins gone, it was seen as having no role, although unhappily, as we shall see, it was informally re-established three months later by some of the army chiefs. Cosgrave was formally elected president of the Executive Council by the Dáil on 9 September.

O'Higgins came back from the army to the department of home affairs and was made vice-president in December. He had seen the revolution primarily as involving Ireland getting its own parliament – and was viewed by the anti-Treaty wing of the national movement as being out of sympathy with the Irish language, autarky, republicanism and militarism.

For his part, Mulcahy saw himself as something of an outsider – remaining during the early stages of the Civil War in Dublin with the army in Portobello, rather than with the other ministers in Government Buildings. He was seen as being primarily loyal to the army.

There were tensions amongst the ministers from the start. O'Higgins, FitzGerald and Patrick Hogan were a group of civilian-oriented ministers who were concerned about parliamentary democracy and the need to establish a democratic system within which the army would be under firm civilian control. All three were French-oriented. They were joined later in Cabinet by Patrick McGilligan, who had been serving in the High Commission Office in London. These four became known to some as the 'Donnybrook set'. Of this group, all but Desmond FitzGerald were UCD graduates. FitzGerald, who had been born and brought up in London, had no third-level education. He had come to live in Kerry in 1913 to participate in what he hoped would become a national movement for independence. He was a poet and had lived for several years in France. Mulcahy, who had studied as a night student at Bolton Street in Dublin (now part of the Dublin Institute of Technology), is said to have disliked FitzGerald.

Blythe was a Protestant from Armagh who, at the age of twenty-four, had gone to Kerry to learn Irish and had met Desmond FitzGerald there. After the September 1923 general election, Cosgrave delegated the finance portfolio to him. In the Cabinet, Blythe was probably closest to Cosgrave, who, however, kept himself somewhat apart from his ministers – as the leader of any government has to do. Eventually, however, at the time of the Army Mutiny, Blythe sided with the civilian ministers.

Professor Eoin MacNeill was by far the most senior of the ministers. Intellectually, he 'towered over all', but he was ineffective as a minister. In fact, he spent much of the early months of the Civil War working on a translation of the Four Masters manuscript!

Finally, Joe McGrath, an activist during the War of Independence, had been appointed by Collins as director of intelligence in 1922 and was put in charge of Oriel House in Westland Row, which had a bad reputation for ill-treating prisoners. He had been appointed to the government later that year when he failed in an attempt to persuade Labour to nominate a minister.

In the very different backgrounds of these men one can find the seeds of the Army Mutiny of 1924.

O'Higgins was to describe the Civil War government as 'Eight young men in the City Hall standing in the ruins of one administration, with the foundations of another not yet laid, and with wild men screaming through the keyholes.' Initially, the members of the government, effectively besieged in Government Buildings, slept mostly on the floor there; only the president of the Executive Council, Arthur Griffith, had a bed. Some were accompanied by their wives, although my mother, Mabel, who was opposed to the Treaty, remained at home in Marlborough Road, Donnybrook with her three children. Some civil servants also lived with the ministers in Government Buildings.

In late September 1922, the government introduced in the Dáil an Army Emergency Powers Resolution, which resulted in the setting up of military courts with the power to sentence to death. After the rejection by republicans in mid-October of an amnesty, the first four executions of arms-carrying republicans occurred; these were followed shortly afterwards by that of Erskine Childers, publicist for the anti-Treaty movement. The government took the view that, having executed four republican 'foot soldiers', they could not exempt from execution one of the leaders of the republican cause. Childers was found guilty of what had been made a capital offence – being in possession of a small revolver that had been given to him by Collins long before this. It is difficult to acquit the government of prejudice against Childers, an Englishman who had, absurdly, been suspected by Griffith of being a British agent, engaged in fomenting a civil war in order to give the British a chance to bring their troops back to Ireland to restore peace in the country!

Immediately after those executions, the republican military leader, Liam Lynch, issued an order for the killing of fourteen categories of people – including Dáil deputies, senators, newspaper executives, 'hostile' journalists and other 'aggressive Treaty supporters'. After the implementation of this order with the killing of Deputy Sean Hales, the government, under pressure from the army, ordered the execution without trial of four IRA prisoners.

It is very hard for us today to accept or justify these acts. But theirs was a very different world from ours – one where the death penalty was universally accepted, although the four executions without trial were, of course, widely condemned. The government firmly believed that only by means of such executions could the State be saved from anarchy. At least some modern historians are inclined to feel that, by thus halting the campaign to murder deputies and others, the republicans were in fact deprived of the only means by which their revolt might have defeated the government.

As far as I am aware, none of the ministers who took these decisions ever expressed any doubts or regrets about them, and executions of convicted IRA men, after trial for murder, continued under de Valera up to the end of the Second World War.

The origins of the Army Mutiny seem to have lain in the fact that, at the outset of the Civil War, Collins appointed to the leadership of the army fellow members of the IRB – but not his own closest followers, the Active Service Unit, or 'Squad', who owed a special loyalty to him, but whom he seems to have seen in a different light from those he put in charge of the army. If Collins had survived, this might not have mattered, but after his death it proved immensely divisive.

Under Collins, the army leaders rapidly built up a force of fifty-five thousand men, many of whom, including half the officers, had served earlier in British forces. As was the case in respect of the civil administration, Collins's concern was always with efficiency. After his death, however, members of his Squad, and others who had not been promoted to high positions in the army, became disgruntled with being sidelined, as they saw it. Although they were at war with the republicans, they were themselves more republican than most of the Cabinet. Seeing former Irish officers of the British army being made senior to them, they became deeply resentful of what they came to see as a 'pro-British' trend in both the army command and the Cabinet.

In December 1922, one of this group, Liam Tobin, called together some anti-IRB officers who formed the IRAO – the Irish Republican Army Organisation. From then on, that body put the Army Command and the Cabinet under pressure. Cosgrave met them several times in 1923, in an attempt to humour them. The Cabinet could not afford to allow this dissent to emerge publicly prior to the September 1923 election, upon which might depend the willingness not merely of part of the electorate but also of the largely unionist banks to support the government. Meanwhile, the generals had responded to this development by reviving the IRB – thus dividing the army between two secret bodies.

Mulcahy, who was supportive of the army chiefs (he himself seems to have been an IRB member, although fairly junior in that organisation), and resistant to the IRAO, finally agreed in July 1923 to support Cosgrave's policy of containment. But when, just months after the election, demobilisation began, Mulcahy ignored requests from the IRAO not to demobilise some of their officers.

When, in November, sixty IRA officers who had mutinied against demobilisation were expelled without pay, the government moved to establish a committee, comprising MacNeill, Blythe and McGrath – the latter being sympathetic to the IRAO – to supervise future demobilisation. After a threat by McGrath to resign from this committee, the government eventually agreed that the committee could act retrospectively and review previous demobilisations.

All of these events undermined the authority of the Army Council, and at the same time the government's confidence in that body was weakened by allegations that it was favouring IRB officers. Meanwhile, the situation was further complicated by the fact that relations between Mulcahy and O'Higgins – the latter of whom, as minister for home affairs, was in charge of the police led by Commissioner General Eoin O'Duffy – had seriously deteriorated. O'Higgins had all along been most unhappy with army indiscipline and with the unwillingness of the army leaders, including Mulcahy, to deal with this problem.

The situation was further complicated by the fact that Mulcahy and the army leaders were also, without the knowledge of the government, contemplating some kind of reconciliation with the defeated IRA – something to which the more hardline O'Higgins was completely opposed.

Late on the night of 3 March 1924, Cosgrave was handed an ultimatum from the IRAO demanding the dismissal of the Army Council, the suspension of demobilisation and a tougher attitude towards the British in relation to implementation of the Treaty provisions. Part of the army was in revolt.

On the following night, Mulcahy, without government authority, ordered his colleague McGrath's house to be searched, and McGrath resigned. Next day, over Mulcahy's head, O'Duffy was appointed GOC (general officer commanding) and Inspector General of the army. A Cumann na nGaedheal parliamentary-party meeting sympathised with McGrath in this affair, and Mulcahy found no support there. But there was a danger that McGrath would make an inflammatory speech in the Dáil.

The IRAO then started to climb down, and the government, fearing the damage that a Dáil statement by McGrath might do, offered an amnesty to the IRAO, and an army inquiry. At that point, Cosgrave retired ill, leaving O'Higgins in charge. Long afterwards, both General Michael Joe Costello and General Sean MacEoin said that what actually happened was that Cosgrave had been hoping that O'Higgins would overreact and possibly leave the government. There is an implication that O'Higgins might have charged him with such a ploy and then required him to retire for a period with a diplomatic 'illness'. Certainly Mrs Mulcahy later said that Mrs Cosgrave had visited her during the crisis and had told her that O'Higgins wanted Cosgrave to resign.

Whatever the truth of all of this, O'Higgins took over *de facto* control of the government. An army raid on Devlin's Hotel (where Tobin and his allies were located), in defiance of the government amnesty (although, it must be said, authorised by Diarmaid Ó hEigartaigh, the Secretary to the Government) gave him a somewhat dubious excuse to sack Mulcahy – consent for this action having first been secured from Cosgrave at home – and with him to sack also the entire Army Council.

O'Higgins then went to the Dáil and made the speech that it had been feared earlier that McGrath would make, announcing that Tobin and his allies would not be returning to the army, which had of course been expected in the light of the earlier amnesty. The boil had been successfully lanced.

Some days later, Cosgrave returned, taking on the defence portfolio, which he retained for the following eight months. O'Higgins's former secretary, Paddy McGilligan, was appointed to succeed Joe McGrath, thus strengthening the group of civilian ministers and O'Higgins's position within the Cabinet.

Nevertheless, by October 1924, faced with pressure from the nine-strong group of TDs that McGrath had brought together after his resignation, and fearing their opposition in the Dáil, Cosgrave was prepared to accept conditions for their support, including party control of policy, the removal of 'anti-Irish elements in positions' of power, resistance to the advice of permanent officials, and the return of Tobin supporters to the army. MacNeill and all the civilian ministers rejected this course of action, however, leaving Cosgrave in a minority of one in his Cabinet.

The 'National Group' then resigned their seats but, in circumstances which will be described below, Cumann n nGaedheal won seven of these seats back in early 1925. What was significant about this entire episode is that it ended so peacefully. The generals accepted their relegation without demur. So did Tobin, who was later appointed to a position in the civil service. McGrath went into business, founding both the Irish Sweepstakes and an Irish glass industry, and he and his family were later very supportive of Fine Gael. And in June 1927, Mulcahy was reappointed to the government as minister for local government and public health – and went on, twenty years later, to become leader of the Party for sixteen years.

For his part, O'Higgins continued to work loyally under Cosgrave as vice-president. He was appointed minister for external affairs in June 1927, in recognition of his remarkable performance at the 1926 Imperial Conference, which advanced movement of the Dominions towards unchallenged sovereign independence. My father was moved from external affairs to defence, where (reportedly following a difficult encounter between Cosgrave and the new army chiefs over their attitude to the feared emergence of a minority Labour–National League government with support from Fianna Fáil) he was given the difficult – and most unpopular – task of completing the process of bringing the army fully under civilian control. The result was that, although there seems to have been some ineffective plotting in 1931 between several army generals and Garda Commissioner O'Duffy, nevertheless, when Fianna Fáil secured a mandate in 1932 to form a government with Labour backing, the army at once accepted the authority of the new government and served it loyally thereafter.

In the final analysis, simple patriotism triumphed over deep personal divisions and any personal ambition. Thus was parliamentary democracy firmly established in our State.

Let me now turn back to the parallel development of the Cumann na nGaedheal political party during this early period. The pro-Treaty government had lost the support of the Sinn Féin Party early in 1922, and a political party supporting the government did not come into existence until more than a year later, on 27 April 1923. This sequence of events proved crucial to the future of both the government and the party, in which, indeed, the members of the government never showed much interest. From the start, the party had a very limited role, and its efforts to influence the government were almost wholly unsuccessful, leading on the former's part to frustration, a measure of alienation, and general ineffectiveness.

From January to December 1922, the pro-Treaty leadership had operated through two distinct but parallel government structures, the Dáil Government and the British-recognised Provisional Government, neither with a political party behind them. The members of the two governments had, naively, envisaged a political system without parties, but instead with small groupings perhaps coming together for particular purposes. They had not envisaged that a split in Sinn Féin would develop into two or more politically opposed parties.

Moreover, faced with the Civil War, the two governments, under Griffith and Collins, saw themselves as leaders of the nation rather than of a party. An attempt was made in the autumn of 1922 to get representatives of the Labour Party to join what the two leaders and their supporters saw as a national government, but Labour, unhappy with many aspects of the war, refused to do so.

Cosgrave, succeeding Griffith and Collins as leader of the parallel governments, saw himself as being above politics and did not want to be a party leader. At that stage, there was no recognition of the fact that the pro-Treaty leadership would need a party organisation to win elections. Elections were simply not high in their list of immediate concerns! Nevertheless, in September 1922 more realistic supporters of the Treaty started the process of establishing a pro-Treaty party, but at the first meeting that was called only two of the five who had been nominated to undertake this task turned up!

At first, it was proposed that each constituency would be autonomous – as is still the case with the Ulster Unionist Party in Northern Ireland. But a second draft proposal wisely provided that locally selected candidates would have to be ratified by a twenty-four-member National Executive. Constituency representation at central level was not to come from a party branch structure, however. Instead, in a kind of merit system, each constituency was to be represented at the centre in proportion to the number of TDs it had elected. From the outset, Ernest Blythe, who was active in this process, endeavoured to limit the role of the new party, fearing, with good reason, that it could become a source of pressure for 'jobs for the boys'.

A preliminary conference of deputies and fifty-eight invitees from around the country – it was remarkable that so many were able to get there given the state of the country at that time – was held on 7 December 1922. The conference decided to revive the name of Griffith's original party, Cumann na nGaedheal. Two TDs, Sean Hales and Padraic O'Maille, who went by horse and trap from that meeting to the Ormonde Hotel for lunch, were shot – fatally, in the case of Hales. This was the event that led to the execution without trial of four republicans that same night.

The party was finally established on 27 April 1923 in the Mansion House at a meeting attended by a hundred and fifty people. After its establishment, the only member of the government who kept in regular touch with it was Mulcahy. Blythe, who had played a leading role in founding it, later described it as 'a snarling organisation', and O'Higgins, FitzGerald and McGilligan (the latter of whom joined the Cabinet in 1924) had little time for it. (Forty years later, W. T. Cosgrave was to tell me that his government had contained 'a half-statesman, Kevin O'Higgins, but no politicians' – specifically mentioning in this latter connection my father Desmond FitzGerald as being 'too busy arguing about theology with Father Cahill' and Paddy McGilligan as refusing 'even go to Cork for a meeting'.)

The secretary of the Standing Committee of the party, James Dolan, demanded that ministers attend party meetings – something they were very reluctant to do. When he asked Cosgrave to make a policy statement to the party, Cosgrave turned up, but spoke in generalities.

The party soon proved itself to be not merely a source of many tensions but also an inefficient instrument. It failed to raise funds – in today's money terms, its 1924 receipts from its members amounted to about €18,000! Within two years of its foundation, it was in debt to the tune of well over €200,000, again in today's money terms.

There was from the start a conflict between the Cabinet and the party over jobs. The party reflected the views of those who expected the whole public administration to change hands with the revolution, believing that the rewards of public office should accrue to those who had fought for independence. The Cabinet, from Collins down, recognising that they faced the huge task of founding a State in the midst of civil war and virtual anarchy, were concerned to draw instead on talent from wherever they could find it – including from the former British administration, something which particularly annoyed the party members. One of the first steps Collins took after the Treaty debate was to get British assistance in the establishment of an Irish version of the UK Civil Service Commission, to make public appointments on the basis of merit only.

Collins also brought agents of his in from the former police force to organise the new Garda Síochána. The Volunteer members of that body mutinied in March 1922 against these leaders at the Curragh, where they were being trained; after a siege by the army, the mutineers had to be stood down. A fresh start in forming an unarmed civilian police force was made in Dublin several months later. Moreover, as explained above, the army itself had eventually to be expanded to fifty-five thousand men, most of whom, including half the officers, were necessarily drawn from outside the ranks of the Volunteers. When the party was formed, all these issues caused great dissatisfaction amongst its members.

Land reform was another major issue of contention. Although, at the time when independence was won, only a handful of landed estates remained to be divided, there were nevertheless tens of thousands of restless landless men, who were ready and anxious to start a fresh land war.

A third source of tension within the ranks of government supporters was the North. Many supporters of Cumann na nGaedheal continued to hanker after a continuation or revival of Collins's interventionist policy there. The Cabinet, even before Collins's death, had decided to terminate this policy – although they had not yet had an opportunity to tell him of this decision.

Finally, in the face of advice from a fiscal enquiry committee of economic experts on industrial protection, strongly backed by the secretary of finance, J. J. McElligott, the government decided to limit industrial protection to half a dozen products: footwear, soap and candles, sugar confectionery and cocoa preparation, table waters and glass bottles. This substantial dilution of Griffith's protectionist policy was also a source of tension between government and party.

In fairness, it has to be said that, from the point of view of the party, its relationship with the government was most unsatisfactory. Its members saw ministers as being remote from, and even hostile to, their concerns, slow to appear at the party's meetings, and generally dismissive of its role. By the standards of political parties elsewhere, they had a point.

Thus, with Dáil opposition, due to abstentions by republicans, limited to the small Labour Party and some farmers' representatives, the Cumann na nGaedheal Party, instead of being a support for the government, became virtually an informal Opposition! The truth is that these tensions between government and party were unavoidable in the circumstances in which the party had come into being. But the consequence was that the party, formed from the top down, never developed strong popular roots – as Fianna Fáil, building from the bottom up a few years later, was able to do most successfully. This remained a problem for Cumann na nGaeheal and its successor, Fine Gael, for more than fifty years, until the late 1970s.

To add to the government's difficulties, whilst public opinion was heavily pro-Treaty, the supporters of the Treaty were mainly passive and had little enthusiasm for the huge task to be undertaken by the new government. Physical and moral courage were at a discount – and with the republicans in the Civil War committed to assassinating fourteen categories of people, including 'aggressive supporters of the government', there was little willingness to defend publicly the new administration.

In the eighteen months after the September 1923 general election, the government, for a variety of reasons, had to contest as many as nineteen seats in by-elections. Only three of these were due to the deaths of deputies. Two were due to the curious practice, which continued through the 1920s, of key figures contesting several seats at a general election and then standing down in the one that could most easily be held in a by-election. Another was due to the appointment of Deputy Hugh Kennedy, the attorney general (himself elected at a by-election a year earlier), as chief justice. Yet another was because of a legal disqualification. The remaining twelve were caused by resignations. Five of the twelve by-elections were held in November 1923, and the other seven, involving nine seats – all which due to resignations over the Army Mutiny – were held on 11 March 1925.

In the event, the government won all but four of the nineteen seats – and topped the poll in seventeen of them. Two of the four republican gains were, from the government's point of view, unavoidable: in the case of two of the nine by-elections arising from the Army Mutiny resignations, there were two constituency vacancies, so the republicans were almost bound to win a seat in each of these. In a third case, the Cumann na nGaedheal candidate, Professor Michael Tierney, later president of UCD, was nominated only at the last minute – and the fourth, in Dublin South, was won by Seán Lemass, a very strong republican candidate.

The Cumann na nGaedheal Party and its Standing Committee had their headquarters in Parnell Square. But because of what the government saw as the party's inadequacies, the government, when faced in late 1924 with the last seven of the nineteen by-elections, established a separate temporary organising committee in December 1924, with premises in Dawson Street, near the Dáil. This committee, effectively without help from the party organisation, succeeded in having the Cumann na nGaedheal candidates top the poll in all seven constituencies. And after the by-elections, the Dawson Street premises were sold at a profit!

All that having been said, the record of achievement of the Cumann na nGaedheal Government in the face of all these difficulties was, by any standards, remarkable. Having successfully ended the Civil War and having within a year released all the many thousands of internees, its new, unarmed Garda Síochána thereafter maintained order while the government set about the physical reconstruction of the country.

In addition to the destruction of parts of O'Connell Street in 1916, and of the Custom House in 1921, other parts of O'Connell Street and the Four Courts had been destroyed in 1922. In addition, during the Civil War, bridges had been blown up and railways and rolling stock destroyed throughout the country. Moreover, independence had ended transfers from Britain in respect of pensions and unemployment assistance, leaving the Irish Exchequer – which, for a period, had to carry the cost of an army of fifty-five thousand men – severely depleted. A new and untried government in the midst of a Civil War and its aftermath was not well-placed to borrow, and so had to pay for almost everything out of current revenue. In those conditions, to have succeeded in completing the huge task of physical reconstruction by 1931 was an extraordinary achievement.

Criticism of civil-service pay cuts and of the temporary reduction in the old-age pension by one shilling (10 percent) in 1924 ignores the fact that the pension, which had been doubled in 1920, had actually increased in value by a further 6 percent between the foundation of the State and April 1924, because of a fall in the cost of living. Moreover, during the remainder of the government's term of office, a combination of a further 10 percent drop in the cost of living and the early restoration, in 1927, of the temporary cut in the pension raised pensioners' purchasing power by 20 percent.

In 1926, the government extended the Civil Service Commission public-appointments system to local authorities by establishing a Local Appointments Commission. This ended a situation which had sometimes involved bribes being paid for local-government jobs: in today's money terms, as much as £50,000 was once paid for an appointment as dispensary doctor!

Inefficiency and corruption in local councils was dramatically diminished by abolishing for various periods the worst offending bodies, and later by putting in city and county managers to undertake much of the decision-making at local level. At the time, Fianna Fáil in opposition criticised these reforms as 'undemocratic' but it has to be said that that party continued this clean-up process when it came to power.

Meanwhile, a huge body of native Irish legislation was introduced, drafted by indefatigable administrative civil servants and lawyers, and an efficient central administration was established. Innovative initiatives included the establishment of the ESB and the building of the Shannon Scheme, the creation of the Agricultural Credit Corporation and the establishment of the Dairy Disposal Company to merge creameries and undertake cattle breeding, bacon curing and broiler production, as well as the establishment of a Medical Registration Council, a Dental Board and a Veterinary Council.

In the international arena, Ireland became an active and respected member of the League of Nations. Despite British opposition, it succeeded in registering the 1921 Treaty with the League and initiated the process of Dominion diplomatic representation abroad. From 1926 onwards, the Irish government successfully led the revolution in the Commonwealth which by 1931 had made all the Dominions sovereign, independent states. As a result, by 1932, nothing remained of British rule in Ireland other than the nominal role of the king in accrediting diplomats to other states – a role which was preserved until 1949 – the oath of faithfulness to the king as head of the Commonwealth, and the right of appeal on certain issues to the Privy Council in London; and the government was preparing to seek the removal of these two latter features.

Finally, as I have earlier mentioned, the Cumann na nGaedheal government went to great lengths from 1927 onwards to ensure that, when the time came to hand over to Fianna Fáil after an election, the army would accept the people's verdict and serve loyally the new government, despite the fact that it was comprised of people they had defeated in arms a mere nine years earlier.

This all made up a remarkable record of achievement. But by 1932, the members of that government were physically and mentally exhausted. Reluctantly, and with many fears for the future, they handed over to Fianna Fáil – for what turned out to be a period of sixteen years – the end of which my father did not live to see.

Deep though the political divisions were between pro- and anti-Treatyites – and also, as I have shown, amongst the pro-Treatyites, and then later, with the foundation of Fianna Fáil, amongst the anti-Treatyites – all those involved on both sides shared a common vision of an Ireland that would re-create a past culture, that was Gaelic and Catholic. They felt that it was of the utmost importance to be faithful to the indigenous Irish tradition, and they gave little thought to how to incorporate into their scheme of things other Irish traditions, whether Anglo-Irish or Ulster Scots.

Both sides felt that they owed a special debt to the Irish language, which had brought so many of them together in the Gaelic League in the years before the First World War. Cumann na nGaedheal sought, somewhat simplistically, to repay this debt by deciding in 1924 to make the Irish language an essential subject for the Intermediate Certificate by 1928, and Fianna Fáil followed through with a similar Leaving Certificate requirement in 1934. Irish was also made an essential subject for entry into and promotion within the public service. The fact that these provisions, *de facto,* excluded the two other non-Gaelic Irish traditions from much of the life of the new State does not seem to have struck either of the two political groups at the time.

Moreover, the members of both of the first two governments – Ernest Blythe apart – were deeply Catholic. While they did not think in terms of creating a Catholic State – three centuries of official established religion in Ireland had made both Catholic clergy and the laity sceptical of such a regime – they passed laws, and later a Constitution, that was deeply influenced by Catholic teaching. The responsibility for creating a non-pluralist State rests almost equally with both sets of politicians – although, eventually, Fianna Fáil went further than Cumann na nGaedheal in this respect.

Looking back on this period some eighty years later, there is not much point in criticising either the first or the second government for having failed to create a pluralist Ireland: that would have been quite outside their frame of reference. They were men of their time, as we are of ours. Our State had to go through several generations of almost exclusive emphasis on the indigenous culture of the majority of the Irish people before coming to terms with the complexity of the country's cultural inheritance.

These two governments differed in some measure on the issue of protection for infant industry – Cumann na nGaeheal being more influenced by the free-trade ideas of their time, and Fianna Fáil by the autarkic ideas of the 1930s. The misguided idea of self-sufficiency seems, however, to have come specifically from de Valera. This approach was abandoned only at the very end of de Valera's years in power, after it had done much harm. The truth is that neither side possessed politicians who had much grasp of economics – although, in the late 1950s both John A. Costello and Seán Lemass finally began to come to grips with the issue of belatedly securing economic development by reorienting the economy outwards. But by then decades had been wasted, and throughout the 1950s, Ireland had, quite unnecessarily, stagnated whilst the rest of Europe and the world were forging ahead.

The members of both the first two governments remained loyal to their revolutionary commitment to the public good: they were all men of probity, seeking nothing for themselves beyond salaries as ministers that were modest by international standards. Fianna Fáil, however, having inherited a State from whose public life they had initially excluded themselves, were less committed to meritocratic as against political appointments, and they undid some – but only some – of what the first government had fought for so determinedly against their own supporters.

The survival of a democratic Irish State through this turbulent period of European history, when most of the rest of Europe succumbed to dictatorship, is the special achievement of those who founded our State. We owe a huge debt to the selfless patriotism, and the toughness, of the members of our first government. I myself am proud to be the son of one of those men.

6

CATHOLICISM, THE GAELIC REVIVAL AND THE NEW STATE

The prevailing Catholic ethos of the new Irish State must be viewed in the context of, and seen as a long-term reaction against, the dominant role in Ireland of the 10 percent Anglican minority and the Established Church of Ireland from 1691 until at least the mid-nineteenth century. For the Roman Catholic majority, the role played by these elements of Irish society was in many ways more significant than British rule itself.

Post–1691, King William III failed to restrain the Anglican Establishment in Ireland from dominating the now fully colonised island – in breach of the Treaty of Limerick. That Establishment controlled public administration, industry and, at least initially, commerce. Moreover, through the operation of the Penal Laws, by 1775, no less than 95 percent of the land – which at that time was still the principal source of wealth in the country – was in Protestant hands.

It is true that, during the latter part of the eighteenth century, tolerance of the practice of Catholicism grew and Catholics began to play a larger role in commerce. But they remained excluded from parliament – in Dublin and later also in Westminster – until 1829. Moreover, all hospitals and schools, as well as the only university, were Anglican.

I estimate that, by the 1820s, Catholic parents, mostly desperately poor rural dwellers, were paying teachers in 11,500 'hedge schools' (schools run by individual masters under hedges, or in barns or mud cabins) an average of about €100 a year per child in today's money to educate their children – around half a million of them in total. Over a period of more than fifty years from the 1830s onwards, however, the British government established a national system of primary schools that was designed to replace the hedge schools, which were seen as subversive.

Although these new national schools were intended to be multi-denominational, by 1850 they had been converted by both Catholics and Presbyterians into denominational establishments, existing in parallel with the Anglican Church's own schools.

From the 1820s onwards, Catholics were for the first time allowed to build substantial churches. What were then the poorest people in western Europe financed the construction not only of all these new churches but also of their own hospitals and many secondary schools. These schools were given state aid after 1878 through a 'results' payment system, based on academic performance in state examinations at three distinct levels.

As British governments became increasingly more willing to use the power they had secured through the Union of 1801 to alleviate the grievances of the Catholic majority, the Anglican community became increasingly dissatisfied with what they saw as their 'betrayal' by successive British governments, for example through the dis-establishment of the Church of Ireland (1869–71) and, from the 1880s onwards, through land reform. The resultant tensions preserved – and for a period even intensified – sectarian tensions, not just in Northern Ireland but throughout the island.

Moreover, the extension of the franchise between the 1830s and the 1880s, as a result of which the Catholic population eventually came to constitute a majority of the electorate, led to growing concern amongst Protestants about any possible modification of the Union of 1801 that might leave them in a minority position within a revived Irish parliament. Faced with these radical changes, Presbyterians as well as Anglicans reacted against what they came to see as a mood of growing Catholic triumphalism. (Many of these negative reactions have since 1969 been replicated amongst the Protestant community in Northern Ireland as they have had to face British reforms designed to place Catholic nationalists in a fully equal relationship with Protestant unionists.)

From the 1880s onwards, Protestant fears of the implications of Home Rule in an Ireland with an electorate that was in the process of becoming 75 percent Roman Catholic led this minority to oppose bitterly any measure of Irish self-government, which, they feared, would lead to reverse discrimination by a Catholic majority against the Protestant minority. This introduced a sectarian element into the political struggle for Irish independence: on the Catholic side, sectarianism was aggravated by former tenants' unhappy memories of their experience of Protestant landlords – memories that persisted long after most of the land had been transferred from these landlords to their tenants.

The origins of today's confessional, i.e. religiously organised, Irish education and, to some extent, also its hospital system thus lie away back in the sectarian structure that was imposed on the island after 1691. In the nineteenth century, this structure became increasingly unacceptable to Catholics, when the earlier Anglican objective of excluding Roman Catholics from any role in society, so as to bolster their own dominant minority position, became more evangelical and missionary in character – and thus, from the point of view of Catholics, fearful of what they saw as attempts at proselytism, even more sinister. The extent to which this led to a counter-sectarianism that came close to a form of racism, may be found in Cardinal Cullen's comment that 'Irish Protestants are foreigners and not part of Ireland' – a phrase that was, somewhat uncharacteristically, echoed on one occasion by Éamon de Valera during the War of Independence, when he remarked that Protestants were 'not Irish people'.

It is therefore scarcely surprising that, although during the period of the War of Independence (1919–21), the members of the Irish Hierarchy were divided in their attitude to that conflict (four Ulster bishops were openly supportive of Sinn Féin, as were several bishops in other parts of the country), some forty-five priests were active members of Sinn Féin – and twenty-four of these were chosen to chair almost 30 percent of the eighty-seven constituency executives – a practice that persisted at Northern Ireland Nationalist Party conventions until the 1960s. During the 1919–21 period, de Valera – described by one observer as 'surrounded by a sombre bodyguard of priests' – was also prone to stressing Sinn Féin's close relationship with the Catholic Church. Against this background, the question in 1921 was not whether a new Irish State would have a Catholic ethos – that was in some measure, at least for the early period of independence, inevitable – but rather how far such an ethos would be subject to self-control on the part of the new nationalist regime.

The British government, concerned to secure the rights of the Protestant minority, substituted in 1920 a form of proportional representation in multi-seat constituencies for the traditional 'first-past-the-post' system. This proportional system was then employed in the 1921 elections to the post-partition northern and southern parliaments. It remained open to these two Home Rule governments, however, to abandon this electoral system later should they wish to do so – as, in the event, the Northern Ireland government did towards the end of that decade. The government of the new Irish State has, however, retained this electoral system ever since. It was in fact embedded by de Valera in the 1937 Constitution, and the electorate twice rejected subsequent attempts by him to return to the first-past-the-post system.

Other protections for the Protestant minority in the Irish State incorporated in the 1922 Constitution included a ban on endowment of religion by the State and a guarantee of private-property rights. In the final draft of the Constitution, this latter provision replaced the first two articles of the original draft – which, at the suggestion of an American socialist member of the drafting committee, had subordinated private-property rights to the public interest.

Moreover, half of the sixty members of the first Senate were nominated in order to ensure that that body would represent the business and professional communities, sixteen being southern unionists – the figure of sixteen to diminish over a twelve-year period. These provisions were all adopted by the Dáil without much debate – for, although at local level there was evidence of sectarianism, the Sinn Féin leadership, whilst for the most part strongly Catholic, was not sectarian, and was concerned to ensure fair treatment of the minority. Despite earlier tensions with some bishops, the Catholic Hierarchy unanimously supported the new government in the Civil War. In fact, on 10 October 1922 it excommunicated anyone who continued to defy the government in arms.

The leaders of the new State were not minded, however, to tackle the confessional structure of the educational system or to monitor caring religious-run social institutions such as reformatories or bodies engaged in dealing with unmarried mothers, nor did they seek to change the structure of the health services, which included a number of 'voluntary' or religious-controlled hospitals. They simply could not afford to take over such institutions, nor had they any appetite for an action would have alienated all the Churches, Catholic and Protestant.

From the foundation of the new State onwards, Irish governments have been careful to avoid any form of religious discrimination – apart from slightly favouring the more thinly spread Protestant community in respect of school-transport arrangements. This provision was challenged only once, when, a few years ago, Catholics in Greystones sought and secured the right to have their children, as well Protestant children, bused to Wicklow as well as to Bray.

Although the Cabinet contained one Presbyterian, Minister for Finance Ernest Blythe (who after 1927 became vice-president of the Executive Council), the new government nevertheless moved at an early stage to remove the previous, very limited provision for divorce by Act of Parliament and also, later in the 1920s, introduced censorship of publications and of films, in line with the wishes of the Roman Catholic Church. It is fair to add, however, that, at this time, the Protestant Churches, and indeed many individual Protestants, were also in favour of censorship, and many were also opposed to divorce – although some were less inclined than Catholics to go along with state intervention in such matters.

In the 1920s, there were, however, some tensions between the first government and the Roman Catholic Hierarchy over public appointments. The president of the Executive Council, W. T. Cosgrave, had to face down the Catholic bishops on this issue, especially in relation to medical appointments – playing on the embarrassment of the Catholic Church over the granting of marriage dispensations that had not been notified to the civil authorities. Cosgrave told one bishop that, to discriminate on the basis of religion with regard to appointments 'would be to conflict with some of the fundamental principles upon which this State is founded.'

In 1931, the Cumann na nGaedheal government also rejected an attempt by the Catholic Church – supported by Fianna Fáil, which was anxious to recover ground with the Church following the excommunication of republicans during the Civil War – to veto the appointment of a Protestant as county librarian in Mayo. Fianna Fáil also claimed to 'represent a big element of Catholicity' and accused the government of being supported by Freemasons. And the party criticised the government for having opened diplomatic relations with the Holy See without having first consulted the Catholic Hierarchy – who were known to be opposed to such a move.

On the other hand, the Cumann na nGaedheal government enthusiastically joined in preparations for the International Eucharistic Congress of 1932: I still possess a Congress flag that was flown over our house during that event. The party was out of office by the time the Congress was held, however, and Fianna Fáil made the most of its participation in the Congress.

In 1935, legislation was introduced by the Fianna Fáil government that included a provision banning contraceptives. There followed the 1937 Constitution, which introduced Church-influenced elements that were notable by their absence from the 1922 Constitution, but, as mentioned earlier, de Valera successfully resisted pressure from the Holy See to declare Ireland a Catholic State.

In 1951, a political crisis arose because of the ham-fisted handling by the coalition government of the day of Catholic Church opposition to a 'mother-and-child' health scheme. The government caved in to Church opposition to the scheme – which, however, was successfully reintroduced in slightly modified form by a successor Fianna Fáil government.

Thereafter, few ministers felt morally obliged to follow Church teaching on social issues – an exception being the votes of Taoiseach Liam Cosgrave and his minister for education, Dick Burke, against a Bill, introduced by the minister for justice, Pat Cooney, in 1974 to liberalise contraception. But, in relation to legislation on sexual issues, politicians naturally had to take account of public opinion, which continued to be influenced, albeit to a diminishing degree, by the Catholic Hierarchy.

The first chapter of this book traced the decline of the Irish language from its position in 1700 as the language of the great majority to its position in the twentieth century as the language of isolated groups of people along the west and south coasts. Brian Ó Cuív has pointed out that 'Perhaps one of the greatest forces of all which hastened the displacement of Irish by English, and which prevented any genuine practical effort to preserve the language, was the involvement of the people as a whole in Irish politics from the end of the eighteenth century. Things in Ireland were never the same again after 1798. Irish nationalism [was] propagated almost entirely through English – [through] ballads [and] speeches from the dock'.

Eventually, this process of anglicisation created its own reaction – one that was initially quite separate from political nationalism, being supported by Protestants as well as Catholics. In 1876, a Society for the

Preservation of the Irish Language was established; the work of this organisation led to something like a thousand English-speakers starting to learn Irish. A couple of years later, the introduction of a system of payment by results in secondary education – designed to offer some support for Catholic schools – helped to encourage Irish teaching in these schools. In 1904, national-school scholarships in Irish were introduced.

In 1893, the Gaelic League had been founded by Douglas Hyde and Eoin MacNeill as a non-political body – within whose branches, however, many future revolutionaries met each other. But in the early 1900s, the IRB, which had already infiltrated the GAA in the 1870s, turned its attention to the Gaelic League, going so far as to install the non-Irish-speaking IRB-man Tom Clarke as its secretary. As a result, by 1914 Pearse felt able to describe the League as 'the most revolutionary influence that has ever come into Ireland. The Irish revolution really began when the seven Gaelic Leaguers met in O'Connell Street. The germ of all future Irish history was in the back room.' He added that it became an 'important tool for adherents of physical force.'

This takeover left both Douglas Hyde and Arthur Griffith embittered, and Hyde resigned the presidency of the League in July 1915, saying that 'These people queered the pitch and put an end to my dreams of using the language as a unifying bond to bring all Irishmen together.' Pearse, however, had come to see the League in its non-political form as a 'spent force and I am glad of it. The vital work will be done not so much by the Gaelic League as by the men and movements that have sprung from it.' Michael Laffan has written of the domination of the Gaelic League by the urban intelligentsia, and Connolly had remarked in 1898 that it 'had not demonstrated the spirit of self-sacrifice – it had not learnt that you cannot teach the language to a starving child.'

Although attitudes to the Gaelic League were mixed, the revolutionaries emerged from involvement in it with a great sense of the debt they owed to the language that had brought them all together, and this became a powerful force, motivating the first two governments in their language-revival policies.

On the eve of independence, in 1921, the INTO produced a National Plan involving one hour a day of Irish teaching, and the use of Irish as a teaching medium for infants. On St Patrick's Day 1922, the Dáil Government came out in favour of Irish teaching if the teacher was competent in the language, remarking that 10 percent of teachers had Irish-language certificates and 25 percent had attended Irish colleges. Crash courses were to be introduced for all teachers under the age of forty-five. Soon, half of all teachers would be competent in Irish, which was to be made a required subject for the Intermediate Certificate by 1928.

In 1924, legislation was passed to establish the new Irish public administration, including a Department of Education. The old system of payment by results was abolished, and replaced by provision for the payment of teachers and capitation grants. The year 1926 saw the emergence of an INTO Second National Programme, with an admission that the first programme had been too ambitious, some teachers being poorly qualified. There was to be a slower transition for older pupils, and time allocated to mathematics and nature study was to be reduced to leave more time for Irish. In the same year, Irish-speaking preparatory colleges were opened in the west, giving an effective monopoly of primary teaching to young people from this area. Finally, in 1934, Fianna Fáil made Irish a compulsory subject for the School Leaving Certificate.

What has been described as 'a lone voice against a consensus' on this subject had been raised as early as May 1919 by my father, Desmond FitzGerald – himself an enthusiast for the language – who pointed out that Irish was in fact dying. English, he went on to say bluntly, was even more the language of Ireland than French was of France: he had earlier spent two years in Brittany. The separation of Ireland from England was more urgent in cultural than in political terms, he argued, but the reality was that modern dances would be cultivated in a free Ireland, and while the kilt might be Celtic, the Irish people would abandon the idea of wearing it. Ireland needed outside influences, and they should be sought on the Continent of Europe rather than in Britain. Irish people should go into the world and choose what was best and most adaptable.

These sentiments contrasted strikingly with de Valera's view, expressed twenty years later in the Senate. He had three aims, he said: the revival of the Irish language, national sovereignty and unity with the North, but even for the sake of a united Ireland he 'would not give up the policy of trying to make this a really Irish-Ireland – not by any means . . . I would say NO and I would say it for this reason: because I believe that so long as the language remains, you have a distinguishing character-

116

istic of nationality which will enable the nation to persist. If you lose the language, the danger is that there would be absorption.'

Eventually, this emphasis on efforts to revive the Irish language led to a reaction, which became a public issue in 1964 when people in Mayo and Galway petitioned against teaching children, many of whom would emigrate, through Irish. That same year, Father MacNamara published his *Bilingualism and Primary Education,* which showed that 42 percent of hours in primary schools were devoted to learning Irish. He attributed to this the fact that Irish primary school pupils were sixteen to seventeen months behind British children in written English and sixteen months behind native Irish speakers in written Irish. Despite the widespread fury his book created amongst Irish-language enthusiasts, the proportion of time absorbed by the language in primary schools was gradually – and quietly – reduced to about 25 percent. Finally, at about the same time, the Language Freedom Movement was established to challenge what was seen as an excessive emphasis on the revival of the Irish language — a development that initially evoked a quite violent reaction from some language enthusiasts.

A decade later, a national coalition government removed the provision under which anyone who failed Irish in the School Leaving Examination was denied a certificate setting out their achievements in other subjects, and also opened entry to the public service to young people who lacked a qualification in Irish. This provided opportunities for public employment in the State to people from Northern Ireland: many Catholics, as well as almost all Protestants, from the North had previously been excluded from such employment by this requirement.

If the island had not been partitioned, it is difficult to see how an all-Ireland State anything like the current twenty-six-county State could have developed. The Catholic Church could never have played such a dominant role in the State, nor could the Irish language have been elevated to such a key position in a State with a 25 percent Protestant minority.

However frustrating it would have been for those who, in the truncated Irish State, sought to create a Gaelic and Roman Catholic society, a united Ireland would perforce have to have been a multicultural one – unless, of course, the nationalist majority had themselves chosen to seek freedom to create such a Catholic Gaelic State by partitioning the island so as to secure the freedom to pursue such a goal.

It seems to me that we in the Irish State have been singularly obtuse about partition. We have never been willing to face the reality of the fact that it was only the British decision to divide our island politically in 1920 that gave us the opportunity to pursue for half a century or so the dream, or chimera, of creating a monocultural society and state – which has eventually turned out to be something of a cul-de-sac. The British did the political partitioning, but it was we ourselves who cut ourselves off in so many fundamental ways from our northern compatriots – nationalist as well as unionist, I believe – by legislating to create a quite different kind of State, one that would eventually need to be substantially dismantled if we were ever to create an all-Irish State.

Despite the way in which, by devious and hidden political tactics, the northern Unionists created a discriminatory social system, they did not in fact substantially change their laws or system of government – as we in the South proceeded to do enthusiastically. If the island had not been partitioned in 1920, we and our unionist fellow-Irishmen in the North would, after an initial period of tension, eventually have had to find some way to create together such laws and structures as might better suit the needs of our small island than those that had been left to us by the British government. But what we and our northern unionist and nationalist compatriots would have thus created together could have borne little resemblance to what actually emerged in our truncated State.

The truth is that politicians in our State have never faced up to the reality of what a united Ireland would have had to be like in order to accommodate peacefully in the political system two very different cultures. The kind of Ireland that our revolutionary forebears envisaged, and which they and we have done our best to bring to pass, could only ever have existed in a partitioned Ireland. When we eventually come to accept this harsh reality, we will have reached a stage at which we will be ready to think seriously about working towards some kind of eventual Irish unity.

Despite the religious neutrality of its earlier Constitution, the overwhelming predominance of Roman Catholics in its population – 94 percent of the total at mid-century – made it almost inevitable that the new State would *de facto* take on some kind of Catholic identity. Patrick Corish, in his book *The Irish Catholic Experience,* remarked that a sore and sensitive post–Civil War Ireland was never in greater need of an identity, which had to be either the Irish language or the Catholic Church (in the event, it was a combination of the two). He added that, in a post–First War Europe that was marked by a conservative reaction to a loosening of traditional values, it was not surprising that the leaders of the new State drew on the conservative Catholic ethos.

Thus, although Protestants in the new Irish State were certainly free from any form of discrimination, Roman Catholic influence on legislation made the country a somewhat 'cold house' for non-members of the Roman Catholic Church. The small Protestant community does not seem ever to have protested about any of these matters, and by the 1930s this community had largely opted out of politics. Pressure for a more pluralist, multicultural approach from the late 1950s onwards came from liberal Catholics rather than from the Protestant community. The passivity of the Protestant community in relation to these matters was accounted for by the fact that, at the outset, they must have been very nervous about their future in the face of a Civil War amongst those who had secured independence for the new State – and were grateful to the new government, which was doing what it could to deal with republican attacks on their property, especially in rural areas, where many of their houses were burnt down.

Allowing for the departure of the British army and the families of soldiers, the 1926 population census data for various age-groups would suggest that, by that year, several tens of thousands of Protestants had left the State for Northern Ireland or Britain. Emigration among Protestants continued thereafter at a higher rate than for Catholics until after the Second World War – following which, the much better-off Protestant community experienced a significantly lower emigration rate than did the poorer Catholic majority. (In 1991, the proportion of Protestants in the top three socio-economic groups, viz. 40 percent, was twice that for Catholics, and in a number of key occupations, as well as on farms of over fifty acres, they were over-represented, in some cases as much as three- or four-fold.)

The superior economic status of the Protestants who remained was never challenged. The fact that there was an evident concern on the part of the new government to protect their interests must have encouraged them to 'lie low and say nothing' about what must in some instances have been unwelcome changes in their social environment.

In Frank Pakenham and Thomas O'Neill's biography of de Valera, he is quoted as stating that he believed that the northern unionists were at bottom proud of being Irish: the history, traditions and culture of the Irish nation could not fail to attract them. One may contrast this romantic view with Nicholas Mansergh's realism: 'The greater their insistence upon the Catholic–Gaelic foundations of Irish nationhood, the more acute the northerners' feeling that they were, and were deemed to be, alien to it.'

7

The Origins, Development and Present Status
of Irish 'Neutrality'

The neutrality of each of the neutral European states has been conditioned by their very different histories. All neutralities are contingent, but perhaps Ireland's is even more contingent than most. Although the roots of Irish neutrality go back to the foundation of the State, in its present form it is largely the accidental, indeed unintended, product of somewhat later events.

From the late sixteenth century to the time of the 1916 Easter Rising, Irish leaders who were engaged in or contemplating revolts against British rule frequently sought military assistance from Continental powers: at different times, the Holy See, Spain, France and Germany. Indeed, in 1915–16, contacts with Germany had gone so far as to involve contemplation of the installation of a Hohenzollern – the kaiser's sixth son, Prince Joachim – as king of Ireland. Patrick Pearse was sufficiently realistic to accept that a German victory, which at that time was seen as a precondition for the achievement of Irish independence, would necessarily entail, as had been the case throughout much of Europe since the early nineteenth century, the installation of a German monarch.

Against this background, any settlement to which Britain might be persuaded, by arms or otherwise, to agree in the aftermath of the First World War would, of necessity, have to be such as would guarantee British security against a threat emanating from Europe via an independent Irish state. Thus, even while the War of Independence was in progress, Éamon de Valera found it expedient to proclaim the principle that an independent Irish state would never be a threat to Britain's security. In his seminal work *Un-neutral Ireland,* Professor Trevor Salmon describes how, in the United States in February 1920, de Valera felt it important to put forward a series of proposals towards this end – despite the danger, which soon became a reality, that this initiative would split Irish-American support for the independence movement in Ireland.

Having stated that 'mutual self-interest would make the peoples of these two islands, if both independent, the closest possible allies at a moment of real national danger to either', de Valera went so far as to suggest a kind of British Monroe Doctrine, under which Ireland's relationship with regard to Britain would be analogous to that of Cuba to the United States. He also suggested that consideration be given to an 'international instrument . . . as in the case of Belgium', as well as to Irish participation in the League of Nations – then in the course of being established – within which all would agree to respect and defend each other's integrity and independence. The Irish should 'see fear in the downfall of Britain and fear, not hope, in every attack upon Britain', he added.

The principle that an independent Ireland must never be allowed to become, or be used as, a threat to the security of Britain had thus been established as a fundamental principle of Irish foreign policy even before the State was founded. And in the negotiations that led to the Articles of Agreement of 6 December 1921 – as well as in the controversy, and eventually civil war, to which this agreement soon led – the issue of Anglo-Irish defence arrangements, including the maintenance of British naval bases in the territory of the new State, was relatively uncontentious.

The Irish negotiators, while accepting these defence arrangements without demur, nevertheless proposed, somewhat contradictorily, that Ireland should be neutral and that Britain should seek guarantees of Irish neutrality from other states. This proposal was, however, rapidly dropped when the British pointed out that no country would recognise as neutral an Ireland that had British bases on its territory.

In 1927, my father, Desmond FitzGerald, told the Dáil that, in the event of a general attack on these islands, it was 'perfectly obvious that the Irish army must cooperate with the British army'. But, when asked if Ireland could be neutral if the United Kingdom alone were attacked, or whether it would be 'bound up in' such an attack by conceiving of itself 'as part of the defence forces of the British Islands', he avoided the question.

Until 1935, the issue was in any event to some degree subsumed in the arrangements for collective security under the aegis of the League of Nations. Because of Ireland's commitment to the concept of collective security through the League, the Irish government under de Valera was prepared in September 1935 to join in imposing military sanctions on Italy following its attack on Abyssinia. This was despite the likely unpopularity of such a move in Ireland owing to the sense of a common bond between Ireland and Italy as two predominantly Roman Catholic countries. The failure of the League to act in this case was seen by de Valera as a 'bitter humiliation', following which Ireland, along with other small states, could, in de Valera's view, resolve 'not to become the tools of any great power' and to 'resist every attempt to force them into war against their will.'

Nevertheless, during the negotiations for the Anglo-Irish Agreement signed in April 1938, de Valera contemplated, and even proposed, a defence agreement between Ireland and Britain, a draft of which at one point came before the Negotiating Conference. With the decision to return the Treaty ports to Ireland, however, the defence agreement issue was apparently not being pursued by the British side and fell into abeyance.

In July 1938, de Valera took a first, very tentative step towards asserting Irish neutrality in any impending conflict, saying: 'Assuming other things were equal, if there were any chance of our neutrality in general being possible, we would probably say that we want to remain neutral.' He added that, nevertheless, 'consultation with Britain might be necessary and advisable' and in the event of an attack by a foreign state, it would be in Britain's interest to help Ireland, and 'we should try to provide in advance so that that assistance would be of the greatest possible benefit to us.'

Against this background, ad hoc cooperation on defence between Britain and Ireland took place in the months that followed, culminating in a proposal made by de Valera after the Munich Peace Conference to appoint a French officer as military adviser to the Irish army, as 'a clear indication to Germany and the world that Éire was on the side of the Western democracies.' This was rejected by the British government on the grounds that Ireland was a friendly country with access to secret military equipment and information, and that Britain could not take the risk that, through such an officer, these might become available to a foreign country. (It was believed in Irish army circles that the officer in question might have been General Charles de Gaulle, but there is no documentary evidence of this.)

In the event, Ireland was a non-belligerent during the war. It is questionable whether Ireland can properly be described as having been 'neutral' in the war, because the scale of assistance that it gave to Britain secretly was scarcely compatible with the concept of neutrality under international law. This cooperation, as set out in a British War Cabinet memorandum in February 1945, included the following:

1   Arrangements that Irish coast-watchers' reports be made *en clair* by radio on shipping movements, and in a code accessible to the British on aircraft movements, so that this information would be available to Britain

2   Agreement on a corridor for flying-boats from Lough Erne in Northern Ireland so as to give them immediate access to the Atlantic across County Leitrim, rather than having to follow a roundabout route around the northernmost point of County Donegal

3   Agreement that the British navy could attack German submarines in Irish coastal waters so as to combat the latest form of submarine warfare

4   No ban on foreign enlistment, such as existed in other neutral countries (this allowed more than forty thousand Irish people to join the British forces, including four thousand who had deserted from the Irish army but were not subject to any penalties for doing so if and when they returned on leave)

5   Close cooperation between the Allied intelligence services and Irish army intelligence

6   The release of British airmen after a period of internment, this internment period being dropped completely in the latter part of war (German airmen were interned throughout)

7 Full assistance in recovering damaged Allied aircraft

8 Close military collaboration in preparation for a possible German attack, including the establishment of a headquarters near Dublin for a British general to command the combined forces of the two states. (This latter aspect was not known to the Irish army.)

9 A ban on the use by the German Legation of its radio, and the confiscation of this radio in 1943

10 Towards the end of the war, the location of a radar station in Ireland

(This list of Irish departures from neutrality omitted the fact that, in 1938, help was sought by Ireland from Britain in establishing an Irish intelligence capacity to deal with German espionage in Ireland.)

As it suited de Valera to give, and after the war to maintain, the impression of Ireland having been strictly neutral, and as it suited Churchill to attack Ireland for the same reason, the nature and extent of Anglo-Irish wartime cooperation was not revealed until the relevant documentation was tracked down by historians several decades later.

On the other hand, in July 1940 de Valera refused a conditional British offer of Irish unity, which would have involved an immediate meeting of the parliaments of Northern Ireland and the Irish State to draft a new constitution, in return for either an Irish declaration of war on Germany, or Irish agreement to British troops being stationed in Ireland in preparation for a possible German attack. A condition was that such a move to the establishment of Irish unity would have to be agreed by the Northern Ireland government – to which, however, the proposition was never put because of de Valera's negative reaction to it. Lord Brookeborough, later Northern Ireland's prime minister, subsequently said privately that, had this proposal actually been put to the northern government, he for one could not have rejected it, in view of the war situation then facing Britain.

The reasons for Irish neutrality during the war are complex. Firstly, neutrality represented an assertion of sovereignty by a new state, the right of which to remain neutral had been contested in Britain during the 1930s – and was indeed rejected by Winston Churchill after the outbreak of war. Secondly, a major factor was, of course, fear of the consequences of involvement in the conflict, and in particular of aerial bombardment, i.e. the same factor that caused all other European states except France and Britain to remain neutral until they were attacked. Thirdly – and this reason is, I believe, greatly underestimated both in Ireland and abroad – there was a deep-seated (but for obvious reasons never publicly expressed) fear that voluntary involvement in the war on the Allied side could lead to a recrudescence of the civil war which had ended only sixteen years earlier. This fear was aggravated by the knowledge of contacts between Germany and the IRA; the IRA had in 1939 declared war on Britain and had been strong enough in late 1939 to capture, even if only temporarily, the entire ammunition reserves of the Irish army from the Magazine Fort in the Phoenix Park.

This consideration influenced not merely de Valera, who doubted his capacity to prevent such a catastrophe were Ireland to enter the war on the Allied side, but also politicians of the Opposition parties, including those who were most committed to the Allied cause – my own father amongst them. The only exception was the deputy leader of Fine Gael, James Dillon, who resigned from his post, and from the party, in 1942 on this issue – but after the United States, to which he was personally strongly committed, had been forced into the war by the Japanese attack on Pearl Harbour and the German declaration of war on the USA.

It should be added that the rallying of the Irish people to neutrality, which included the voluntary enlistment of almost fifty thousand men in the Irish army and a hundred thousand in the Local Defence Force, in addition to the more than forty thousand who volunteered for the British forces, was a powerful uniting force amongst the Irish population during these years.

In the post-war period, the success, as it was almost universally seen, of neutrality during the war led to the conversion of the pragmatic decision to remain a wartime non-belligerent into a myth of traditional neutrality. The establishment of the North Atlantic Alliance in 1948–49 coincided with the emergence in Ireland of a coalition government in which the post of minister for external affairs was held by Seán MacBride – who before the war had been a member of the IRA and, briefly in 1936, the IRA's chief of staff. Believing that the Atlantic Pact offered a possible opportunity to exert pressure on Britain to end the partition of Ireland, MacBride persuaded the government to make Irish reunification a precondition of Irish membership of the Alliance, on the grounds that 'no Irish government could participate with Britain in a military alliance while this situation continues, without running counter to the national sentiment of the Irish people.' This scheme failed: the British and Americans were unwilling to force Northern Ireland into the Irish State against the wishes of its people as a quid pro quo for securing bases in Southern Ireland.

At no stage in the prolonged discussions on participation in the Alliance was it argued by the Irish government that neutrality prevented it from joining the Atlantic pact. The government stated, indeed, that it was in agreement with the general aim of the proposed treaty and that 'the sole obstacle to Ireland's participation in the Atlantic pact was partition.' Moreover, shortly afterwards, in 1950, a proposal for an Irish/American defence pact was supported by Seán MacBride as minister for external affairs – but was rejected by the American government. This rejection was due in part to a concern not to weaken the alliance by setting an example of bilateral arrangements with a European country, but in part also to British opposition to a pact: the British government feared that such a pact might later be used by the Irish government as a means of rallying American support on the issue of partition.

There the issue of Irish neutrality lay until 1961, when the Irish government decided that, in the light of Britain's impending application for membership of the EEC, Ireland should also apply for membership. This decision was taken by a government headed by Seán Lemass, who had succeeded de Valera as Taoiseach in 1959 and had little sympathy with neutrality. Six months before the Irish application, in December 1960, Lemass had stated that 'there is no neutrality and we are not neutral', asking rhetorically whether, if help from Ireland were crucial to an Allied victory, 'Could we in the last resort refuse it?'

From 1961, when Ireland applied for membership of the European

Community, until 1981, the thrust of statements by successive Irish Taoisigh of both the main parties and by other ministers was to the effect that there were no reservations whatever about Ireland's membership and that, whenever the defence of Europe arose as an issue in a more integrated Europe, Ireland would play its part. Nevertheless, the Irish public remained attached to the concept of neutrality and was reassured from time to time that the issue was not likely to arise in the near future in view of the lack of progress towards a common foreign policy and full political union.

In March 1981, the Dáil debated the issue. In the course of this debate, the Taoiseach, Charles Haughey, rejected the suggestion that the Dáil reaffirm the 'principle of the neutrality of Ireland in international affairs and declare that our foreign and defence policies will continue to be based on this principle.' Haughey also rejected the view that, in accordance with the 'traditional policy of neutrality', it was necessary to establish without doubt the reality of Irish neutrality. Both of these affirmations were rejected by his Fianna Fáil government on the grounds that 'political neutrality or non-alignment is incompatible with membership of the European Community and with our interests and our ideals.'

In that debate, Haughey for the first time linked Irish involvement in Community defence to specific future developments, viz. the achievement of Economic and Monetary Union, and the raising of Irish per capita income to at least 80 percent of the Community average – from 61 percent, as it was at that time. (Ireland subsequently entered EMU, and the country's per capita disposable income now exceeds the Community average.)

It should, perhaps, be added that this debate followed Anglo-Irish discussions between Haughey and the British prime minister, Margaret Thatcher, in 1980. It is widely believed that, during these discussions, the Taoiseach had made proposals to Thatcher involving Anglo-Irish cooperation on defence. The fact that his government felt it necessary to reject an amendment to a Dáil motion on defence declaring that no such discussions had taken place was seen at the time as confirming that the matter had in fact been raised between the Taoiseach and the prime minister. Such a proposal was, however, ruled out by Thatcher in March 1981, when she stated that 'if Ireland wished to discuss defence, it would presumably do so with a much wider group of nations.'

It would therefore appear that, despite Ireland's purported commitment to neutrality, at two different points in time since the establishment of the North Atlantic Alliance, approaches have been made on behalf of Ireland to the US and British governments, respectively, proposing bilateral defence arrangements – and that, on both occasions, such arrangements were rejected by the other governments involved. It is interesting that these two approaches are associated with the two leading politicians most strongly identified in the public mind with traditional nationalist attitudes: Seán MacBride and Charlie Haughey.

The period 1981–87, during the bulk of which I led a Fine Gael–Labour coalition government, with Fianna Fáil in opposition (although Fianna Fáil were back in power between March and December 1982), was one during which the position of the Fianna Fáil Party on neutrality was radically, although not necessarily permanently, modified to one of apparent hostility to any involvement in European defence, or in NATO. In October 1981, discussions within the Community on options with regard to political cooperation led to controversy on whether these discussions prejudiced neutrality in the current context. My government was put on the defensive by the Opposition on this issue, although I argued that it was Fianna Fáil in government that had allowed the issue to be opened up at a meeting at Venlo in the Netherlands before the change of government in July 1981.

More seriously, in April and May of the following year, when Fianna Fáil were temporarily back in power, the conflict between Britain and Argentina led to a sudden reassertion by Haughey of Irish neutrality in the EC context. His government at first supported the EC sanctions against Argentina, specifically stating that this policy had no implications for the issue of Irish neutrality. But the government subsequently warned that Irish neutrality would be maintained in the event of a formal declaration of war by Britain against Argentina, and on 4 May, the Irish government withdrew its support for sanctions on the grounds that, 'as a neutral nation, Ireland . . . has always refrained from military alliances of any kind'. During the second half of May 1982, Ireland and Italy opted out of further sanctions.

During the period of my second government, from December 1982 to March 1987, I maintained, without giving special emphasis to it, the post-1961 Irish position that, with the evolution of the Community into

political union and economic and monetary union, Ireland would be prepared to undertake the defence commitments appropriate to such a stage
of political development. At the same time, I took care to ensure that,
pending such developments, current decisions made by the Community
did not prejudice our existing position as a non-member of a military
alliance.

Moreover, in view of the political sensitivity of the issues involved,
both within the Government and vis-à-vis the Opposition, and in order
to be able to rebut any accusations of prejudicing our neutrality, I
refrained from joining in – while nevertheless listening attentively to –
informal discussions on defence matters, including disarmament, at
European Council meetings between heads of government. From the
Opposition backbenches in 1987, during the debate on the constitutional
amendment to enable Ireland to adhere to the Single European Act, I suggested that the new Fianna Fáil government should not feel bound by this
self-denying ordinance. To give but one example, it seemed irrational to
be willing to discuss disarmament in arenas where such discussions would
have relatively little effect, such as the United Nations, while refraining
from doing so in the councils of the Community, where we might be able
to influence the policy of members of NATO in a positive and constructive direction.

There is, I think, some reason to believe that, in the mid-1980s, there
was a certain evolution in Irish public opinion on the issue of neutrality,
arising from a growing acceptance of the desirability of both political
union and economic and monetary union within the Community. There
is concrete evidence for this in a public-opinion poll, conducted in
December 1988, that showed 60 percent of Irish people supporting, and
only 19 percent rejecting, the proposition that a common organisation for
defence should be created between the twelve countries of the European
Community by 1992. This contrasted markedly with polls showing more
than 80 percent support for Irish neutrality – although this disparity may
reflect in some degree the fact that this question on European defence,
and earlier ones on neutrality, were posed in different terms.

Nevertheless, the neutrality issue remains capable of arousing
controversy. Thus in March 1989, when a motion was put down by independent members of the Seanad urging the government 'to reject calls for
involvement in so-called European defence commitments and to reaffirm

unequivocally the national policy of non-participation in military alliances', the Fianna Fáil government chose to accept it rather than to have any doubts cast on the party's credentials in the matter of neutrality – and, it has to be said, other parties followed suit.

Finally, the former Fianna Fáil minister for foreign affairs, Ray Burke, opposed Irish participation in the Partnership for Peace (involving members of NATO, Russia and associated states, as well as all the neutrals), which the previous Fine Gael–Labour–Democratic Left coalition government had been contemplating joining. As a result, Ireland for a time shared with war-torn Tajikistan in Central Asia (and, after its withdrawal from the Partnership, Malta) the eccentric distinction of being the only member state of the Conference on Security and Cooperation in Europe to abstain from participation in the Partnership.

It will be evident from what I have said that Irish neutrality does not conform to classic definitions of neutrality. Nor is the Irish situation similar to that of other neutral European states such as Switzerland, Austria and Sweden, which, in their different ways, have had much more clear-cut concepts of neutrality than Ireland has demonstrated since the State was founded. This confusion about Irish neutrality clearly reflects a divided public, an important section of which remains strongly influenced by a desire to remain detached from anything that can be represented as involving a military commitment outside the compass of the United Nations.

The fact that the current Fianna Fáil–led government has failed to maintain its unambiguous pre-1982 rejection of neutrality and its acceptance of eventual Irish participation in European defence has contributed to the present confusion. This confusion may, perhaps, persist until and unless developments in relation to European defence reach a stage where an Irish decision on the matter can no longer be avoided.

What we in Ireland have been slow to recognize – or perhaps have been slow to admit even to ourselves – is that, just as throughout the cold war we depended on NATO to deter, and to defend us from, possible Soviet aggression, so also do we depend today on NATO and, within NATO, most particularly upon our neighbour Britain, for our security in relation to external threats. Such external threats could take the form of threats to our energy security, possible nuclear threats from rogue states with missiles capable of reaching north-western Europe, nuclear pollution deriving from further reactor disasters in the former Soviet Union, or a breakdown of peace in Europe arising from an international conflict in the Balkans. In this acceptance of exclusive dependence upon others for our security against external threats, we have differed notably from states such as Finland and Sweden – countries that have been less fortunate in their near neighbours than we have been since we achieved independence more than eighty years ago.

If I may add a personal note at this point, I have always deplored this Irish form of 'dependent' neutralism since, in 1949, my elder brother Fergus (a former Irish army officer) and I initiated a correspondence in the *Irish Independent* in favour of NATO membership. I could never regard our decision to opt out of western European defence and to rely for our defence exclusively on a combination of other states in the formulation of whose policy we have no say as being in accordance with our dignity as a state, or with our moral responsibilities. Of course, as a realistic politician, working in government with another party committed to the policy of non-participation in a military alliance, and opposed by a party that adopted an opportunistic stance in relation to European defence, I had no alternative but to accept the status quo. But my personal beliefs on this matter have never changed since the North Atlantic Alliance was established in 1949.

8

THE ORIGINS AND RATIONALE OF THE

ANGLO-IRISH AGREEMENT OF 1985

On one issue in particular, my views have remained constant throughout my life: that is, the futility of attempting to achieve Irish political unity by force or by constraint, or otherwise than with the free consent of a majority of the people of Northern Ireland. A logical corollary of this stance has been a concern to develop a constructive dialogue between the Irish State and the unionist community in Northern Ireland, which needs to be linked to a move to create conditions within the Irish State that, economically, socially and culturally, would be attractive rather than repellent to northern unionists.

Such a policy, however, must not be pursued at the expense of the nationalist minority in Northern Ireland. Indeed, the truth is that an improvement in relations with unionists, had this been attempted, could have opened the way to the removal of discrimination against the northern minority by reducing unionist fears, which arose from a sense of being a threatened minority in the island as a whole. Nevertheless, there can be no disguising the fact that, in the pursuit of such a policy, tensions would have arisen from time to time between a proper concern for the right of the nationalist population in Northern Ireland to be free from discrimination, and efforts to improve relations with the unionist community.

In 1968–69, the inability of unionism to react constructively to the civil-rights movement – which involved the nationalist minority seeking, belatedly, to opt into the Northern Ireland system on a basis of equal treatment – created tensions that led to the suspension of devolved government in Northern Ireland in 1972. The aftermath of these events provided an opportunity for the Irish government that took office in 1973 to seek to pursue a constructive relationship with the unionist leadership under Brian Faulkner. This effort, which contributed to the signing of the Sunningdale Agreement, ultimately failed because of the resistance of important elements of unionism to the provisions of that agreement for power-sharing in Northern Ireland and for a new North–South relationship through a Council of Ireland. The experiment collapsed after the Ulster Workers' Council strike of May 1974.

In the aftermath of those events, the future of Northern Ireland was clouded in uncertainty. The new British Labour government was less than candid with the Irish government about the review it then undertook of its policy on Northern Ireland. This review – as our government then suspected, and as we now know to have been the case – included consideration of a possible withdrawal from Northern Ireland, and the British government sought to mislead the Irish government about their discussions with Sinn Féin in early 1975.

During that year of uncertainty, the Irish government pursued a dual policy of seeking to reassure the nationalist minority while avoiding any specific commitment as to the course of action it would pursue in the event of a British withdrawal, and at the same time seeking to establish a constructive, unofficial relationship with the unionists who had recently been involved in the process of undermining the Sunningdale Agreement. During 1976 and the first half of 1977, these contacts with Official Unionists proved particularly friendly and fruitful. They do not appear to have been maintained following the change of government in the South in June 1977, however.

In 1979, Fine Gael, in opposition, produced a policy document on Northern Ireland. This included a suggestion for a possible loose confederation of two Irish States that would devolve upwards – to a confederal government in which both parts of Ireland would be *equally* represented – a limited range of powers in relation to external affairs, security and monetary matters, and some financial matters. The two States could have different heads of state to whom, and by whom, ambassadors could be accredited. Northern Ireland, sharing equally in this confederal structure, would have the right to alternate with the Southern State in key positions in the confederal government, and also in Irish representation in the European Community.

This proposal was received by unionists in Northern Ireland without hostility. While describing the document as 'of no interest', Harry West, who was then leader of the Official Unionist Party, nevertheless said that his party would be willing to have talks on it. The leader of another small unionist party of that period, Ernest Baird, said that it would be wrong to dismiss it, and Ian Paisley avoided committing himself either way on the proposals set out in the document.

The Fine Gael–Labour government elected in June 1981 was deeply preoccupied during its early weeks in office with the Hunger Strike, but in August a Northern Ireland review conference of ministers and officials decided to give priority to developing contacts between Irish government officials and leading unionists, including, if at all possible, Ian Paisley, with a view to seeing how they could become involved in structures that might flow from the joint-studies process that had been initiated following the summit meetings in 1980 between Charles Haughey and Margaret Thatcher. It was also agreed at this conference that it would be desirable, if possible, to modify the provisions of Articles 2 and 3 of the Constitution with regard to Northern Ireland, with a view to creating more favourable conditions for discussions with unionists. It was following this that I as Taoiseach launched the idea of a constitutional review in a radio broadcast in September 1981.

Meanwhile, I had taken steps to secure a presentation of the unionist case to public opinion in the Republic by encouraging a visit to Dublin by a unionist group led by Bob McCartney. The aim of this visit was to alert public opinion in our State to the issues that would have to be confronted in any negotiations with the unionists.

At that stage, the full impact of the Hunger Strikes on nationalist opinion in Northern Ireland had not become clear. But during 1982, it became evident that the handling of the second Hunger Strike by the British government had radicalised a significant proportion of nationalist opinion in Northern Ireland, leading to considerable additional support for Sinn Féin and the IRA. Consequently, I came to the conclusion that, despite my own personal commitment to seeking progress by dialogue with the unionists rather than by talking over their heads to the British, I could not in conscience persist with such a policy if, as then seemed likely, such persistence in an approach that showed no signs of yielding any results in the foreseeable future would merely play into the hands of the IRA, increasing even further, perhaps to a dangerous degree, support for that organisation in Northern Ireland. Nor, in the circumstances, could I reasonably reject the need to combine some kind of 'Irish dimension' with our internal Northern Ireland devolution policy, for to do so would have merely contributed further to a possibly disastrous radicalisation of northern nationalist opinion and to an erosion of the position of the Social Democratic and Labour Party in favor of Sinn Féin.

These issues were now emerging as potential threats to the security of the whole island. If the IRA were to become able to claim, credibly, that it enjoyed majority support within the nationalist community in Northern Ireland, it might be emboldened to raise the threshold of violence to the point of risking outright civil war in the North – something from which it had always hitherto drawn back when its activities had seemed in danger of producing such a result.

Nevertheless, in the Dimbleby Lecture 'Irish Identities', which I delivered on BBC television in May 1982, when I was leader of the Opposition, I placed the main emphasis on the need to seek common ground between the two traditions in Northern Ireland, with a view to the emergence of political structures that would respect their diversity. Moreover, I added that we should seek to create in our own State the kind of pluralist society that might have evolved if Ireland had not been divided sixty years earlier.

I also suggested in that lecture the introduction of an all-Ireland policing and judicial system that would help both the British and ourselves to ensure that members of the IRA could not evade arrest and conviction by passing rapidly from one jurisdiction to another. And with regard to an eventual political solution, I suggested that we look for a structure, however novel, that would enable the people of Ireland to tackle together things that could not be done as well separately, such as security and the pursuit of the interests of all the Irish people in the European Community in cases where these interests differed from those of Britain. I also proposed that Ireland and Britain move towards a form of common citizenship.

This lecture thus foreshadowed some of the themes that were to be taken up in the New Ireland Forum in 1983–84 and in the Anglo-Irish negotiations of 1984–85 – although, at the time of that lecture, I had not come to a firm conclusion as to the details of the approach I would adopt in relation to these issues when returned to government.

Later, in October 1982, SDLP leader John Hume told me of his intention to propose the establishment of a nationalist Council for a New Ireland. I saw merit in seeking to establish common ground amongst nationalists, north and south, as a preliminary to negotiations with the British government directed towards reducing the alienation of the minority in Northern Ireland. However, it seemed to me desirable to provide an opportunity for a wider discussion that might involve unionists as well as nationalists, although I recognized that it was most improbable that the Unionist political parties, as such, would join in such an enterprise.

In a speech in October 1982 in Pittsburgh, Pennsylvania, whilst still in Opposition, I therefore proposed consultations involving all the parties in the Dáil, together with 'all in Northern Ireland who might be willing to talk to us, however informally, whether they be organized in political parties or not, and whether they sought, opposed, or (less probably!) were indifferent to the development of a new political relationship between North and South.' The discussion should be 'with all in Northern Ireland who may see merit in reducing tension within our island, and should be designed to seek the help of those concerned in identifying those aspects of the Constitution, laws and social arrangements of our State which pose obstacles to understanding amongst the people of this island.'

On my re-election to government in December 1982, these ideas began to take more concrete shape in my mind. The fact that, in the assembly election in October, Sinn Féin had secured 10 percent of the vote in Northern Ireland – more than a quarter of the total nationalist vote – and the likelihood that it would build upon this to increase its share of the vote still further, imbued me with a sense of urgency about securing arrangements that would reduce the alienation of a large part of the nationalist minority from the institutions of Northern Ireland. I believed that this might be achieved by seeking some form of involvement by the Irish government in a manner that might reduce the alienation of the nationalist minority, and make it possible to secure nationalist support for the institutions of government and policing in Northern Ireland.

I recognised, however, that such a move could be seen or represented by Fianna Fáil as an unacceptable compromise that fell short of the aspiration to Irish unity. I also realised that opposition from this source might make it impossible for me to secure the necessary public support for my objective of creating the conditions in which peace and stability could be restored to Northern Ireland and in which the IRA could be marginalized.

It was in this context that I presented to the government my idea of a 'New Ireland Forum', which would both provide a platform for the presentation of the unionist case to public opinion in the Republic, with a view to generating a more informed public approach to the Northern Ireland problem, at the same time hopefully securing a sufficient measure of support, or at least of acceptance, by Fianna Fáil for my proposed approach to the problem of the alienation of the minority in the North. The initial reaction of the Cabinet to my proposal was strongly negative; only two ministers supported me. The next day, however, through personal contacts with ministers, I secured a reversal of this initial negative reaction. I then presented my proposal to John Hume, making it clear to him that I was not prepared to accept his narrower concept of a nationalist Council for a New Ireland, and seeking his support for a New Ireland Forum open to all parties. Once he accepted my proposal, I asked him to assist me in securing acceptance by Fianna Fáil of the establishment of this Forum – acceptance that I felt might not be withheld once the SDLP had agreed to participate. This tactic was successful: Charles Haughey accepted with only minor textual changes the terms of reference of the Forum, from which I had deliberately excluded any direct reference to Irish unity, so as not to exclude unionist parties from its deliberations, and in particular so as to encourage the Alliance Party to participate. In the event, the Alliance Party decided not to take part because, I believe, of the terms of unilateral statements made about the role of the Forum by Charles Haughey, then leader of the Opposition. Nonetheless, several non-political unionists eventually made presentations to it.

I hoped to secure two things from the deliberations of the New Ireland Forum, which started work in May 1983. First, I hoped that there would emerge from it a set of principles for the achievement of peace and stability in Northern Ireland – the stated aim of the Forum – and that these principles would provide a common basis upon which the Irish and British governments could proceed to negotiate. The second result I hoped to achieve was the emergence of a number of 'models' for a possible eventual resolution of the Northern Ireland problem. These would include, as well as a unitary state and a federation or confederation, the idea of joint sovereignty or joint authority – explicitly leaving open, however, other possible models that could emerge from negotiations. By securing acceptance of a joint-sovereignty or joint-authority model in the report of the forum, I would, I believed, have eliminated, or at any rate greatly weakened, a possible Fianna Fáil objection to whatever might eventually emerge from an Anglo-Irish negotiation – which would inevitably be something other than a united Ireland. These twin objectives were in fact secured in the report of the Forum, even though this outcome was somewhat obscured in the public mind by the attempt of the Fianna Fáil leader, Charles Haughey, when presenting his views on the report, to suggest that the parties to the Forum had agreed that a unitary state was 'the only solution' – a view the other parties had specifically and unwaveringly refused to accept.

Meanwhile, in the summer of 1983, I authorised a 'deniable' approach to the British government that was designed to attract the attention and interest of Prime Minister Margaret Thatcher as she prepared to establish the priorities for her second term of office. This approach involved the suggestion of a willingness on our part to assist in defusing the alienation of northern nationalists through the direct involvement of the Irish government in the security process in Northern Ireland, should that commend itself to the British government.

In November, at a summit meeting with Margaret Thatcher, I explained my rationale for the New Ireland Forum and what I hoped would emerge from it. I confirmed our willingness to consider joint action in Northern Ireland, should the British government be open to this. But the issue of joint action was not pursued between us at this meeting because of the prime minister's sensitivity to the possibility of questions being asked in Parliament on this issue as a result of a recent airing of it in the media. I also reluctantly agreed that no negotiations would take place between the two governments until the Forum's report had been completed and publicised. My approach secured the prime minister's interest and was in fact followed in March 1984 by a British initiative along lines which, however, did not commend themselves to us.

After presentation of the Forum Report in May 1984, we initiated formal discussions with the British government at official level, presenting the three models set out in the report and filling out the joint-authority proposal. This latter proposal of ours provided for the exclusion of defence, foreign policy and finance from the scope of joint authority, although there might be consultations on these issues, and certain functions, such as representation of some or all of Northern Ireland's interests in the European Community could, by agreement between the two governments and after consultation with the Northern Ireland Assembly, pass from the British to the Irish authorities.

Joint authority, the establishment of which we saw as an *exercise* of sovereignty rather than a *cession* of sovereignty by the United Kingdom, was proposed, involving a full-time Cabinet minister from each government; it would directly control certain reserved areas until such time as responsibility for these were transferred to a Northern Ireland Executive. In the security area, a system of joint command was proposed, with alternating command at the highest level, and an all-Ireland court was also envisaged. As a basis for negotiations along these lines, we proposed early agreement on a public statement that the two governments based themselves on the principles set out in the 'Present Realities and Future Requirements' section of the Forum Report. These proposals had been formally authorised by our government after a full discussion in Cabinet. In the light of a reported negative initial reaction from the British prime minister to our suggestions, however, I came to the conclusion shortly afterwards that, if my initiative were not to founder very quickly, we should indicate at least a possibility of movement on Articles 2 and 3 of our Constitution, in return for a major package involving some form of joint authority.

In early July 1984, we received the formal British response to our proposals, which involved rejection of the unitary state and the federal and confederal models. We were told, however, that the British government had been much more cautious about rejecting the joint-authority proposal, although the issue on which it had really concentrated was our openness to other views, which had been expressed in paragraph 5.10 of the Forum Report. There was acceptance of the need for some sort of joint action in security operations. The British, however, saw insuperable difficulties with anything that looked like joint sovereignty and felt that the distinction we had made between joint authority as an exercise of sovereignty and the actual sharing of sovereignty would seem very fine indeed to unionists in Northern Ireland. The British government had, however, been trying to find a way around this, and they wondered if a system of government in Northern Ireland in which the Irish government would have a part, but which would not seem to involve a derogation of British sovereignty and yet would be seen by the nationalist minority as an effective means of protecting its interests, would be possible. An Irish government presence involving civil servants, in Belfast, could be an element in such a package.

It was on this basis that negotiations proceeded in the months that followed. But with the involvement of the Northern Ireland Office in the British negotiating team from September onwards, and the appointment of Douglas Hurd as Northern Ireland Secretary, there was a noticeable retreat on the part of the British negotiators. At a summit meeting in November 1984, the British government not only pulled back from positions that had hitherto been under active discussion but also played down the value of amending Articles 2 and 3 – the importance of which I had stressed in a private discussion with Margaret Thatcher at the outset of this meeting. They pressed the view that the more limited proposals it was now putting forward could be implemented without our having to change our Constitution.

Although the discussion at this meeting had thus taken an extremely negative turn, the agreed communiqué nevertheless had a positive tone, and at a subsequent press conference the British prime minister went to considerable trouble to present our discussions in a most positive light. Unhappily, the tone of voice in which, towards the end of her press conference, she responded to a particular question about the three Forum models had a negative impact on the minds of the journalists present, who came to the erroneous conclusion that the negotiations were effectively at an end.

The tone of Margaret Thatcher's response to the three Forum models evoked amongst a media and public who were, of course, unaware that, since July, our discussions had gone beyond these three models to examine other possibilities, a very negative response, not merely in Ireland but also in Britain and elsewhere. So much so, indeed, that when we met shortly afterward for a bilateral discussion in the margin of a European Council meeting in Dublin, Margaret Thatcher was moved to ask me: 'Garret, what did I do wrong?' Moreover, we were able to get US president Ronald Reagan to raise the matter at a meeting with her shortly afterwards in Washington and to ask for further discussion of it at their next bilateral encounter in February 1985.

All of this led to a radical reconsideration of the British stance, and on 25 January the British government presented proposals of a much more substantial character than those that had been adumbrated at the November summit, making it clear at the same time that they were not seeking or expecting an amendment to Articles 2 and 3 as a quid pro quo for what they were now suggesting. The new British proposals involved the establishment, within the Anglo-Irish intergovernmental framework set up in 1981, of a joint body to discuss Northern Ireland legal matters, relations between the police and the community, prisons policy, security coordination, and political human rights questions, as well as other topics that might be agreed. Within this joint body, every effort would be made to resolve differences rather than simply to report these differences to the two governments. There would be a joint secretariat in Belfast, with ministers from the two governments as joint chairs of the body. The question of joint or mixed courts for terrorist crimes would be considered by a subcommittee. In relation to policing, the body would put in hand a program of action that would include, among other things, the establishment of local consultative machinery, improvements in the handling of complaints, and action to increase the proportion of Catholics in the Royal Ulster Constabulary. The main object of all this was to make the police more readily acceptable among the nationalist community. There was to be a new structure to protect human rights and to prevent discrimination, and our views would be taken into account in appointments to a number of bodies. Finally, the proposal for a British–Irish parliamentary tier was described as 'still open'.

It was on this basis that the negotiations proceeded during early 1985. By the end of April, however, it was becoming clear that our proposals for 'confidence-building measures', as they were then described, which would involve the RUC and the Ulster Defence Regiment and would include a possible review of prison sentences related to a reduction of violence, were not being given adequate attention on the British side.

When I met Margaret Thatcher in the margins of the June European Council meeting in Milan, our discussions centred on these issues. In response to her reaction – that, in effect, on their side they were already afraid they had gone too far – I made it clear that our government had come to the conclusion that unless these 'associated measures', as they were by now being described, were implemented simultaneously with the signing of the agreement, our government could not back the agreement. After a very heated discussion, in which I was moved to go back at some length over the past performance of British governments in relation to Northern Ireland, the prime minister conceded that steps could after all be taken in respect of these matters. She suggested, however, that these steps should be described as 'implementing part of the agreement' rather than as involving 'associated measures'. In the months that followed, agreement was reached in relation to issues such as the accompaniment of the British army and the UDR by the police, and the appointment of additional Catholic judges to the higher courts in Northern Ireland, with a view to modifying a religious imbalance in these courts.

The primary concern of the Irish government throughout the negotiations had been to secure an outcome that was likely to have a significant impact on the alienation of much of the nationalist population from the political and security systems in Northern Ireland. While the outcome of the negotiations, in relation to security matters in particular, fell somewhat short of our objectives – with the result that it seemed unlikely that the particular aim of achieving a full identification by the minority with the policing system in Northern Ireland would be achieved – we judged that the proposed new structure would significantly enhance support among the nationalist community for constitutional politics and would have a noticeably adverse effect on support for and tolerance of the IRA within that community.

From early 1985 onwards, there had been concern on the part of some members of the Irish government as to the possible reaction of unionists to an agreement along the lines that seemed to be emerging. In contacts with unionist politicians around that time, we formed the impression that, especially in the case of the Official Unionist Party, some of those concerned had a very good idea of what was being prepared as a result of informal briefings by British officials – without, however, having seen the actual language proposed – and that they did not seem to find these ideas as alarming as expected. When we had passed on this impression to the British in February, they had responded by saying that there was not a monolithic unionist view – although they wondered whether the Official Unionists would 'come up to scratch', and whether they could deliver the electorate if Paisley sought a massive vote of disapproval. Several months later we were somewhat reassured on this issue when we were given further information by a senior unionist politician concerning the briefing on the negotiations which he had received from a Northern Ireland Office official.

The question of unionist attitudes to the impending agreement was raised again by members of our government at a meeting in mid-September at which further information was sought on the contacts we had been having with representatives of the different parties and other interests in Northern Ireland. A report on this was furnished to a government meeting at the beginning of October. In this report, the government was told that an important factor in assessing the current mood in Northern Ireland was that there had been widespread leaking by the British side of the progress that had been achieved, and about the discussions that were taking place between the two governments. These leaks had included information on the possibility of some form of Irish presence in Belfast, of significant changes in the security area involving the RUC and the UDR, and of a proposal by us for a mixed court for the trial of terrorist offences. Our officials also understood that, as James Molyneaux, leader of the Official Unionist Party, was a Privy Councillor, the British government had probably kept him well informed, on a Privy Council basis, as the talks had progressed. Reference was also made to numerous contacts that our officials had had with members of the Official Unionist Party and the Democratic Unionist Party, which had indicated that briefings of varying content had been given to a number of members of these two parties.

The report went on to say, however, that there were nevertheless indications that there would be significant opposition to the agreement from some unionists. A leading DUP member had told us that the argument the British government would use in trying to sell an agreement to the unionists, to the effect that it would help to defeat the IRA, would not be enough to compensate for what unionists would see as an infringement of sovereignty. Moreover, leading members of the Official Unionist Party had told us that their party would oppose any role for Dublin other than a minimal consultative one. If a ministerial or official presence in Belfast were to be involved, it would, we were told, be 'very difficult' for unionists to see this as other than an infringement of sovereignty.

The document continued that it was widely believed by serious observers and among middle-class moderate unionists with whom we had been in touch that the vast majority of the unionist population wanted peace and stability and would be prepared to accept a role for the Irish government and some form of power-sharing with northern nationalists, if the result were to be peace in Northern Ireland. Some unionist politicians had been more forthcoming and less belligerent in private than in public.

In a verbal briefing accompanying the memorandum, I told my colleagues that we had indicated to the British government that we had felt that there might be a case for a more formal briefing of the unionist politicians on the agreement but that the British had made the point that there was a great difference between the unionists and the SDLP, whose leaders we had fully briefed. The latter wanted the negotiations to succeed if the outcome was right, in their view, but there was no similar guarantee as regards the unionists. Our response to this had been that any such briefing would require the use of judgement and discretion but that, if possible, a situation should be devised such that the unionists could not say afterwards: 'Of course, if you had told us what was going on . . . ' We had made clear to the British that, while it was the view of our ministers that the British should consider briefing the unionists, we recognised that, of course, they might judge that it was better not to do so. In response to this, the British had said that they had in fact thought about it, and that 'something had been given to Molyneaux in his role as a Privy Councillor' but not to the DUP on the same scale, because, of course, its leader, Ian Paisley, was not a Privy Councillor.

On the basis of this information, and in the light of hints to us from some unionist sources that public indignation about an agreement would be accompanied by a measure of private acquiescence, I offered some reassurance to the members of the government who were concerned about the possible political reaction from unionists. At the same time, however, I told them that the best information we had suggested that there could be a significant violent backlash from paramilitaries on both sides.

It later became clear that we had overestimated the extent of briefing that had been provided by the British to Molyneaux personally and had also underestimated his unwillingness to face the realities of the situation – encouraged in this, we heard later, by Enoch Powell. It was only after the agreement had been signed that we were told that it had come as a great shock to Molyneaux, that he had refused a Privy Council briefing, contrary to what we had earlier understood, and that his contacts with Enoch Powell, and perhaps with a member of the British Cabinet, had led him to believe that there would be no agreement, or at any rate that there would be no agreement that did not include an amendment of Articles 2 and 3. Accordingly, he had discounted all the media leaks that had been intended to alert him and his colleagues to what was likely to emerge. My own efforts to make personal contact with Molyneaux during the negotiations had eventually proved fruitless; he had withdrawn agreement to meeting me privately.

From all this, it will be clear that the agreement was never envisaged by the Irish government as an attempt to 'downface' the unionists, as they subsequently alleged. From the inception of the process that led to the agreement, the objective had been to weaken support for the IRA by reducing the alienation of the nationalist minority in Northern Ireland and to stabilise the position in that area by creating conditions in which this minority could identify with the system of authority there, as it had not previously been able to do.

It should, of course, be added that, until the eve of the signing of the agreement, we were uncertain also about the nature of the reaction to it that we could expect from northern nationalists. From an early stage, the SDLP leader, John Hume, had been kept in touch with developments, and during the first half of 1985 the party's deputy leader, Seamus Mallon, and two other leading members of the party were brought into our confidence. They, however, quite properly retained their independence of action, pending consultation with their colleagues when the agreement was finally settled. In terms of ending nationalist alienation and securing nationalist acceptance of the institutions and security structure in Northern Ireland, the form the agreement eventually took was less helpful than we had originally hoped. In fact, until a couple of days before the agreement was signed, we were not certain that it would secure the support of all the leading members of the SDLP.

In the final discussion that took place with the SDLP leaders, I told them that what had emerged fell short of our aspirations and that, in signing the agreement, the Irish government realised that it was taking a considerable risk – as, of course, the SDLP would be doing in supporting it. But within the agreement there was, I believed, a potential for much more progress – and, even if we failed to swing nationalist opinion back from Sinn Féin to the SDLP, I was in no doubt that it had been worth trying. The four SDLP leaders then gave the agreement their unanimous support.

It should be said that both governments anticipated a significant increase in violence from both the IRA and loyalist paramilitaries in the aftermath of the agreement and made preparations to deal with such a contingency. In the event, however, there was no significant upsurge in violence in the period immediately following the agreement, and the level of violence during 1986 was no greater than in 1985 – contrary to the impression subsequently fostered by some interested parties.

One further point should, perhaps, be added by way of a footnote. In the early months of 1985, there were indications that support for the IRA had already started to wane and that the danger that had led us to initiate these negotiations – that the IRA might be encouraged by increased support among the nationalist minority in Northern Ireland to raise the level of violence to a civil-war level – was diminishing. Nevertheless, although the urgency of securing an agreement was somewhat reduced as a result of this apparent drop in support for the IRA, we remained convinced that the alienation problem among the nationalist community continued to be a major one and that an agreement along the lines that eventually emerged remained desirable with a view to overcoming this problem.

So much for the facts of what happened during the negotiation of the Anglo-Irish Agreement – at least as seen from the Irish side. Let me add a few additional remarks. Tribute should be paid to the principal negotiators. On the Irish side, the key political figures guiding the negotiation under my overall leadership were the Tánaiste, Dick Spring; the minister for foreign affairs, Peter Barry; the minister for justice, Michael Noonan; and successive attorneys-general, Peter Sutherland and John Rogers. At civil-service level, the Irish negotiators were led by the Cabinet secretary,

Dermot Nally, supported by the secretaries-general of the departments of foreign affairs and justice, respectively Sean Donlon and Andy Ward; assistant secretary Michael Lillis; the Irish ambassador in London, Noel Dorr; and the head of the attorney-general's office, Declan Quigley.

9

THE FUTURE OF NORTHERN IRELAND

Partition proved to have a powerful internal dynamic, as each part of the island pursued its own very different goals. In the nature of things, southern governments moved to divide the island more deeply by means of effecting a radical change in the ethos of the area under their jurisdiction, through an Irish-language revival initiated in the schools and the public service, and also by giving its Constitution and laws a Catholic tinge whilst rejecting a 'Catholic State', such as the Vatican wished to see. Everyone involved grossly underestimated the extent to which loyalty to the new Irish State on the part of its inhabitants would quickly replace any real, as distinct from sentimental, sense of an all-island Irishness. By contrast, the North changed much less, although Protestant fears there perpetuated Catholic alienation.

Paradoxically, while southerners lost their sense of an all-Ireland Irishness as a result of their loyalty to their new State, northern Protestants never lost the feeling that they were a threatened minority in the island rather than a secure majority in their own polity. And the peoples of both areas were eventually left with a sense of guilt about the way they reacted to their new situation.

In the South, for decades this sense of guilt was easily assuaged by Anglophobic anti-partition irredentism – which was given free rein until the outbreak of violence in the North forced a fundamental rethink by the political class between 1969 and 1972. This violence soon led to a belated recognition (public on the part of some, private on the part of others) that the interests of the Irish State lay in seeking jointly with Britain to create a stable and peaceful Northern Ireland, remaining within the UK until such time as a majority in the North might decide otherwise. And recognition also grew of the fact that there was a need to rethink the neo-Gaelic and Catholic uniculturalism that had marked the new Irish State from its foundation

Twenty years were, however, to elapse – between the early 1970s and the early 1990s – before all political parties in the Irish State felt able publicly and unambiguously to adopt both the concept of pluralism as the ethos of their State and the principle of consent as a necessary basis for Irish unity – and for a British government to recognise the futility of seeking an end to the violence primarily by security measures and instead faced up to the political steps that needed to be taken to secure an end to republican violence. The final acceptance by all but a tiny minority of republicans, north and south, of the principle of consent has now created the conditions for the belated emergence of a stable Northern Ireland polity that is accepted and endorsed by all its people.

The reality is that, to an even greater extent than in the cases of Scotland and Wales, the domestic needs of Northern Ireland are different from those of England – in respect of such issues as strategic investment, industrial development, agriculture, regional policy and education, and also in relation to the need to carry through a transition from a security-dominated to a 'normal' society. To someone from the South, the revived form of developed government of Northern Ireland that was briefly established some time after the Belfast Agreement seemed to work well at what may be called the 'operational level'. The successful preparation of the Third Draft Programme for the future, the constructive ways in which ministers tackled their tasks, and the positive spirit in which the new North–South relationship began, were all encouraging developments. The subsequent prolonged hiatus has obscured these positive aspects of the new devolved system of government.

The fact that a constructive approach marked the early work of this new devolved administration – despite the fact that one party in it was still linked to a paramilitary body, and that another felt unable to join with its partners at executive meetings – suggests that, with the resolution of the political crisis, a re-formed executive, responsible to the assembly, will eventually prove to be a dynamic force in the future development of Northern Ireland. As it is a new and contemporary development, and not burdened by a historic heritage of customs and precedents – as are the governments of Britain and the Republic – a devolved executive in

Northern Ireland seems to me to have a huge potential capacity for innovative action, based on a very close relationship with the people of Northern Ireland.

As to the North–South relationship: freed from the shadow of Articles 2 and 3 of the Irish Constitution, this relationship has, I believe, great possibilities for constructive action, especially in areas where neither part of the island is large enough on its own to maximise its potential – energy and tourism, for example. This has indeed already been demonstrated by the work of the North–South Ministerial Council and its implementation bodies.

I have to say, however, that I regret that industrial development was not included in the brief list of areas agreed for North–South action. This is an area of activity where the Republic has a remarkable record of achievement, through the work of the highly sophisticated IDA. It has long seemed to me that a single, all-Ireland IDA, organised on a basis that would ensure equal treatment for both areas, could have a powerful impact on industrial development in Northern Ireland.

It is important that residual unionist fears about closer relations with the Republic, which, logically, should have been removed by the acceptance of the consent principle by the Republic as well as by republicans in Northern Ireland, should not inhibit joint action in the economic sphere in cases where Northern Ireland would be a net beneficiary. The Republic has the capacity – and, I would hope, the will – to assist the Northern Ireland economy, helping it to catch up with both the South and the United Kingdom in the years ahead – a point to which I shall return. This potential should be fully exploited.

Of course, there remain many problems to be overcome in 'bedding down' this new polity. But I want to turn at this point to three longer-term issues facing a Northern Ireland that has its own devolved government. First, as the Alliance Party never tires of pointing out, the political foundations of the new structures are essentially sectarian. The Constitution of Northern Ireland as it emerged seven years ago is based on balancing politically two distinct communities. It discourages the emergence of normal political divisions along the lines of divergent views as to how far the initial distribution of resources arising from the working of a capitalist system needs to be modified by redistributive action – which is the issue that provides the key element for normal politics in most democratic societies.

In Northern Ireland, such issues will have to be fought out and decided within a government structure that is predetermined by quite different forces – forces that cut right across conventional socio-economic divisions. How will this work? And how, if at all, can this system ever become normalised within a Northern Ireland context? This issue must in time come to preoccupy all those who wish to see Northern Ireland becoming a normal democratic society.

The second issue to which I want to draw attention is the potential impact of demographic change in Northern Ireland. It is clear that, in justifying the abandonment of violence and future reliance on the democratic process, the Sinn Féin leadership has relied heavily on what it has claimed to be the prospect of an emerging Catholic majority – perhaps, they suggest, as early as 2016. Earlier in the current decade, this approach was accompanied by rumours spread about the 2001 Census, suggesting that it would reveal that people of a Catholic background already constituted between 46 and 47 percent of Northern Ireland's population. That particular balloon was punctured by the publication of the 2001 Census results, which, when allowance is made for the very small number who refused to state their religious background, indicate that about 44.5 percent of today's population come from a Catholic background – as do about 42 percent of the adult population, viz. the electorate.

Projected forwards, these figures suggest that, even if the fertility rate of Catholics continues to be higher than, or at the very least equal to, that of Protestants – an assumption upon which recent trends in Catholic countries in southern Europe cast considerable doubt – some thirty years would be likely to elapse before the electorate could contain a majority of voters from a Catholic background. This timescale could, however, be somewhat foreshortened if, despite a political settlement and the return of normal conditions to Northern Ireland, the proportion of Protestant young people going to Britain for higher education, and staying away thereafter, remained about twice as high as in the case of young people of a Catholic background.

Whether Northern Ireland remains in the United Kingdom or unites with the Republic will not be decided by a simple religious headcount, however. Throughout much of the 1990s, annual surveys of opinion in

Northern Ireland showed that a significant majority of Catholics – usually close to 35 percent – expressed a preference for remaining in the United Kingdom. Since the Belfast Agreement, this view has also been expressed by a smaller proportion of Catholics polled – around 20 to 25 percent. On this latter basis, for a majority in favour of Irish unity to emerge amongst the Northern Ireland electorate, it would be necessary both for the Catholic fertility rate to remain indefinitely at or above that of Protestants and also for those Catholics who have hitherto favoured remaining in the United Kingdom to change their minds on this issue.

The fact that a majority in favour of Irish political unity is thus not likely to emerge within the next quarter of a century, and might not emerge even thereafter, does not mean, however, that concern about such a development might not, in the period ahead, be a destabilising factor amongst elements of the Protestant community, especially as republicans will have an interest in keeping this particular pot boiling. On the other hand, this changing demographic situation should also offer a strong incentive to unionists to act in such a way as to encourage elements in the Catholic community to maintain their support for continued participation in the United Kingdom.

A third issue affecting Northern Ireland's future is that of its capacity for economic growth. In the second half of the 1960s, the economies of both Northern Ireland and the Republic were growing at a rate of more than 4 percent a year – much faster than that of Britain, where the growth rate was then about 2.25 percent. Writing about Northern Ireland in 1972, in a book entitled *Towards A New Ireland,* I was emboldened to suggest that, if this disparity between the Irish growth rates, north and south, and the growth rate in Britain continued, both parts of this island could catch up with Britain within a quarter of a century. I was nearly right about the Republic, for, despite the mess made of our economy at the end of the 1970s, which took eight years of pain to put right, Irish GNP per head is now within 5 percent of the UK level.

Northern Ireland was less fortunate. From the early 1970s onwards, its growth rate slowed, partly because of the gradual disappearance of its declining industries, but also because of the Troubles. Nevertheless, although growth there slowed, during those thirty years the economy of Northern Ireland caught up slightly with Britain, reducing the shortfall on the overall UK level of output per head from 30 to about 25 percent.

Most strikingly, however, because of the very much faster growth in the Republic, Northern Ireland's share of the total output of the island of Ireland dropped to 23 to 24 percent – as against the 37 to 38 percent of total Irish output for which it was responsible half a century ago. Northern Ireland's output per head is 21 to 22 percent below that of the UK.

Recently, the Northern Ireland economy has been showing some resilience. During the recession of the early 1990s, its growth rate was very little lower than that of the Republic, but it is not matching the 4 to 5 percent-plus growth rate achieved by the Republic since 2003.

For Northern Ireland to catch up with the rest of the UK in terms of output per head will not be easy. The Republic did so in the 1990s because of an unexpected combination of circumstances: a uniquely rapid 4.5 percent annual growth of labour supply – due to demographic factors – coinciding with exceptional demand for Irish labour in Ireland on the part of external investors. These factors increased the rate of growth of labour productivity to double the average European rate.

Some major factors that have contributed to this exceptional outcome are not currently available to Northern Ireland – most notably the 12.5 percent corporate tax rate, but also the non-specialised secondary education system and the supplementation of the university system with a network of regional technical colleges which has enabled the Republic to achieve an overall domestic rate of entry into third-level education of as much as 60 percent. Partly because of this extensive third-level-education structure, the Republic does not suffer form the kind of brain drain at third level that is such a disturbing feature of Northern Ireland.

Devolution will offer Northern Ireland the possibility of addressing some, although not all, of these problems. While it may be difficult for it to catch up with the rest of the UK in terms of output per head, as the Republic has virtually done, there is certainly room for a further significant narrowing of this gap.

What has already been achieved in difficult circumstances is impressive, e.g. the increase of one-quarter in the numbers at work since 1986 – almost twice the British increase for that period. Although the low level of unemployment means that an available labour supply no longer offers a significant source of additional workers, the number of eighteen-year-olds in the Northern Irish population is one-sixth higher than in the rest of Europe, and a final peace settlement should release workers from the security sector.

Even more striking has been the huge increase in manufacturing productivity in Northern Ireland between 1996 and 2001 – although, as in the Republic, this naturally came to a halt in the face of the recent slowing of global economic growth.

A peaceful and stable Northern Ireland, enjoying widespread external goodwill, with its own devolved government in which representatives of both communities work together harmoniously, would have an opportunity substantially to break out of debilitating over-dependency on very large-scale transfers from Britain. Of course, transfers from richer to less-well-off parts of any state are a normal feature – in the Republic, some counties derive between 4 and 6 percent of their disposable income from net transfers (the excess of social transfers over taxes paid). But beyond a certain point, over-dependence on such transfers debilitates the local economy, depressing initiative. In the case of Northern Ireland, the scale of its dependence on transfers from the UK may be judged from the fact that, although its output per head is now 17 percent lower than in the Republic, its living standards probably remain somewhat higher.

Another way of measuring this excessive dependence is by reference to the proportion of output that is absorbed by private consumption. The European average ratio of private consumption to GDP is 58 percent. In Britain, which invests a very low proportion of its output in its future, the figure is 65 percent. In Northern Ireland, the ratio of consumption to output is 80 percent – which means that a very large proportion of its investment and public spending has to be financed by Britain.

With an effective devolved government, Northern Ireland could perhaps start to break out of this over-dependence and recover some of the self-reliance and economic dynamism of earlier times, for its economy is no longer being pulled down by the decline of its older industries – shipbuilding and traditional engineering, textiles and clothing. That process has effectively been completed.

10

THE NORMALISATION OF THE BRITISH–IRISH RELATIONSHIP

The Irish–British relationship is usually seen in exclusively politico-cultural terms. This approach ignores the existence of a fundamental economic imbalance between the islands.

In my view, the emergence of a normal relationship between Ireland and Britain required the elimination of historic economic inequalities between the two peoples. And, for reasons that I shall explain, this could not have been achieved without a combination of two developments. First, the achievement of Irish political independence, the objective case for which was not – as it has often been presented – merely politico-cultural, but also economic. And second, participation of both Ireland and Britain in a wider European single market within which Ireland could achieve a more balanced and equal relationship with its neighbouring island, and catch up with it in economic terms. The new State's experience during the fifty-year period from 1922 to 1972 demonstrated that the first development without the second provided an inadequate basis for such a normalisation.

In addition to the elimination of economic inequality, a further crucial factor in this process had to be a settlement, involving both the two States and the two communities in Northern Ireland, of the problem posed by the conflicting identities of those two communities.

Even if Irish independence had not been preceded by a partition of the island, the first two preconditions would have applied. However, by intensifying the post-independence Irish–British tensions that were inherent in a continuing unbalanced economic relationship, partition seriously exacerbated what was, in fact, a fundamental economic problem between

Ireland and Britain, and led eventually to a bitter conflict within the confined area of Northern Ireland.

The preparation of what is likely before long to become a widely accepted political settlement of the Northern Ireland problem has been facilitated by common Irish and British membership of the EU. A basic problem, however, remains, in relation to the domestic economy of Northern Ireland, viz. the debilitating character of its continued very high degree of economic dependence upon Britain, which was discussed at the end of the last chapter.

The validity of my argument concerning the first two preconditions for normalisation of the British–Irish relationship clearly depends first upon the existence of what can fairly be characterised as an objective Irish need for political independence, and subsequently on demonstrating that such political independence provided an inadequate basis for a normalised Anglo-Irish relationship unless it was accompanied by the ending of economic dependence on Britain – an outcome which could be secured only through membership of a European single market by both States. Finally, my thesis depends on demonstrating that the achievement of economic parity with neighbouring Britain was necessary for the normalisation of Irish–British relations – a less tangible, because basically psychological, point.

Before looking at the underlying economic issues, it is, however, necessary to refer briefly to what eventually became a hugely complicating factor in the whole Anglo-Irish relationship – to wit, the Ulster settlement element of the gradual conquest of Ireland by England, which had climaxed in the late seventeenth century.

Unlike the simultaneous conquest of North America, the British conquest of Ireland was necessarily very incomplete. In North America, a combination of the technological superiority of the conquerors and the genetic vulnerability of the indigenous population led to the almost complete disappearance of the latter. But in Ireland, the indigenous and settler populations had historically shared a common epidemiological experience, having survived similar European infections over preceding millennia. For that reason, and despite a certain technological advantage enjoyed by the conquerors, in the Irish case the whole indigenous Irish population survived conquest. This was true even where, as in the north-east of Ireland, conquest was accompanied by extensive settlement, involving an element of local displacement of the indigenous population to neighbouring poorer land.

In most of the remainder of the island, the indigenous population was not displaced: conquest there generally took the form of a transfer of the ownership of land rather than an actual land settlement. The problem that was thereby created in the larger part of the island was thus capable of eventual resolution by land reform – a process accomplished at con-siderable cost by the British government in the late nineteenth and early twentieth centuries. In the northern province of Ulster, however, most good land had, in fact, been taken during the course of the seventeenth century by Scots or English – amongst them my own maternal ancestors from Scotland, who settled in Down and Antrim.

The Union of 1801 led to a century-long flow of resources from Ireland to Britain amounting to between 2 and 5 percent of Irish GDP annually. This arose from the fact that, until the twentieth century, gov-ernment spending of taxation resources drawn from the whole of a poli-ty was almost exclusively concentrated on central administration and on defence of the State: there were then no transfers to local level for edu-cation, health, housing, social welfare or local administration. The disap-pearance in 1800 of an Irish government, however narrowly based it may have been socially or religiously, thus imposed a debilitating drain on what had always been a much poorer economy than that of Britain.

This problem of perverse financial transfers was resolved during the first decade of the twentieth century by a combination, first, of Tory transfers from Britain to foster economic activity with a view to discour-aging demand for Home Rule (or, worse still from Britain's viewpoint, independence), and second, the subsequent Liberal government's intro-duction of old-age pensions and unemployment insurance. As a result, by 1911, for the first time in history, England was subsidising rather than exploiting Ireland. (Was the disappearance of this traditional nationalist grievance, which had the potential to diminish support for independence as against Home Rule, perhaps subconsciously a factor in the minds of some of those who organised the 1916 Rising?)

At this distance in time – and in the light of Northern Ireland's recent experience of the negative economic consequences of over-dependence on financial transfers from Britain, which within the past half-century have helped to reduced that region's share of total Irish output from about 37.5 percent to 23.5 percent of the total for the island – we can see that, in fact, this development made more urgent than ever the achievement of Irish independence. For, had the greater part of Ireland not become independent in the 1920s, the emergence of the welfare state in the UK in subsequent decades could have left what is now the Irish State dependent on Britain to the tune of 20 percent or more of its national income.

That scale of financial dependence might well have made a move to political independence by Ireland too costly in the short term for the Irish people to risk it. And, without the power to develop its own economy – as the Irish State eventually proved capable of doing by deploying control of its own taxation and economic policies successfully towards that end – Ireland might never have been able to become a viable and prosperous State, with a GNP per head now virtually equal to that of Great Britain. This is an aspect of Irish independence that has been completely ignored by Irish political historians.

In addressing the normalisation of the Anglo-Irish relationship, something must be said briefly about the impact on the British–Irish economic relationship of joint Irish and British membership of the European Community, now the European Union. Although this was not understood at the time when Ireland became independent, the fact is that, since the 1890s, Britain had become the slowest-growing economy in Europe – and this was to continue to be the case until about 1980. For half a century after independence, this sluggish British market was the only one in Europe open to Irish exports. Moreover, for the great bulk of Irish agricultural exports – which, even as late as 1972, constituted almost half of the country's export trade – Britain was the worst market in the world. Since 1846, successive British governments had opened the country to food imports from all over the world, in a successful attempt to keep down prices, and thus wages, so as to give Britain an artificial advantage in world trade.

Irish political independence thus failed to change the unfavourable economic situation in which Ireland had found itself as a result of various British policies over the centuries, and the Irish economy remained depressed throughout almost all of the half-century that followed independence. Only the opening of Continental European markets to Irish agricultural and industrial products could boost the Irish economy, by offering remunerative prices for farm products and by providing an opportunity to attract industrial investment by foreign – especially US – firms that were interested in serving the Continental European market. So, in those years, to the political grievance of partition was added the reality of a debilitating neo-colonial relationship of almost complete economic dependence upon the former colonial power, Britain.

At the end of the 1950s the hope of breaking out of this situation by joining the newly established European Community – a development that, in the event, was postponed until 1973 – led to a dramatic outward reorientation of the Irish economy, which enabled Ireland for the first time to achieve a growth rate comparable with that of its Continental neighbours. Emigration fell – and was indeed temporarily replaced by net immigration in the 1970s – and for the first time in a hundred and twenty years the population rose quite rapidly in the 1960s and 1970s as the younger generation, now remaining at home instead of emigrating, married and had children.

Until the mid-1980s, this population growth absorbed so much of the increased Irish output that it was only in the 1990s that the level of per capita Irish output and incomes began to catch up with that of the rest of the EU, raising Irish GNP per head from 60 to 100 percent of the fifteen-member EU average within just a decade. That is the fastest economic catch-up by any country in European history.

Membership of the EU helped to transform the Irish economy; this in turn had a positive impact on the Irish–British relationship in a number of ways. First, it gave Irish agriculture – which in 1972 still accounted for 18 percent of GDP – a major, if temporary, boost that helped greatly to offset the short-term negative effects of the transition from industrial protection to free trade. This was because British membership of the European Community required that country to abandon its more-than-a-century-old cheap-food policy, which had debilitated the Irish economy. (The negative impact of this policy had, in fact, been intensified at the end of the 1940s by the introduction of direct subsidies to UK farmers.)

Second, alone amongst the northern European beneficiaries of the EU Common Agricultural Policy, Ireland also benefited significantly from EU structural funds, which were designed to help develop the social and physical infrastructure of less-developed parts of the Community. Between 1974 and 1996, transfers through the Community Budget to Ireland from these two schemes added an average of 4 percent each year to the country's GNP.

Third, and by far most important, the opening of the Continental European market to Irish industrial products enabled Ireland for the first time to attract large-scale foreign industrial investment as a result of a combination of its natural advantages – an English-speaking labour force, political stability and low social costs – and of its chosen policies of low corporation tax, sophisticated industrial promotion, and free education to university level. Aided by exceptional flows into the Irish labour market – employment rose by 62 percent between 1991 and 2005, more than seven times faster than in the rest of the EU – the Irish economy expanded by 8.5 percent a year between 1993 and 2000. These developments ended Irish economic dependence on the UK, to which Ireland now sends less than 18 percent of its exports.

The partition of the island of course also had a serious negative impact upon the Irish–British relationship. The 1921 Treaty, which created an independent Irish State, included a right for Northern Ireland to opt out of this State within a month of its formal establishment – on the basis that the boundary of Northern Ireland would then be determined by a Commission 'in accordance with the wishes of the inhabitants, so far as may be compatible with economic and geographic conditions'. The Irish negotiators, ignoring the qualifying sub-clause, seem to have thought that this would involve large-scale transfers of parts of Northern Ireland that would make its survival politically impossible. In 1925, however, the South African chairman of the Commission interpreted the economic and geographic sub-clause as limiting boundary changes to ones that would not interfere with the economic hinterlands of local towns. His adjudication, while adding very few parts of Northern Ireland to the Irish State, would, quite unexpectedly, have put some parts of the Irish State into Northern Ireland. In the event, the two governments decided to leave the boundary unchanged.

Following the failure of the Boundary Commission in 1925 to yield the kind of major changes to the North–South frontier that had been hoped for, successive Irish governments seemed to ignore the Northern Ireland issue, failing thereafter to pursue with vigour aspects of discrimination by northern unionist politicians against the Catholic nationalist minority. In the Irish State, partition was in fact demoted to a domestic political football at election times, becoming the subject of inflammatory irredentist rhetoric.

Right up to the outbreak of violence in Northern Ireland in 1969, British governments, for their part, felt inhibited from carrying out their responsibilities there because of fears that they would be dragged back into Irish affairs as a result of a northern government resigning in protest at British intervention to restrain abuses. Such a mass resignation had in fact been threatened at an early stage of the existence of the new Northern Ireland polity. Those British fears also no doubt contributed to the extraordinary, and very dangerous, decision to rule out any parliamentary questions on Northern Ireland affairs in the House of Commons.

Let me turn now to the political relationship between Britain and an independent Ireland. During the 1920s, Ireland participated in and then came to lead successfully a movement to secure unfettered sovereignty for the Dominions of the British Commonwealth. This movement laid the foundations for the later, somewhat tortuous, emergence of Ireland in 1949 as a republic outside the Commonwealth. But from the moment when Ireland left the Commonwealth (*de facto* although not yet *de jure* – that is to say, after the Ottawa Conference of 1932) until, together with Britain, it joined the EU in 1973, the relationship between the Irish and British States was tenuous and often tetchy.

During the Second World War, there were of course contacts at ministerial, civil-service, army and secret-service level, as Ireland, despite being nominally neutral, worked closely with Britain (and, separately, but only at secret-service level, with the United States). In peacetime, however, there were a surprisingly limited number of occasions when members of the two governments met each other. These meetings were usually to negotiate improved trade arrangements, as in 1938, 1948 and 1965 – although it has to be said that the first of these negotiations involved more than trade, viz. the return of the naval bases which Britain had retained when the 1921 Anglo-Irish Agreement conceded political independence to Ireland.

In between these occasional negotiations, there was extraordinarily little contact between the two governments; such contacts seem to have been confined to informal meetings between ministers for agriculture, health and labour respectively at annual Food and Agriculture, World Health and International Labour Organisation conferences, and perhaps also casual contacts between their respective ministers for foreign affairs, meeting at the UN in the years after Ireland's belated admission to that organisation in 1955.

Irish wartime neutrality had a long-lasting, negative impact on British political and public opinion. This was despite recognition by the British chiefs of staff of the advantage of not having to extend the protection of British forces to the neighbouring island, and of the avoidance of the risk that Irish entry on the side of the Allies would have sparked off unrest, or even a renewed civil war, in Ireland – a development from which only the Germans could have benefited.

Given the close cooperation of the Irish security authorities with their British opposite numbers, including the assistance of one key Irish expert with the breaking of German codes, Irish neutrality at the operational level was seen in a quite positive light by both British and US officials – but not by most of those countries' politicians. I believe that, right up to the 1990s, the shadow of Irish wartime neutrality remained a negative factor in both the political and popular relationships between the two countries. It was only with the emergence in Britain in the 1990s of two prime ministers, John Major and Tony Blair, who were both members of a generation that had no negative memories of Ireland's wartime neutrality that a serious psychological barrier on the British side to a normalised relationship between the two States finally disappeared.

The longer-term consequences of the persistent failure on the part of the British to tackle the problem of discrimination in Northern Ireland were the emergence in the late 1960s of the civil-rights movement, the subsequent breakdown of order in Northern Ireland, the introduction of the British army in partial replacement of a discredited and demoralised Royal Ulster Constabulary, and eventually the emergence of the Provisional IRA.

In the Republic, these events produced total confusion. No one in politics or the civil service, except for a couple of senior civil servants, particularly T. K. Whitaker (despite having moved from the key post of secretary to the department of finance to the governorship of the Central Bank six months before the violence of August 1969), seems ever to have given any serious thought to the Northern Ireland problem.

Moreover, unhappily, in 1969 and early 1970 the Taoiseach, Jack Lynch, did not command the loyalty or respect of two ambitious ministers, who took it on themselves to help split the northern, extreme nationalist wing of the IRA away from its left-wing leadership – to the philosophy of which these ministers were ideologically antipathetic – and who then backed the breakaway Provisional IRA group with money and attempted arms imports. When this plot was exposed by the leader of the Opposition, Liam Cosgrave, Lynch was forced to act by immediately sacking the ministers in question. The government and the State survived this alarming crisis.

Several years were to elapse, however, before the Republic's political system came firmly to grips with the northern situation and the Irish government began to work with the British government towards establishing a power-sharing government in the North, as well as confronting the IRA and its many supporters in the United States – as the Irish government was already doing at home. Meanwhile, although reforms were introduced in the North, and although in March 1972 the unionist government was replaced by direct rule, the handling of the emergency in Northern Ireland by the British army and by local security forces left a good deal to be desired, especially in terms of the negative relationship that developed from 1970 onwards between the British army and the minority nationalist community.

In this matter, the British ministry of defence seems to have exercised a *de facto* veto on restraint in relation to the army's behaviour, which might have prevented the dangerous strengthening of the IRA through the resultant increased tolerance of, and indeed in some measure support for, that terrorist body on the part of an increasing proportion of the nationalist population. This problem of the British army was not finally and fully brought under control until the advent of the Labour government in 1997.

The years from 1973 to 1981 saw several failed attempts to find a political solution to the way in which Northern Ireland should be governed, but the short-lived joint government of 1974 was brought down by unionist extremists, whose workers' strike was not confronted in time by a nervous British Labour government which was apparently unsure of its command of army loyalty. Moreover, in 1980–81 a new and initially insensitive Tory government failed to head off, and then handled ineptly, two IRA hunger strikes, which for the first time won the IRA sufficient political support amongst the nationalist community to encourage its political wing, Sinn Féin, to adopt an 'armalite and ballot box' policy – that is to say, putting forward candidates for election whilst continuing with a campaign of violence that eventually cost the lives of some 3,500 people, only a small minority of whom were members of the British security forces.

In early 1983, faced with a rise in electoral support for the IRA in Northern Ireland, which might in time have encouraged that organisation to increase its violence to such an extent as to start a civil war, and increasingly unhopeful of any positive political movement by deeply split unionist politicians, I was moved, as Taoiseach, to establish a New Ireland Forum.

My hope was that this would establish some common political ground in the Republic as a basis for a later negotiation with the British government that would be designed to achieve two objectives: first, a significant modification of counter-productive British security policies in Northern Ireland, and second, the introduction of an element of Irish-government involvement within Northern Ireland designed to facilitate acceptance by the local nationalist minority of the continued participation of Northern Ireland in the UK so long as a majority in the North continued to reject Irish unity. A combination of these elements would, I hoped, swing nationalist support back from Sinn Féin/IRA to the SDLP, on a scale sufficient to make the IRA rethink its policy of violence.

Through this process, after fifteen years of a strained Anglo-Irish relationship, the common interests of the two governments in securing the peace and stability of a Northern Ireland that would remain within the UK unless and until a majority of its population decided otherwise led eventually to a meeting of minds by the British and Irish governments in 1985, which produced the Anglo-Irish Agreement of that year. As foreseen, that agreement led to a decline in nationalist support for and tolerance of the IRA, and consequently, after much debate within Sinn Féin/IRA, to that organisation's 1993 decision to abandon its stalemated campaign of violence.

Five years later, the Belfast Agreement was signed. This agreement involved fudge and ambiguity around the issue of the decommissioning of IRA arms and explosives, and around the ending of all violence by the IRA. Because of problems within their own ranks, the leaders of Sinn Féin/IRA, Martin McGuinness and Gerry Adams, were for many years unable to announce unambiguously the republican movement's abandonment of all violence, including criminal activity.

The two governments showed exemplary patience with the apparently eternal political wrangling within and between the Northern Ireland political parties, and worked closely together to restart the stalled political process. The major Belfast bank raid of December 2004 temporarily set this process back, and at the time of writing the restoration of a power-sharing administration remains uncertain even if Sinn Féin were to accept the role of the police in Northern Ireland.

Factors relating to Northern Ireland that have aided the normalisation of Irish–British relations include the following:

1   By the 1990s, the gradual acceptance by the security forces in Northern Ireland, and especially by the British army, that, while they could contain the IRA threat in Northern Ireland, they could neither defeat that organisation nor prevent attacks by it on targets in Britain. This led to a decision by the British government that the possibility of a political solution should be pursued.

2   Greater involvement in the Northern Ireland problem by the British foreign office and the cabinet office, balancing the narrow, and often very short-term and security-oriented, approaches of the ministry of defence and of the Northern Ireland Office of the British government.

3   Acceptance in 1985 by Margaret Thatcher of the seriousness of the approach to this issue by the Irish government of 1982–87, which I led, together with the subsequent emergence of two British prime ministers who, in contrast to their predecessors, had no negative memories of Irish wartime neutrality and were prepared to treat Irish governments as equal partners.

On the Irish side, positive factors have included:

1   In the context of European Union membership, the gradual disappearance of the traditional inferiority complex vis-à-vis Britain which in the past had inhibited some Irish governments from negotiating self-confidently with British governments.

2   In the face of the violence carried out by the IRA, an evolution of Irish opinion away from traditional irredentist nationalism. This gave Irish governments increased room for manoeuvre in seeking a Northern Ireland settlement, so that in 1993 even an Irish prime minister of the more nationalist Fianna Fáil Party felt able explicitly to abandon the traditional Irish irredentist claim on the territory of Northern Ireland, which had long since been dropped by the other two main parties.

3   Early realistic recognition by Irish governments of the seriousness of the IRA decision of 1993, arising from initiatives by John Hume, to seek a resolution of the problem on a basis that would involve *de facto*, even if not perhaps explicitly *de jure*, acceptance of the principle that Irish reunification could take place only with the consent of a majority in Northern Ireland.

Of great importance also was the fact that, although during the 1970s and 1980s there had been tension between the two governments on issues relating to the handling of security in Northern Ireland, British ministers and officials eventually came to realise and accept that the Irish government's concerns in relation to Northern Ireland were motivated neither by irredentism nor by Anglophobia, nor by atavistic support for Northern nationalism. Instead, the British government came to understand that, in the face of the appalling tragedy of Northern Ireland violence, and the risks all this posed to the Irish State itself, Irish governments had reformulated their position in terms of a dual commitment: first, to rectifying the many, justified grievances of the northern minority, and second, to protecting the security of the island of Ireland, which was threatened by the growing strength of the IRA, especially in the period after the hunger strikes. The key objective of Irish policy could thus be seen by British governments to have become the achievement of peace and stability in a Northern Ireland that would remain within the United Kingdom until such time as a majority of its population expressed a wish to unite with the rest of the island.

From 1993 onwards, the two governments sought together to build on these new, positive factors by addressing together the change of stance by the IRA in relation to violence. Inevitably, there were times when their different perspectives on the precise approach to be taken to unionist and nationalist protagonists respectively gave rise to some temporary tensions between them. But as time went on, increased mutual understanding, respect, and trust gradually developed between the two governments, to the point where the frequency and intimacy of communications between them has come, right up to prime-ministerial level, to surpass anything that has previously been seen in terms of bilateral relations between European states.

It should be said that it is unlikely that the two governments would have succeeded in working together so closely on this thorny issue had not the members of successive Irish and British administrations come to know and eventually to trust each other in the context of European ministerial councils. Even though, on many specific EU issues, Irish and British governments have found themselves on opposite sides, the positive impact of the involvement of the two States in the European Union institutions upon the quality of Anglo-Irish inter-governmental relationships at the personal level must not be underestimated.

Behind all this lies a paradox that has yet to be recognised by public opinion in either country. The unique, and seminal, achievement of the IRA has been to have brought Ireland and Britain, and particularly the governments of these two States, closer together than had seemed possible in the past, in a common search for a solution that would end IRA and reactive loyalist violence and give peace and stability to Northern Ireland within the United Kingdom until and unless its people decide otherwise. The Northern Ireland problem, which throughout the entire history of Irish independence had bedevilled the relationship between the two neighbouring States, thus became in the end the catalyst for a positive transformation of the Irish–British relationship. History sometimes develops very surprising turns and twists!

The different experiences of the two countries and their peoples in relation to the European Union has obviously been another important factor in normalising the Irish–British relationship. In economic terms, EU membership has enabled Ireland virtually to catch up with its larger neighbour in terms of both per capita output and living standards. The 40 percent gap in both these measures that, until as recently as fifteen years ago, divided the two countries has now been largely bridged.

Ireland was always bound to benefit disproportionately from EU membership: quite apart from the special importance of access to the EU market for a state with a vocation to become a high-tech exporter, Ireland was also the only EU state able to benefit from *both* arms of EU social policy, viz. the Common Agricultural Policy and structural funding. By contrast, Britain was never going to gain as much from EU membership, or to be as comfortable as Ireland within the institutional structure of the EU.

From the outset, Britain was a net financial contributor to the Union – heavily so, because of the Common Agricultural Policy. On joining the Community, Britain had to abandon its traditional cheap-food policy and, whilst accession gave it better access to Continental European markets, its relatively low productivity level limited the gains it could secure from that access. Moreover, at the time of accession, Britain was still traumatised by the recent loss of its Empire and was psychologically unprepared for the sharing of sovereignty that was involved in EU membership. Its history since the Reformation had also made it hesitant about any permanent engagement with Continental Europe, especially with a group of states that included the Latin countries – most particularly its historic enemy, France.

This sharp contrast between Irish and British experiences in the EU tended to increase Irish self-confidence and contributed greatly to the disappearance of the Irish inferiority complex that had been inherited from the period of British rule. Irish people quickly came to realise that, far from being less able than the British to participate successfully in an international forum such as the EU, Ireland was in fact better equipped to play a positive and successful role in this new enterprise – within which the people of the Irish State felt just as comfortable as the British felt uncomfortable. An important factor there was the widely acknowledged success of all six Irish presidencies of the EU, the last of which saw both the enlargement of the Union from fifteen to twenty-five member states, and a most successful Irish-led negotiation of agreement on a new European Constitution – although this subsequently rendered futile by French and Dutch repudiation of the Constitutional Treaty. Together with the massive diversification of Irish trade, and the consequent ending of economic dependence upon the UK, all this has contributed to the much more relaxed and positive relationship that now exists between the two States.

The joint approach of the governments of Ireland and the UK to the Northern Ireland problem would not in itself have been sufficient to normalise Irish–British relations. Had Ireland remained an economic poor relation of Britain outside the UK as it had previously been within that Union, it could not have developed the self-confidence it needed to become comfortable in its relationship with its larger neighbour. And if Ireland had remained a poor country, Britain would not have come to respect and to develop a relationship of relative psychological equality with its smaller neighbour.

11

THE EU AND THE US

DIVERGING VALUES

First of all, it needs to be said that there is nothing new in the existence of tensions between Europe and America. Some of these tensions derive from history and some from geography, whilst others again are secondary effects, arising from the ways in which those two elements have, over several centuries, modified the outlooks of the peoples of these two regions, gradually differentiating their respective perceptions of their interests and their value systems.

Later, I will return to one aspect of this early development – its impact on the way in which democratic government is structured on the two sides of the Atlantic. That issue is, I believe, much less important, however, than the very significant value shifts that took place, most strikingly in Europe and not in the United States, during the second half of the twentieth century.

The scale and intensity of the differences that arose between the peoples of the United States and Europe over Iraq surprised and disturbed people on both sides of the Atlantic. Some of these differences were explicable in terms of the different intensity of the impact of the September 11 terrorist attacks upon a US population that was directly affected by this catastrophe and upon a European population that was external to the action – people who, although clearly horrified by the attacks and deeply sympathetic towards America's plight, remained nevertheless observers of, rather than victims of, that traumatic event.

But this is far from being the whole of the story. I believe that a second important, but generally overlooked, factor has been the way in which hitherto unrecognised divergences between the European and US approaches to international relations came to be suddenly and dramatically highlighted by the Iraq crisis. In part, this reflects the fact that, although the location of the main land-war front-lines of both the Second World War and the subsequent prolonged cold-war stand-off lay largely in Europe, creating in both cases conditions of mutual dependence between the United States and Europe, in the aftermath of the collapse of the Iron Curtain the US no longer needed Europe in quite the same way as it had before. This affected the underlying attitude of the US towards Europe and, more subtly perhaps, that of Europe towards the US – in ways which became readily apparent only in the dramatic context of the Iraq crisis.

But another more long-term factor was also involved, of which Americans may be almost wholly unaware – the quiet revolution that had been taking place in underlying European attitudes towards international relations during the post–Second World War period.

What seems to me to have been happening during that half-century is that, with regard to international relations, the American and European political systems have been responding to quite different stimuli. The lesson that was finally drawn by Europeans from centuries of conflict was that cooperation between neighbouring states on a basis of mutual respect and something like equality is the best, indeed the only, way to manage their affairs. By contrast, American political attitudes to the outside world were influenced rather by that country's subsequent experience of the cold war, and more recently by the emergence of the US as the sole global superpower. This seems to have suggested to many in that country that the interests, and perhaps also the values, of the United States can best be protected through the exercise of power.

The cold war was, of course, a period during which Europe and the US were jointly engaged in countering threats from an expansionary totalitarian regime to certain fundamental values and interests shared by people on both sides of the Atlantic. And it was precisely because both Europe and America were defending deeply held, shared values that the gradual emergence of these differences in respect of some aspects of their political value systems passed almost unnoticed during the second half of the twentieth century. It is well-known that intellectual revolutions tend to be imperceptible to those who are engaged in them.

One way or the other, it was only with the Iraq crisis of 2002–03 that fairly deep fissures between the respective reactions of the US and Europe to a new kind of global crisis emerged, revealing the extent to which their value systems in relation to international affairs had drifted far apart over previous decades.

Before addressing what can be fairly described as a fundamental European revolution in political attitudes towards international relations, let me say something about the position of the United States. The role in which the United States found itself placed in the second half of the twentieth century inevitably led it in quite a different direction from that on which Europe was embarking.

By the start of the twentieth century, the United States had already become the world's strongest economy. But despite its brief involvement in the First World War, it did not engage fully with the rest of the world until mid-century. The same was true of the Soviet Union – albeit for quite different reasons. By the late 1940s, the stage was set for a confrontation between the West and the Soviet Union which might have destroyed the globe, but the skill and good judgement with which successive US administrations managed this situation over many decades, in conjunction with their European partners, ensured that peace prevailed until the Soviet Union eventually collapsed.

From these global events, the United States inevitably drew lessons very different from those that Europe was continuing to draw retrospectively from its traumatic experience during the Second World War. The unique geographical situation and global role of the US made it unnecessary for it to contemplate any sharing of sovereignty with other states. Moreover, its relative geographical isolation left it fairly impervious to external influences of the kind that every European state was encountering daily.

It is, of course, true that, during the cold war, a North Atlantic Alliance had been necessitated by the front-line geographical situation of western Europe, but once the collapse of the Soviet Union left only one superpower in existence, the US was no longer so dependent upon allies for the protection of what it saw as its global interests. Allies remain useful to the US, of course, and worth being supported by them, primarily with military rather than civil aid programmes – but the United States had become strong enough to be open to the temptation in certain extreme circumstances to go its own way, even against the broad thrust of world opinion.

The use of power in this way has its limitations, however. Power can readily be used to destroy – but much more than the exercise of power is needed in order to rebuild, as we have seen in Iraq. Moreover, the exercise of power has a dangerously distancing effect on those who hold and deploy it. The powerful find it difficult to empathise with the weak – and the weak can become fearful and resentful of the strong, agreeing with them out of fear rather than conviction.

By contrast with the overwhelming strategic power of the United States, the UN is a weak instrument. Its Security Council is often crippled by the veto of one or other permanent member, and its Assembly has often been dominated by states that are hostile to the United States' close ally, Israel. To the US, the UN can consequently appear mainly as a break on its capacity to pursue its interests.

But dangers to the United States deriving from the temptations posed by its new role as the world's first superpower are primarily matters for Americans to debate and to come to terms with amongst themselves. As a European, my concern is rather with the changes that have been taking place during the past half-century in European values affecting inter-state relations – changes that may not yet have impinged on American consciousness and which, I feel, may have contributed to some of the transatlantic tensions that have been exposed by the Iraq crisis.

There are certain moments in history, rare enough perhaps, when the terrible consequences of some past attitudes or policies may lead peoples and their leaders consciously to reverse what may have seemed until then to have been the irresistible tide of history. In Europe, the immediate post-war period was one of these moments.

Perhaps I should say that, in Ireland today, we are more conscious than most peoples of this kind of 'reversal of history' phenomenon. For between the 1950s and the 1990s, the Irish people underwent a double process of this kind – first economic, then political. The first such reversal occurred at the end of the 1950s. Prime Minister de Valera's quarter-of-a-century-old attempt to make our small country economically self-sufficient had proved a disastrous failure – ensuring the continuance of under-development and emigration, which cost Ireland half of each successive age cohort of its population. In the late 1950s, this failure precipitated an abrupt reversal of economic policy in favour of liberal free trade. Within fifteen years, this had transformed Ireland into an economically successful member of the European Community; within a further fifteen years, it secured an eight-year period of economic growth at a rate that had never before been seen in Europe.

The second fundamental policy reversal occurred during the two decades following that revolution in economic policy, as the appalling consequences in Northern Ireland of Irish irredentist nationalism, reacting against sectarian unionism, required the leaders and most of the people of the Republic – and eventually also even the most militant nationalist elements in Northern Ireland itself – to reverse the engines of that nationalism. Irish nationalists finally abandoned a decades-old irredentism that implied the imposition of a monocultural post-Gaelic identity upon the descendants in north-east Ulster of those who, in the early seventeenth century, had chosen Ireland rather than North America as their refuge from Anglican religious domination in Britain. Yet another example of how, after a national disaster, a people can, with wise leadership, reverse their political 'engines' is Germany's re-emergence as a stable democracy in the aftermath of the Nazi period.

In Europe, within a very few years of the end of the Second World War, a reaction against the disastrous mid-twentieth century experiences of extreme nationalism precipitated just such a dramatic, and ultimately remarkably successful, attempt to reverse history's tide. Successive attempts to dominate Europe, by the Austrian/Spanish Hapsburg dynasty in the late fifteenth and sixteenth centuries, by France under Louis XIV in the seventeenth century and under Napoleon in the early nineteenth century, and last of all by Germany in the first half of the twentieth century, all ended in failure, at a constantly rising cost to human life – as also had Britain's attempt, which was less costly in human terms, to control the seas around and beyond Europe with a view to dominating world trade; that was finally successfully challenged by the United States in the late 1920s.

By 1945, much of Europe's productive capacity had been destroyed, its peoples were in a state of despair, with many near starvation level, and there was a realisation that two hitherto internally focused extra-European states had suddenly emerged as global superpowers: a benevolent United States and an ideologically and militarily threatening Russia, in the guise of the Soviet Union.

The culturally complex patchwork of European states that had been the eventual outcome of several millennia of successive settlements mainly by different groups of Indo-European tribes coming from areas around or beyond the Black Sea had shown, over many centuries, both extraordinary intellectual vitality and a stubborn unwillingness to cohere under the domination of any one of its peoples. Had these peoples now reached the end of the road – or did there still exist sufficient intellectual energy for Europe to re-create itself in a new, quite different, and constructive shape?

The challenge for this apparently failed Europe of 1945 was to find a way to exploit its intellectual inheritance in a manner that would provide its inhabitants with a reasonable future in the new bipolar world of the later twentieth century. Attempts at domination of Europe by one or other of its ethnic groups having all failed to yield anything other than mutual destruction, Europe's salvation could now lie only in the reversal of history's tide through the sharing of state sovereignties. By contrast, the two recently emerged superpowers experienced no such need to share sovereignty with other states. On the contrary, they saw their future rather in the assertion of their sovereignty vis-à-vis each other.

The pursuit by Europe of its objective of the sharing of sovereignty necessarily involved the development of new values appropriate to this new mission. In the chronological order of their development, these new values are: first, a commitment to international law, combined with a concern to protect the role of the newly established United Nations, which, whatever its defects, was and is seen as offering the best available protection against global anarchy; second, within Europe itself, the subordination of each state's sovereignty vis-à-vis its own citizens to a supranational Court of Human Rights; third, the creation of a zone of peace, as well as a single market, in western Europe, within which the rule of law would replace war as the ultimate arm of policy; fourth, the abolition of capital punishment throughout the Continent; fifth, together with the post-war moral rejection of colonialism – a feature of Europe's past that had always been a bone of contention with the libertarian United States – the emergence of large-scale development cooperation, involving extensive civil-aid transfers to developing countries, many of them former colonies, especially in Africa; sixth, deriving from Europe's extensive development cooperation and trade relations with the rest of the world, a commitment to global ecology, in cooperation with the developing world; and seventh, most recently, a willingness to reinforce the role of Europeans as potential peacemakers overseas by making the actions of their soldiers subject to a code of criminal international law. These developments in Europe's approach to international affairs have taken it along a very different path from that of the United States, which has never experienced the kind of pressures of history that have revolutionised European thinking during this half-century.

Of course, not all of these developments bear directly on Europe–US relations, to which, however they provide an important backdrop. Some of them, however, have proved important in the context of the Iraq crisis – for example, the strong European commitment to international law and to the United Nations and its procedures; the partial – in some states almost complete – reorientation of European armies towards peacekeeping; and perhaps also the European commitment to human rights, which has felt itself challenged by the holding by US armed forces of suspected members of al-Qaeda, outside the rule of law, in Guantánamo Bay.

From the point of view of the United States, which has undertaken the lead role in the effort to deal with international terrorism, the overall thrust of this changed European approach to international affairs may seem at times to be 'wimpish', or even irritatingly self-righteous. Where the US has clearly been in error, however, is in its use of the term 'Old Europe' in this connection. For, whatever one may think of all this, we are dealing here with a New Europe, one that has rejected many of the values of pre-1945 Europe. Because the public stances of some of the European governments differed on the issue of the Iraq war – some supporting the US and others withholding such support – there is a danger that the extent to which most Europeans in fact share these seven values may be underestimated in the US.

The truth is that, in almost every western European country, public opinion was instinctively opposed to the initiation of the Iraq war at the time it was launched, without explicit UN authorisation. Of course some western European governments ignored public opinion in their countries: the British prime minister seems to have done so by conviction, although he and his government were clearly also influenced by Britain's traditionally close ties with the US. Other western European governments may have taken a pro-US line for reasons of expediency, in order to remain on good terms with the United States. Others again simply remained silent on the issue in the hope of avoiding negative US reactions.

Eastern European governments were more genuinely supportive of the United States, because they have yet to overcome their security concerns vis-à-vis Russia and, consequently, at this stage are strongly oriented towards the US as an ultimate guarantor of their security – perhaps even more than towards the EU. But none of this should delude Americans into failing to take due account of the significance of the quite radical underlying changes that have taken place in European values and attitudes to international relations during the past half-century.

There are two principal aspects to the issue of international law in relation to Europe and the UN. First, at international level, there has been a strengthened European commitment to the global institutional structure created in the aftermath of the Second World War, and more generally to international law. And second, there has been the creation, initially within western Europe, of a zone of peace under a supranational legal system that imposes the rule of law on all relations between members of the Union, definitively eliminating, for the first time in history, war as an instrument of policy between neighbouring states.

In the wider sphere of global relations, the refusal by the United States in the mid-1980s to accept the World Court ruling against its mining of Nicaraguan ports revealed clearly for the first time a hitherto largely unrecognised transatlantic divergence in attitudes towards international law. Americans may not have realised the significance of this factor. In that connection it is, perhaps, significant that two decades ago, even as close an ally of the US as Margaret Thatcher rejected, on grounds of international law, a request by Ronald Reagan to join him in supporting the Israeli bombing of the PLO headquarters in Tunis. 'What would you say if I bombed the Provos in Dundalk?' was her response to this request, she told me afterwards. (I might add that, just after the US invasion of Grenada, she said to me heatedly, twice: 'The Americans are worse than the Soviets, Garret'! Of course she did not really mean this, but the remark illustrated the extent to which even the greatest friends of the United States can sometimes be tempted to reject unilateral US actions that are seen as conflicting with international law.)

To Europeans, the apparent reluctance of the United States to accept international law as binding has been disturbing. For many, this concern has been intensified by the United States' recent attempted extension of the right of national self-defence to the taking of pre-emptive armed action against a distant state, Iraq, on the basis of unproven and, it subsequently emerged, unfounded allegations that it possessed weapons of mass destruction capable of immediate use.

Justification of the invasion of Iraq on the quite different grounds of the character of its regime also poses problems for many Europeans who are aware of US tolerance, and even past support, of that same malign Iraqi dictatorship twenty years earlier – and also of other dictatorial and repressive regimes elsewhere in the world. It is, of course, true that there has been an international shift in recent times towards modifying past insistence on non-intervention in the internal affairs of states where they are engaged in activities such as genocide, but such exceptional international action is generally seen as being beyond the remit of any individual state, and as requiring, therefore, explicit authorisation by the United Nations. (Of course, on this issue Americans are perfectly entitled to point out that, during the Kosovo war, Europe accepted the bombing of Serbia without UN authorisation. Europe is not exempt from applying double standards, where it suits it!)

Inevitably, opinions will differ on just where lines are to be drawn in specific cases of this kind. But it is clearly important that, on both sides of the Atlantic, legitimate differences of opinion should be treated in good faith and not made into occasions for mutual recrimination. Thus, US impatience with Saddam Hussein's foot-dragging over admitting the absence of weapons of mass destruction deserved more understanding than it received from some European states and peoples – but so also do European sensitivities with regard to international law deserve more respect from the US.

As for the United Nations, however imperfect its workings may be, Europeans see it as all we have at present to protect us from international anarchy. And it is in no way clear that the longer-term interests of the United States, which has itself often wielded a Security Council veto in protection of its interests or values, have been best served by unilateral (or even, with Britain, bilateral) attempts to designate as 'unreasonable' certain vetoes by other permanent members, which the US may have found inconvenient to its interests. If the Security Council veto power of some large states is to be retained, it needs to be universally respected, whichever state chooses to exercise it.

One could, of course, make a case for changing the UN system so that a veto by a single permanent member would no longer be valid and that, instead, a veto would be required by two permanent members in order to block a resolution that would bind member states. I doubt if such a change would be acceptable to the United States, however! What clearly cannot be defended, and would be universally rejected in the rest of the world, would be a proposition that only the United States would have an unchallengeable veto on UN action, the vetoes of other permanent members of the Security Council being capable of being dismissed and ignored if the United States decided to regard them as 'unreasonable'.

Turning now to the situation inside Europe, the first effort in 1950 to create a supranational European entity largely foundered because of the reluctance of Great Britain and the Protestant states of Scandinavia (supported by predominantly Roman Catholic, but at that point still strongly autarkic, Ireland) to share economic, still less political, sovereignty – despite the fact that, through NATO, they had effectively shared sovereignty in the much more sensitive matter of national defence.

But, curiously, a sharing of sovereignty in respect of human rights was in fact agreed at that very early stage by all the states of western Europe except Switzerland. These states agreed to grant to their citizens a right of appeal to a supranational court in Strasbourg in respect of any case where citizens believe that their own national courts have failed to vindicate one of their human rights.

Subsequently, this European emphasis on human rights came to include a rejection of capital punishment, which was abandoned throughout Europe between the 1950s and the 1970s. No country retaining capital punishment could today become a member of the European Union, and it has even been suggested that US observer status at the Council of Europe might be called into question because of the continued use of capital punishment by some US states.

Amongst a more limited and far-seeing group of six Continental European states, in the 1950s a sharing of economic sovereignty was also under way. After a series of accessions by most other western European states to the newly created European Community, now the European Union, the Union has now been be extended to incorporate a total of twenty-five European states – with only Iceland, Norway and Switzerland amongst western European states remaining outside it.

Romania, Bulgaria and Turkey are next in the queue, with the western Balkan states of Albania and the former Yugoslavia anxious to follow, as they eventually stabilise politically and economically. The rejection of the proposed Constitutional Treaty by the electorates of France and the Netherlands has, of course, cast a shadow over further enlargement of the Union.

The economic aspects of this process are largely outside the scope of this analysis, although, of course, trade issues between the United States and this new major European trade bloc are the source of some occasionally quite acute tensions between the US and Europe.

What *is* relevant to my main theme (viz., that European political value shifts have affected in a significant way Europe's relationship with the United States) is the manner in which the creation of a Community that was initially designed to obviate any possibility of yet another war between France and Germany came to evolve into a Europe that is imbued with a much more general and widespread vocation for peace.

For as long as the cold war continued – during which most western European states were of course participating in the US-led NATO – the contemporaneous shift towards a European vocation for peace, including peacemaking and even peace enforcement in certain situations, remained little noticed. This process was in any event less than universal, for Britain and France, in particular, retained armed forces that were capable of some modest scale of independent armed action outside Europe.

But in the aftermath of the disappearance of the Iron Curtain in 1989, the emergence within a supranationally organised western Europe of what was seen as a zone of peace, within which war has ceased to be a potential means of settling disputes, soon proved its worth throughout north-eastern and central Europe and the eastern Balkans. Influenced by the pacific example of the European Union, as well as by their own concern to join both NATO and the EU as soon as possible, the states in these regions, a number of which throughout the first half of the twentieth century had engaged in persistent territorial conflicts with each other, pointedly eschewed any repetition of those events.

Only in one small part of this region, the western Balkans, did nationalist passions prove too strong to resist the influence of the zone of peace that had been created in western Europe during the decades immediately before the fall of the Iron Curtain. This reflected the inherent instability of the seventy-year-old Yugoslav state, which had been brought into existence in controversial circumstances in November 1918, in reaction to an Italian threat to the coastal territories of Hungarian Croatia and Austrian Slovenia.

Of course, the reluctance of most European states, including France and Great Britain, to take on Serb forces during the Bosnian war of the 1990s reflected the downside of this European shift towards a more pacific approach to problems in Europe. Lessons have, however, been learnt from that experience. For example, the inability of European forces in Bosnia to protect some designated 'safe areas' without US helicopter airlift capacity, which the US at one point was unwilling to supply, probably contributed to the idea of a 'European Rapid Reaction Force' for peacekeeping and peace-enforcement purposes, separate from, but linked to, NATO.

Finally, the much greater European emphasis on development aid for civil rather than military purposes (in relation to its GDP, Europe has been contributing at least four times as much as the US), and the clearly much stronger European commitment to global ecology, e.g. in relation to the Kyoto Agreement, further emphasise the extent to which, in recent decades, Europeans have been pursuing a very different international agenda from that of the United States.

Another quite different issue that in some measure influenced the way in which the Iraq war affected public opinion in Europe and the United States is the difference between the system of governance of most European states and that of the US.

Because, more than two centuries ago, English colonies in North America led the way in the process of democratisation of systems of government, Americans have a particular pride in their democratic heritage. However, as their revolution took place in the eighteenth century, and because of the need at that time for a unifying political element in this novel, experimental federal structure, executive power was vested by the founders of the United States in an elected head of state, chosen by voters at intervals of four years, rather than – as was then beginning to emerge within Europe's evolving monarchical systems – in a prime minister who, in time, would cease to be responsible to the monarch and would instead become answerable to an elected parliament. By contrast, the role of European heads of state, whether they are surviving hereditary monarchs or non-executive presidents, is now merely formal and decorative – except in France, where a presidential system, albeit one that is somewhat closer to the general European parliamentary norm, was reintroduced at the end of the 1950s.

A consequence of these different historical evolutions is that the US presidential and the European parliamentary systems differ markedly in the extent to which the exercise of executive power in the two systems is open to scrutiny. European heads of government are normally subject both to persistent challenges in parliament and, increasingly, also to journalistic scrutiny – including vigorous and fairly uninhibited questioning by reporters at press conferences. US presidents have hitherto been largely protected from all this by the aura that still surrounds the office of head of state.

It should be added that, in most European states, heads of government act to some degree as *primus inter pares* rather than as chief executives – although in Britain, the role of the Cabinet as distinct from that of the prime minister in the process of government has in recent decades clearly been declining, with a form of semi-presidential government emerging.

These are important differences between European and American forms of democracy, of which many citizens of states on either side of the Atlantic are perhaps unconscious. And they became more evident during the Iraq crisis, when European heads of government found themselves under much more pressure from their legislatures and the media than was the case in the United States.

The US–Europe relationship that was built up during the Second World War, and was sustained by mutual dependence during the cold war, was bound to come under pressure after that global stand-off had ended and the United States had emerged as the sole superpower. But it has been unfortunate that this relationship came to be severely tested at such an early point in the post–cold war period, in political conditions that were unfavourable to its smooth continuance, viz. in the aftermath of the election of a new US administration with a strong fundamentalist element, which was followed by the shock of September 11. Europe's instinctive reaction in such a situation is to try to get the US–Europe relationship back on to an even keel again as quickly as possible. Has the US the will, as well as sufficient capacity for empathy with its European partners' concerns, to respond to this effectively?

It is not easy to see how Europe's internationalist vision, based on its commitment to international law and its internal success in building a new model of relationships between neighbouring states which share sovereignty, can be reconciled with what has seemed to be the approach of the present US administration. For this administration has seemed to favour a world within which order is maintained and the global economy organised by the exercise of power from above, under what America may see as its benevolent authority.

It is clear, however, that there are strong pressures within the United States favouring a return to multilateralism – pressures that are being reinforced by the experience of that country in Iraq in the aftermath of the recent war.

12

A Triangular Relationship

Ireland, Britain and the United States

The triangular relationship between Ireland, Britain and the United States has been little discussed, even in Ireland. Yet during and after the Second World War, US policy towards Ireland was strongly influenced by Britain, while during two important periods – 1916–21, and again from 1968 to the present – British policy in relation to Ireland has had to take account of, and has been substantially affected by, US opinion and policy, which in turn has been influenced by Irish-America. The complexity, ambiguity and, in very recent times, potentially constructive character of this triangular interaction in respect of the Northern Ireland crisis clearly merits study and reflection.

Of the three basic components, the US–Ireland relationship is the simplest and easiest to grasp. The Anglo-Irish relationship is complex and subtle, and to an Irishman, and I suspect to others who are neither British nor American, aspects of the British-US relationship appear the most mysterious. Let me start with the Irish-American relationship.

Historically, the early-seventeenth-century British settlements in Ulster and on the north-east coast of North America were closely related, not merely in time but also in character, and to a significant degree in the origins and motivation of those involved. In both cases, there were some settlers drawn from the Anglican establishment: Derry, for example, became Londonderry because it was settled by Anglican City of London companies, and in Virginia and the Carolinas the Anglican Church was established from the outset. Nonetheless, the bulk of both groups of settlers were Dissenters of one kind or another, drawn from outside the Anglican establishment: Presbyterians in Ulster and a variety of Protestant sects in the case of America, who sought greater freedom to practice, but also to impose, their own brands of Protestantism.

A crucial difference between these two settlements lay in the fact that, whereas in the east of the United States, the indigenous population had been largely eliminated by the end of the eighteenth century, and in the west before the end of the nineteenth, in Ulster, as in the rest of Ireland, the native population, although subdued and deprived of its land, survived. In other words, the Irish colonisation was incomplete – to the point where, in Ulster, the survivors broadly held their own numerically vis-à-vis the colonists and elsewhere in the island remained greatly superior in numbers.

Although trade between the Irish and American colonies was inhibited by protectionist British legislation, settlers in Ireland and their descendants were free to move westward to America, and in the eighteenth century very many Presbyterians from Ulster chose to escape in this way from the established Anglican Church in Ireland. As well as depriving Catholics of their land and of their right to worship, the regime established by the Anglican Church also excluded Presbyterians from access to public office, and required all non-Anglicans to support the established Irish church.

The close ties between Presbyterians in Ulster and the Dissenter tradition in America contributed to the enthusiasm with which Ulster Presbyterians greeted the American Revolution and in 1798 sought to emulate their American cousins by rising in arms against British rule in Ulster. And on the other side of the Atlantic, those who had possessed the resources to emigrate in the eighteenth century, together with their descendants, were sufficiently numerous and influential to have provided a significant proportion of the signatories to the Declaration of Independence, as well as nine of the presidents of the United States in the nineteenth century.

In the early nineteenth century, however, Presbyterians in Ulster won their freedom from Anglican discrimination, and thereafter largely found a common cause with Anglicans against the Catholic political majority in the island that was emerging as a result of Catholic emancipation and the widening of the electoral franchise. With the industrialisation of much of Ulster, the flow of Presbyterian emigrants from there to America was reduced, and those who had settled there rapidly became assimilated into the WASP (white, Anglo-Saxon, Protestant) majority and ceased to be an identifiable ethnic minority.

Meanwhile, the rapid growth of the indigenous Catholic population of the island of Ireland and the lack of industrial development in the predominantly agricultural South had created population pressures which, especially after the Famine of 1845–47, in which one million died of starvation or disease, provoked an emigrant flow of millions, mainly to the United States. This flow to the US was halted only by the Depression which followed the Crash of 1929. These virtually destitute Catholic emigrants could not easily assimilate to a WASP culture from which, unlike their Ulster Scots predecessors, their religion as well as their social condition excluded them. Over the greater part of two centuries, these emigrants and many of their descendants retained a distinct cultural identity – and from generation to generation their memories of the atrocious conditions from which they had been forced to flee kept alive a bitter resentment against Britain, the country whose incomplete colonisation of Ireland was the source of their discontent.

If, earlier in this century, the whole island of Ireland had become an independent state, these resentments amongst Irish-Americans might have faded gradually for lack of a continuing grievance upon which to feed. But the retention of Northern Ireland within the United Kingdom, with an artificially contrived local majority achieved by hiving off six of the nine Ulster counties from the rest of the province and island, was accompanied by an abuse of power in that area vis-à-vis the local nationalist minority that Britain allowed to endure for half-a-century. This helped to keep Anglophobia alive amongst many of the Irish in America, as it did amongst many members of the Catholic nationalist majority in Ireland. Moreover, in the last third of the twentieth century, the problems created by the character of the security measures taken by the British authorities in Northern Ireland provided ample ammunition to re-stoke continually the fires of Irish-American resentment of and hostility towards Britain.

Nearer to the scene, the people of the Irish State have been able gradually to develop a more balanced view of events in Northern Ireland, and in particular of the IRA's role in the creation and continuation of violence there. But for Irish-Americans, far removed from the scene, and in many cases living in a nineteenth-century time warp so far as the Anglo-Irish relationship is concerned, this has been much more difficult.

I shall return later to the problems this has posed not just for British but also for Irish governments during the past quarter of a century. Let me turn now, necessarily briefly, to the Anglo-Irish relationship.

The Anglo-Irish relationship is unique: certainly I am not aware of any other colonial relationship between culturally distinct neighbours that has endured so long – one in which, despite the virtual extinction of the native language of the colonised and its replacement by that of the coloniser, the sense of a separate identity has survived in such a resilient way. To these special features of the Anglo-Irish relationship, three others must be added: the scale of the size disparity between the two peoples and the states that eventually came to incarnate their identities, the religious differentiation between them, and the scale of the population movements that have taken place between them in both directions.

When to all these elements is added the continuation of the former coloniser's sovereignty over part of the territory of the colonised, at the instance of the descendants of settlers in that area, it is scarcely surprising that the relationship between two peoples who have had, and indeed still have, such an intimate, but chequered, experience of each other should be complex – and full of paradoxes.

My own family experience illustrates a few of these paradoxes. Although I am a native of, and have held high public office in, the Irish State, I have almost no close cousins here – because of emigration, including the emigration of my paternal grandparents to London in the mid-nineteenth century. All my Irish relatives are in fact Ulster-Scots Presbyterian unionists. My father, a Londoner born of Irish parents, who came to live in Ireland and who spent four periods in jail as an Irish revolutionary, found himself at the age of forty-two the senior minister of the Crown at the Imperial Conference of 1930 – the only minister of any country present who had attended the Conferences of 1923 and 1926. At the end of his life, he spent more than a year in east London, running for the benefit of the British war effort a chemical factory owned by one of his brothers, who had been killed in an air raid.

My mother, the daughter of a Presbyterian, freemason, unionist businessman in Belfast, was a socialist, suffragist republican who, in a moment of revolutionary fervour, told her former employer, George Bernard Shaw, that she would bring her eldest son up to hate England. Not only did she fail to fulfil this promise, she brought her youngest son up to respect and admire Britain and its institutions and to share her — and my father's — deep affection for its capital city, where they had met, fallen in love, and married.

Without descending to stereotypes, there are in fact significant differences between the generality of Irish and English people, and these sometimes impede mutual understanding. Perhaps because of the way their survival required the Irish over recent centuries to acquire a command of the English language, Irish people tend to be more verbal than English native speakers — more verbose, some would say! — as well being perhaps more outgoing and gregarious. (My father once remarked humorously that, in his experience as Ireland's first minister for external affairs — as the department of foreign affairs was known until 1969 — misunderstandings sometimes arose because the English were so laconic that the Irish could not discover what they really meant, while the English had the same problem because they did not know which bit to take seriously of all that the Irish were saying!)

Second, the disparity in relative size between the two countries makes an equal relationship between them very difficult. Together with the nature of the historic relationship, this tended to produce on the British side an unhappy combination of an unhelpful superiority complex and an incapacity for the empathy necessary to understand Irish problems sufficiently well to resolve them. On the Irish side, a corresponding inferiority complex produced a tendency to assume that any British mistake or stupidity (of which there have been quite a few!) were actually diabolically clever moves designed in some unidentifiable way to damage Irish interests!

Third, on a whole range of issues, not merely in relation to Anglo-Irish affairs but to the role of an army, the working of intelligence services, and indeed world affairs generally, the instinctive attitudes of a former imperial power and of a former colony tend to be not merely different but diametrically opposed.

Fourth, the differences in constitutional provisions between Ireland and Britain are profound, and these have powerful, if often unrecognised, influences on national attitudes. In Ireland, a written Constitution is strongly protective of human rights vis-à-vis the executive and legislature, and the courts are seen as – and indeed act as – vindicators of the people's rights against these institutions, rather than as part of the machinery of government. Moreover, because the attorney-general has the duty of protecting the government against the danger of unintentionally impinging on human rights, *de facto* his role is protective of these rights.

In Britain, by contrast, there has until recently been no judicial protection of rights against legislation passed by the executive's parliamentary majority, but only protection against abuses of this legislation. The courts are Her Majesty's courts, not the citizen's courts. And the English attorney-general seems to have no function in regard to the protection of human rights vis-à-vis the executive and legislature. These fundamental constitutional differences are one area in respect of which Ireland is in fact closer to the United States than to Britain.

These profound differences between Ireland and Britain and between the Irish and British peoples would, under any circumstances, make the relationship between them somewhat problematic, even if Northern Ireland had never come into existence. But there is also another and very positive side to the relationship between the two countries: the many debts that Ireland owes to Britain. For Ireland has also been deeply, and in most cases positively, influenced in a number of important ways by its experience of British rule and also by its contact with the British liberal tradition. Its parliamentary system is modelled on that of Britain – with two variants, a proportionally representative electoral system introduced by the British before they left, and a hemicyclical layout of parliament, in contrast to the British system of opposing sides.

Ireland's basic law is British common law – with the important additional element of the constitutional protection of rights. Ireland's trade union system, professional bodies and financial institutions, and indeed to some degree the structure of society itself, are all largely modelled on those of Britain – albeit with much less marked class divisions.

Finally, the common language, and the easy movement of people between the two countries, and in particular of Irish people going to live and work in Britain – many of them now virtually commuting between the two countries – has provided a dimension of social intimacy that is, I think, unique between two neighbouring states.

As to Britain and America, I shall not presume to say much about that relationship but shall simply permit myself a couple of observations on an aspect of the relationship that seems puzzling to an outsider. That American intervention in the First World War swung the balance in Britain's favour and that it did so decisively in the Second World War is self-evident, and many in Britain understandably feel further indebted to the United States because of the extension of American protection to western Europe, including Britain, during the cold war. Earlier in this century, however, there had been several offsetting negative factors in the relationship between the two countries. First, the uninhibited and indeed ruthless manner in which the United States extracted every last penny of Britain's external assets as well as bases in some of its colonies in payment for the help it gave Britain before US entry into the Second World War and, second, the hostility of the United States to Britain's imperial role at that time, which was notably unhelpful to British interests in the immediate post-war period.

Given that, in all events involving human relations, dependence of one upon another frequently evokes resentment rather than gratitude for help received, these negative elements might have been expected to produce some negative sentiment in Britain vis-à-vis the United States during the past half-century. Instead, Britain's attitude to the United States has been almost sycophantically positive; the British have seemed actually to take pride in their dependence on the USA – a dependence which Britain has indeed dignified with the positive-sounding term 'special relationship'. Some have even seen this special relationship of dependence as a substitute for past Empire!

That is why, at the outset, I described the Anglo-American relationship as seeming to an outsider to be mysterious. It is not surprising that Britain should have been so consistently concerned to pursue its vital interests through an American alliance, for that has made excellent practical sense, but it is surprising that, in doing so, the British people should have been so remarkably free of hang-ups or complexes!

I must now turn to the part that Ireland has played in the Anglo-American relationship during the past eighty years. One theme runs through this whole period: British concern lest its Irish involvement should adversely affect its relationship with a United States within which Irish-Americans exercise considerable political influence, especially in Congress. And, throughout much of the period, there has been a corresponding concern on the part of the US government to ensure that this Irish-American political factor should not damage its relationship with its most loyal European ally.

In the late nineteenth century, the Irish-American organisation Clan na Gael financed the Irish Republican Brotherhood in Ireland and helped to defeat in the US Congress both extradition and joint arbitration treaties between the US and Britain. Moreover, during the First World War, American neutrality up to 1917 was strongly supported by Irish-Americans. An emissary of those organising the Easter 1916 Rising was able to visit Germany via the US in early 1915 to coordinate plans with the German government, and subsequent contacts were maintained through Clan na Gael in New York.

In the aftermath of the Rising, after the execution of the leaders in Dublin and following the sentencing to death of Sir Roger Casement in July 1916, the US Senate adopted a resolution urging the British government thenceforth to exercise clemency. Because of delays in the transmission of this resolution by the White House, it did not reach the foreign secretary until just after Casement had been executed. The confidential circulation of the sexually compromising Casement Diaries to the US ambassador in London, among others, had been designed to head off this kind of US pressure.

Then in April 1917, shortly after the United States had entered the war, President Wilson, who was not personally sympathetic to Ireland but was concerned about Irish-American attitudes to the conflict, sent a confidential message to Lloyd George saying that 'if the people of the United States could feel there was an early prospect of the establishment for Ireland of substantial self-government, a very grave element of satisfaction and enthusiasm would be added to the cooperation now about to be organised' between the United Kingdom and the United States. It was this initiative that led to the establishment of the Irish Convention, which later that year foundered on the rejection by Ulster unionists of the form of Home Rule that had been agreed at the Convention by both the nationalist Irish Parliamentary Party and the southern unionists.

Next, in 1918, a proposal to extend conscription to Ireland, which was opposed by the whole of nationalist Ireland, was dropped by the British government, partly because of opposition from the United States. And, following the establishment of a separate Irish parliament and government in January 1919 by the Sinn Féin MPs, who, with the support of half the island's electorate, had won 70 percent of the Irish seats in the December 1918 Westminster election, the US House of Representatives voted by 216 to 45 for a resolution urging the Versailles Peace Conference to 'consider the claims of Ireland to self-determination'. Shortly afterwards, the Senate requested the US delegation at Versailles 'to secure a hearing for the representatives of the Irish Republic.' Wilson's response – to the effect that this would require the unanimous consent of the four Great Powers – swung Irish-America, and with it the Senate, against US participation in the League of Nations – although this was in fact contrary to the wishes and interests of the underground Irish government.

The prospect of a formal ending to the First World War with the signature of the peace treaties faced the British government in 1919 with a legal requirement to make a decision on what to do about the Home Rule Act, the implementation of which had in the autumn of 1914 been postponed until the end of the war. Concern for US and Dominion opinion ruled out a repeal of that Act. Interestingly, the eventual decision to deal with this situation by making provision for two Home Rule parliaments, one for six of the nine Ulster counties and the other for the rest of the island, leaving the question of Irish unity to be settled by these two Irish legislatures, seems to have been strongly influenced by a feeling that this would demonstrate to the United States, and to the Dominions overseas, with their large Irish populations, the sincerity of Britain's commitment to Irish self-government. And so, ironically, Irish-America bears some indirect responsibility for the emergence of the Stormont government!

It is also ironic that, having been influenced to some degree in 1800 to unite Ireland and Britain in order to remove the power of the Protestant establishment in Ireland to block steps to erode discrimination against Catholics, the British government of 1920 should have so modified the Union as to restore, in practice if not legally, this very power of

193

discrimination to a local Protestant majority in a corner of the island.

Throughout 1919 and 1920, the British Cabinet was concerned about the impact on American and Dominion opinion of its drastic Irish security measures, in particular its use of reprisals against the civilian population. In the case of the United States, British concern was influenced by the crucial importance to Britain of U.S. policy on naval armaments and war debts.

It is a moot point whether the eventual British decision to negotiate with the underground Irish government was more influenced by the attitudes of the United States or of the Dominions, whose leaders were present in London in June 1921 for an Imperial Conference. But negotiate the British government finally did, and although the signing of the Treaty on 6 December 1921 led to a civil war in Ireland, the settlement that was then reached effectively removed Ireland as a source of contention between Britain and the USA for many decades thereafter.

The scale and significance of American influence on the events that led to the eventual emergence of the Irish State will be evident from this bare recital of facts.

In early 1938, during the negotiation of the Anglo-Irish Agreement that settled a long-running economic dispute between Ireland and Britain and returned to Irish control Britain's naval bases in its territory, Éamon de Valera endeavoured without success to enlist American support for the unification of the island. He subsequently told the American ambassador that a defence pact with Britain was ruled out because of the continuance of partition, adding, however, that the position of Ireland in a future war would be one of neutrality but that Ireland would never take sides with any enemy of Britain.

The ambassador's report of de Valera's comments continued: 'In external affairs, Ireland must by necessity of events take a course parallel to England. This was made manifest by the recent events in Austria, and he [de Valera] was satisfied that Ireland on the Continent would suffer a fate similar to Austria. England acted as a shield against the Continent threatened with war, and he was convinced that the international political outlook of Ireland would more and more fuse with that of England.'

This assurance – one which had been foreshadowed even before independence by de Valera's February 1920 proposal that Britain declare a kind of Monroe Doctrine for the two islands – has, of course, represented the consistent policy of all Irish governments since independence, whatever their feelings about partition. This stance was later reflected in de Valera's statement to the German minister on 31 August 1939 that Germany should understand that, in a war, 'Ireland would have to show a certain consideration to Britain' and in his warning to Germany at that meeting not to interfere in the partition issue through the IRA – a warning that some elements of the Nazi government ignored.

In the event, of course, Irish neutrality was operated secretly in Britain's favour, as was explained to the British Cabinet in a February 1945 memorandum from Lord Cranborne – a man not personally sympathetic to Ireland – who listed fourteen significant Irish departures from neutrality in Britain's favour, adding that the Irish government 'have been willing to accord us any facilities which would not be regarded as *overtly* prejudicing their attitude to neutrality.' (My italics.)

Nevertheless, despite de Valera's March 1938 assurances to the US ambassador, an Irish military mission to the US in May 1939 met with some reticence in Washington. The Americans first sought and secured an assurance from the Irish mission that the arms would not be used against the North – and then sought British approval for the arms sales, which was given 'without reservations'. (It had in fact been the British, unable to supply arms themselves, who had suggested that the Irish turn to the United States for assistance.) Almost everything sought by the Irish mission was agreed, but in the end the deal fell through because of objections by the Irish department of finance to the cost. This short-sighted decision was of course bitterly regretted by the Irish government during the war.

During the Anglo-Irish discussions held in June and July 1940 (when a British offer of Irish unification in return for British troops being stationed in Ireland to help repel a German invasion was turned down by de Valera), part of the proposed deal involved substantial arms shipments to the Irish army. When the proposed deal fell through, Churchill vetoed the arms deliveries, and in January 1941 Treasury permission for sterling for the purchase of arms from the US was refused. An Irish arms mission to the United States in April 1941 returned empty-handed as far as arms were concerned – although the delivery of two cargo ships was arranged.

(These ships were both later sunk by the Germans.)

Immediately after this, Britain itself started supplying the Irish army with some weapons, a process that continued throughout the rest of 1941. But the British withheld knowledge of these deliveries from the Americans, as indeed they seem to have done about the whole range of covert cooperation between Ireland and Britain during the war. This secrecy may have reflected concern that knowledge of these moves might make the United States more sympathetic to post-war Irish efforts to secure an end to partition. On the other hand, Irish cooperation in maintaining this secrecy may have reflected concern lest knowledge of Anglo-Irish wartime cooperation might, through the US, reach German ears – and might also, if word of it got out, encourage Irish-American support for the IRA.

The continued secrecy for decades after the war about the phoney character of Irish neutrality seems to have reflected a combination of concern on de Valera's part to maintain for domestic purposes the myth of strict Irish neutrality and, on Churchill and Attlee's part, resentment against Ireland's failure to enter the war, and a corresponding reluctance to give it any credit for the help it had in fact given secretly during the war. By the time historians discovered what had been happening, the myth of wartime neutrality was too well-established to be disturbed by mere facts, and it has accordingly largely survived until the present day.

During the war, Anglo-Irish secrecy vis-à-vis the United States had a most negative effect on Irish–US relations when, from early 1940, the United States was represented in Ireland by David Gray, a relation by marriage of President Roosevelt, who notably lacked the kind of understanding of Irish nationalism of which the British representative, Sir John Maffey (later Lord Rugby), often showed he was capable.

In February 1940, just before Gray's arrival, Roosevelt, strongly supported by the British ambassador to the United States, Lord Lothian, had intervened, without success, to suggest clemency for two IRA men who had been sentenced to death in Britain. This kind of action was not to be repeated thereafter, however. Even before the United States was dragged into the war by the Japanese attack on Pearl Harbour, sympathy with Britain in its struggle against Nazism understandably took precedence over any concern for Irish – or indeed Irish-American – feelings.

Thus when, in 1941, well before Pearl Harbour, the Irish government enquired about a naval and air base being built by the Americans for the British in Northern Ireland, it was firmly told that, the territory concerned being recognised by the United States as part of the United Kingdom, any enquiries on this matter should be addressed to the British government. Pearl Harbour itself provided the occasion for that curious message from Churchill to de Valera, delivered in the middle of the night: 'Now is your chance. Now or never. "A nation once again". Am very ready to meet you at any time.'

But if Churchill thought America's entry into the war would change de Valera's approach, he was quite wrong. Indeed, as, at Britain's instance, US troops started to replace British forces in Northern Ireland, this was the occasion for new tensions to arise between Ireland and the United States. De Valera protested against 'this unreserved recognition of British sovereignty over the North', and the Irish ambassador in Washington told the US authorities that his government feared that US forces would be used to attack the South. This evoked an assurance from Roosevelt that the United States had not 'the slightest thought of invading Irish territory or threatening Irish security'.

In February 1943, David Gray – unaware, of course, of the nature and scale of secret Anglo-Irish cooperation – started a campaign to put pressure on the Irish government to provide air, land and port facilities to the Allies, to expel Axis diplomats, and to clarify whether Ireland was or was not in the Commonwealth – the latter a curious concern for an American diplomat! His stated motivation for this initiative had nothing to do with the war: it was, he explained to the state department, designed to secure an Irish *refusal,* so as to 'forestall the attempt which de Valera would otherwise undoubtedly make to represent to the world [after the war] that he was, all along, helpful and friendly'.

Although Gray's proposal was taken up by Roosevelt and Churchill at their August 1943 meeting in the United States, on reflection the British government pulled back on the issue. They feared that de Valera might accept the demands, and thus increase his post-war leverage on partition. For his part, Cordell Hull, the secretary of state, was reluctant to get involved in Anglo-Irish affairs without adequate reason, and a report prepared at his request by the American chiefs of staff showed limited military enthusiasm for Irish bases. It would have been impossible to route transatlantic shipping around the southern coast of Ireland because of the German occupation of France; this had made the southern ports valueless, whilst those in Donegal offered little real advantage vis-à-vis neighbouring Derry.

While none of this prevented Roosevelt from pursuing the matter further with the British government, it did eventually blunt the edge of American enthusiasm for the project. Moreover, Gray's initiative suffered a further setback in September 1943, when, foreshadowing the British reaction to the US invasion of Grenada forty years later, the foreign secretary, Anthony Eden, warned the Americans against making a direct approach of this kind to a country that was a member of the Commonwealth! By December 1943, the British had killed off the proposal to seek bases in Ireland.

Gray then reformulated his proposal so as to focus on the Axis missions alone, and this was eventually reluctantly accepted by the British, who agreed to support a US initiative confined to this issue. But when it was presented in February 1944, this 'American Note' turned into something of a diplomatic disaster. By purporting to see in it an ultimatum, de Valera forced the Allies to back off and actually to give a guarantee against an Anglo-American invasion! Moreover, when, several weeks later, the episode was leaked in Washington, de Valera was immediately seen in Ireland, even by people who were strongly pro-Allied, as having staved off such an invasion. As a result, in a general election that was unwisely precipitated by the Opposition some months later, he recovered the overall parliamentary majority that he had lost a year earlier.

The long-term strategic lesson the United States derived from its wartime experience with Irish affairs was that Northern Ireland's continued presence in the United Kingdom was of great strategic importance to it and that, accordingly, the US had no interest whatever in supporting Irish unification – in fact, quite the contrary. When, in March 1948, a new US ambassador, George Garrett, proposed US support for the ending of partition, he was told firmly by the State Department that, if Dublin controlled the North, military facilities available to US forces during the war might be withheld, whereas so long as the North was part of the United Kingdom, the US had every reason to count on bases there in the event of need. This was a powerful argument, Washington said, for the

US favouring the continued control of Northern Ireland by the United Kingdom.

Against that background, it was not surprising that when, in January 1949, the North Atlantic Alliance was proposed, the US government accepted the British government's request that, if the Irish government raised partition as a barrier to participation in the Alliance, it should say that this issue was beyond its competence and had nothing to do with the proposed North Atlantic Treaty. In the event, the Irish response to this invitation did in fact make membership of the North Atlantic Alliance conditional on the ending of partition – a foolish attempt at arm-twisting that inevitably failed.

A year later, George Garrett, the sympathetic US ambassador to Ireland, raised with Washington – with the consent of the Irish foreign minister, Seán MacBride – the possibility of a bilateral defence agreement with the United States. But after consultation with the British government, which opposed the idea, this was turned down by the United States – again because of British fears that such an alliance might later strengthen Ireland's hand on the partition issue. And there the whole matter rested until, twenty years later, Northern Ireland re-emerged dramatically on the world scene with the advent of the civil-rights movement.

The events of 1968 to 1972 in Northern Ireland – from the civil-rights march of 5 October 1968 that was batoned off the streets of Derry, up to the Parachutists' killing of thirteen civilians in the same city on 31 January 1972 – created a new crisis in Anglo-Irish relations. It also reawakened dormant Anglophobe passions among Irish-Americans.

By the latter year, the Provisional IRA was well launched on its campaign of violence, which threatened not just the peace of Northern Ireland but also the maintenance of law and order within the Irish State itself. The support evoked by the IRA amongst Irish-Americans was thus becoming a serious problem for the Irish as well as the British government – especially when that support started to reach the highest level of the US legislature.

This posed very difficult problems for Irish diplomacy in the 1970s, facing it with the unenviable dual task of countering intermittent British briefings in Washington that were hostile to the Irish government on issues such as extradition and cross-border security, and enlisting the support of US opinion in favour of more sensitive British handling of security within Northern Ireland, whilst at the same time combating the IRA's propaganda and fund-raising campaign in the US and seeking to persuade Irish-American organisations and politicians to support its own policies.

Facing this dual challenge, successive Irish governments had crucially important support from the constitutional nationalist Social Democratic and Labour Party in Northern Ireland – in particular from John Hume, the party's deputy leader, and later leader. It was in fact Hume who in 1972 swung first Senator Ted Kennedy and then Speaker Tip O'Neill in favour of the constitutional nationalist approach to the Northern Ireland problem. Thereafter, able Irish diplomats and visiting Irish ministers, working closely with Hume, reduced very substantially the moral and material support the IRA had been receiving from Irish-American organisations. The Irish government also mobilised a wide range of leading Irish-American politicians in support of its policies, largely marginalising the IRA's supporters in Congress. Indeed, by about 1976 the congressional support that had been secured by the Irish government was second only to that which was traditionally available to Israel.

All this had a curious outcome in 1980, after the replacement of Jack Lynch by Charles Haughey as leader of Fianna Fáil and Taoiseach. Some of Haughey's more republican supporters within the party who had been responsible for his success in the leadership contest, as well as Neil Blaney – a former ministerial colleague sympathetic to the IRA who was now an independent member of the Dáil – were unhappy with the success of the Irish ambassador to Washington, Sean Donlon, in marginalizing support for the IRA in the United States. Although this was contrary to the interests of the Irish State, in order to keep them happy Haughey decided to shift Ambassador Donlon to another post, but Donlon had by then won such respect from the Irish-American congressional leadership that they publicly denounced this decision, and Haughey was forced to climb down and to retain Donlon in Washington. Meanwhile, Irish diplomacy had persuaded President Carter in 1977 to promise US financial support for Northern Ireland if violence ended – a promise that was implemented sixteen years later by President Clinton following the IRA cessation of violence in that year.

Despite his close relationship with Margaret Thatcher, White House interest in Ireland was substantially maintained thereafter under President Reagan. In 1981, Reagan responded negatively to a request by me for him to intervene in favour of the reinstatement of a cancelled British decision that would have ended the hunger strike on a basis that would not have involved acceptance of all IRA demands. But in December 1984, when the Anglo-Irish negotiations were in difficulty, Reagan, at the insistence of the Irish government, raised this matter with Margaret Thatcher, placing it formally on the agenda for the next meeting, which was to take place in February 1985. This contributed to the eventual successful outcome of those negotiations.

When the negotiations concluded in November 1985, a joint Anglo-Irish team presented the outcome in Washington, and the president agreed to welcome the signature of the agreement jointly with his opponent, Tip O'Neill – who, for his part, secured congressional approval for a $250 million aid programme to Northern Ireland and the border areas of the Republic. This support from the president was given despite the fact that the American administration was unhappy with the Irish government's stance on US involvement in Central America. Throughout this period, however, the state department remained more resistant to Irish concerns, maintaining its traditional Anglophile stance.

The Clinton presidency, the first post–cold war US administration, was also the first administration for many years to come to office in circumstances of friction with the United Kingdom, due to the unwise support that had been given by the British Conservative Party to the re-election campaign of George Bush Senior. There had, however, been nothing to suggest that Clinton would take a particular interest Irish affairs.

When, in response to Irish-American pressure, and to the emergence of moves towards peace in Northern Ireland, the Clinton administration began to show such an interest, both the British government and the unionists in Northern Ireland became alarmed. In the event, however, the sophistication and impartiality of the US approach to the issue eventually impressed all the participants, especially on the occasion of a Clinton visit to London, Belfast, Derry and Dublin.

The fact that the Northern Ireland peace process was initiated several years after the cold war had ended meant that British and US concerns about the possible strategic role of Northern Ireland in a war situation – already greatly diminished with the development of nuclear weapons – had ceased to be a factor. The rationale for the state department's traditional bias on Irish matters had thus disappeared, facilitating the emergence of a more coherent approach to Northern Ireland by the various arms of the US government.

The peace process also had implications for the split in Irish-America, including congressional Irish-America, between supporters of the Irish government and supporters of the IRA. The united stance thus made possible was, however, completely dependent on the continuance of the cessation of violence. If the IRA had resumed violence, the consequences for Sinn Féin might have been bitter hostility not only from the US administration but also from some in Irish-America who in the past had been supportive of Sinn Féin/IRA. The fact that this was made abundantly clear by the US was a most helpful development in terms of increasing pressure on the IRA to restore the cessation of violence which had been interrupted on 9 February 1996.

That Britain, Ireland and the USA, between the three of which Northern Ireland has so often in the past been a source of contention, were now at one on how to move ahead towards peace in Northern Ireland proved to be a crucial factor in securing an end to the IRA campaign.

13

Europe's Role in a Globalised World

I should like to start with some general reflections on globalisation, which has been described simply as 'interdependence at intercontinental distances' – but has also been defined more precisely, and more technically, as 'the rise of autonomous transnational spaces and the general decline in transaction costs due to the reduction of institutional and communication barriers.'

The process of globalisation is driven in part by technology and in part by policy decisions. The technology factor is irreversible, but the policy decisions that generate globalisation are in principle capable of modification and even of reversal. Indeed, in the second quarter of the twentieth century, the process of globalisation was temporarily reversed, and it did not regain its full momentum again until the 1970s. The inequalities that had been created in the nineteenth and early twentieth centuries between beneficiaries of globalisation and those who lost out from this process may have played some part in the rise of communism and fascism.

Even today, it remains possible that a world recession will provoke a revival of protectionism. If a policy of protectionism spread from country to country, as in the 1930s, peoples around the world could once again be impoverished. But there is a good chance that this danger can be avoided.

The changes brought about by economic globalisation in recent decades have undoubtedly generated greater prosperity in the world, but it must also be accepted that, in the short term, there can be a downside to this process, as, for example, where the removal of protection leads to the loss of traditional jobs in regions with older employment patterns where alternative jobs are not readily available. Moreover, whilst globalisation has helped more advanced countries to become more prosperous, some – although not all – developing countries have lost ground, especially those that are dependent on demand for unprocessed agricultural products and other natural resources, which can fall sharply during recessions.

I don't think it is possible to discuss usefully the relationship between Europe and globalisation without first addressing some of the criticisms made of organisational aspects of economic globalisation – touching on bodies like the World Bank, International Monetary Fund and World Trade Organisation. The accusation that these institutions are subject to what is described as a 'democratic deficit' seems to me to derive in some measure from earlier criticisms of the decision-making system within the European Union. How legitimate and democratic is the process by which decisions in relation to economic globalisation are taken?

These decisions are the responsibility of ministers of national governments – whether these be ministers of trade or finance or, in particular specialised sectors, ministers of transport, communications, agriculture and so on. These sectoral negotiations have been described as 'islands of governance'; most of these 'islands' have developed in the second half of the twentieth century.

It can, of course, be argued that there is no real 'democratic deficit' here, as each of these ministers acts under the authority of the government of which he is a member – and in democratic countries, these governments are responsible in turn to their parliaments, and ultimately to their electorates. Realistically, however, this system involves a long, and somewhat weak, chain of democratic control – one that may be inadequate to balance the globalisation dynamic that seems to be a feature of almost all international organisations.

In practice, ministers who deal with international negotiations have a good deal of autonomy in their activities, and in some cases they seem to be more concerned to protect the interests of the sector of the economy for which their ministry is responsible than to advance the general good of the people of their state. Thus, in relation to EU domestic farm policy, and also in the part the ministers play in preparing the EU mandate for global trade negotiations, the ministers for agriculture of those EU member countries that have significant farm sectors are often powerful advocates of farming interests.

Second, few parliaments – and this is even more true of electorates – concern themselves much with international negotiations, and parliaments have a very limited role (and sometimes none whatever) in ratifying treaties, still less in approving negotiating mandates in advance. And even where parliaments have a role in preparing a negotiating mandate – as in Denmark – this cannot in practice completely bind the minister, who, in the course of the negotiating process, must be able to do 'package deals' that involve winning on some issues by conceding ground on others. (In Denmark, parliament is notified in advance of impending negotiations in relation to EU Commission proposals, giving it the opportunity to make an input into the preparation of the national government's position in relation to them.)

The truth is that international negotiations are inherently unamenable – there is such a word: it was used by Jeremy Bentham! – to democratic control of the kind that exists at national level where there is a government that can be monitored. There is no prospect of a world government in the foreseeable future, still less of a world parliament to exercise democratic control over the world's national governments. Such control is possible only at the national level – and, it has to be said, is not always very effective even there.

This is true even at the level of the European Union itself. Ninety-five percent of the decisions made by the EU's Council of Ministers (which can act only on proposals made by the independent European Commission) now require to be endorsed by the European Parliament. But that body, although elected directly by the peoples of Europe's states, is of limited effectiveness. And, so far as national parliaments are concerned, with almost all EU Council decisions now to be taken by qualified majority voting rather than by unanimity, national parliaments have no practical means of influencing these decisions.

What steps might be taken to mitigate this unavoidable democratic deficit in the decision-making process on globalisation issues at international level? First of all, democratic parliaments could – and should – follow the Danish practice. Second, where ministries other than the lead ministry in a negotiation have an interest in the matter under negotiation, they should ensure that they are also represented at it. Third, parliamentarians could be included in negotiating delegations. (Some countries already do this, but others – particularly the civil-servant element in government systems – tend to resist such an arrangement.)

Fourth, responsible NGOs could be kept informed of what is happening and allowed to submit their views on the negotiation. Some of these bodies may have specialised information which would enable them to make useful inputs. It should be borne in mind, however, that in certain cases their capacity to make such an input may be limited either by the fact that they are lobbyists for a vested interest or by virtue of their being ideological opponents of the market system, with a hostile rather than reforming mission.

We should, however, recall that one of the longest-established and most successful international organisations is the International Labour Organisation in Geneva, where governments, employers and unions are all represented. (There would, incidentally, be much to be said for transferring to the ILO the discussion of labour standards which are currently debated in the World Trade Organisation. For, in the WTO, some at least of the pressure for higher labour standards is self-interested – motivated by the protectionist concerns of vested interests in some wealthy countries rather than by genuine concern about labour standards in the developing world.)

It should be said that at least some of the complaints made about international economic organisations, including the European Union, are misplaced, because responsibility for these decisions rests with the governments who take them, who are then often content to hide behind the international organisation which has the task of implementing their initiatives. This is especially the case with the European Union: the European Commission is blamed for everything that happens, despite the fact that, except for decisions of an administrative kind (which are, of course, made under the authority of laws that have earlier been adopted by the Council of Ministers and the European Parliament), all new laws are made by the Council of Ministers and the European Parliament. True, these laws are the result of proposals made by the Commission – but most of these proposals (I have heard a figure of more than 90 percent mentioned) ultimately derive from suggestions emanating from some member state or states.

Politicians from member states are often more than happy to allow the Commission to carry the blame for unpopular consequences of the laws they have passed – and which, in many cases, they have themselves initiated. And the same is true of international organisations engaged in activities associated with globalisation.

Finally, it has to be said that many decisions of both the EU and international organisations are necessarily the result of compromises, in which each party concedes something that is of lesser importance for it, in order to secure an objective that is more valuable to some of its citizens. But those entering into these compromises are often unwilling to admit their responsibility for whatever loss may have been suffered by a particular interest is part of the process of gaining a bigger advantage for some other interest.

Recognising that, in the absence of a world government and parliament, it is impossible to create a fully democratic framework for international decision-making in relation to the process of globalisation, there have been efforts to explore ways in which this deficit might be tackled. Recently, such an attempt has been made through a cooperative, bilateral effort on the part of the governments of Finland and Tanzania, under the auspices of what is described as the Helsinki Process.

This approach has recognised the fact that attempts to enforce international norms often prove ineffective (vide the European Growth and Prosperity Pact), both because bigger powers take special privileges and because all states do not have an equal capability to monitor and implement agreements. For that reason, this report suggests that dispute settlement and persuasion, rather than economic and other punishments, be used as a means of global governance capacity development.

Next, this report suggested that, because of a tendency to treat governance as an instrument of control that aims to prevent the rise of alternative forms of thinking and organization, it should be clearly recognised that the 'governist commitment' must not be accepted as a neutral, technical approach. Consequently, because of their incomplete transnational capabilities and also because of their outright partiality in some areas, governments cannot be the sole agency of global governance.

The report noted, realistically, the indispensability of the United States to the management of the globalisation process, for, without its cooperation, global governance is often not possible. Nonetheless, there are of course some areas where the rest of the world has felt it possible and necessary to go ahead without the agreement of the US, e.g. in respect of Kyoto and the code of International Criminal Law. It should perhaps be added that within Europe itself, as distinct from globally, there now exists an element of external accountability in respect of the actions of states, in the form of the European institutions.

To me, this appears to be a rather disappointing initial response to the problems of globalisation; one must hope that the Helsinki Process eventually bears more fruit. I have to add, however, that it would be helpful if critics of globalisation were to formulate their complaints more coherently and to propose specific practical and feasible measures that could limit the negative effects of globalisation on some developing countries. I have found the dearth of such concrete proposals amidst current anti-globalisation rhetoric quite depressing; this has certainly made it difficult to include here effective suggestions for reform of the international capitalist system.

The international agenda has in recent times been expanded to include such issues as the environment, technology, human rights, gender issues and organised crime. Moreover, the expansion of trade and investment is shaping labour standards, food safety, rules of origin, and competition law, whilst information technology is affecting privacy, the monitoring of information flows, and intellectual-property rights – the international protection of which many now think has been pushed too far to protect various vested interests.

The positive reactions to all these developments include signs of the emergence of a new type of relationship that brings together intergovernmental and non-governmental organisations, e.g. the World Bank and environmental organisations, as well as the International Union for the Conservation of Nature, which involves around seven hundred NGOs and roughly a hundred government agencies.

Let me now turn to the role of the European Union in globalisation. With a population that is only 7 percent of that of the globe, the EU is responsible for almost a fifth of the world's exports of goods and for a quarter of the world's exports of services. It is a greater source of foreign direct investment than the US, and, after that country, is the second largest recipient of this form of investment. Moreover, the EU's trade with the rest of the world accounts for a higher proportion of its GDP than is the case with its transatlantic partner.

The emergence in the 1950s of the European Community, later the European Union, was part of a much wider process through which western Europe set out in the immediate post-war period to reverse the tide of its history. At least since the fifteenth century that history had been permeated by a series of attempts by different dynasties or states to dominate this small, but hugely dynamic and influential, western peninsula of Eurasia.

The European Community emerged as something of an unintended by-product of the earlier Coal and Steel Community, which had been designed to secure permanent peace in Europe by merging permanently what were then seen – how the world has since moved on! – as the sinews of war of France and Germany. And it was the failure in 1953 of an attempt to pave the way for political union by establishing a European army that led, two years later, to six governments embarking on an alternative economic route to European union.

It is this deep-seated political motivation – more profoundly felt in Continental European countries than in Britain, and perhaps Ireland – that has helped bind Europe's states together in their complex process of economic integration. It also explains why repeated forecasts of a collapse of the Union under the pressure of inter-state commercial rivalries have always been proved wrong by events.

Politics has also influenced the scale and character of Europe's development-aid activities. These activities have been primarily directed towards former European colonies and, of course, include neocolonial as well as disinterested elements. The disinterested element has been most marked in the case of northern European donors such as the Scandinavians and the Dutch, who are also the most generous – as well, of course, as the Irish and to a considerable extent also, it should be said, the British. Both the character and the volume of European civil aid compare very favourably with that provided by the US, which has been both more sparing and more selective in the assistance it has given to other countries, with much of its civil and military aid going to a single country, Israel.

In general, Europe has been more sensitive to criticisms relating to the downside of globalisation and more willing to make concessions to developing countries in trade negotiations. In its 2003 paper on globalisation, the European Commission makes no bones about the fact that, although globalisation can boost economic growth, 'it can also be disruptive. . . . By pitting unequally developed economies against one another, globalisation may, if unharnessed, widen the gap between rich and poor countries and further sideline the poorest economies.' The paper adds that, 'when business goes global, the rules of fair play must also be set globally.'

The Commission adds that 'EU trade policy goes beyond trade liberalisation; it is about updating and improving international rules and giving them a wider coverage to ensure fair trade and harness globalisation. . . . One of the key challenges today is to ensure that world trade rules take account of non-market concerns, particularly the environment, public services, food safety, agriculture and culture.' It should perhaps be added that, contrary to widespread belief, the EU does not seek deregulation or privatisation where public-interest considerations apply, for instance in the health-care and education sectors, and it is committed to maintaining cultural diversity.

Europe is not just a free-trade area; it has from the outset been a full customs union, the external tariff of which was required, by GATT rules, to be no more protective than had been the tariffs of its member states before it came into existence. And it has since then been very active in promoting reduced protection during global trade rounds. Its tariffs are now amongst the lowest in the world; in fact, most of them in recent times have disappeared under the terms of the Uruguay Round of trade negotiations.

Furthermore, Europe is a genuine single market, within which not only have visible barriers to trade been removed but also steps have been taken, through the single-market legislation of the late 1980s and early 1990s, to tackle the much more complex problem of non-tariff barriers to trade. These barriers include health-and-safety requirements, which are often abused for protective purposes, as well as a preference on the part of governments to use domestic suppliers.

An extremely important feature of the European Union is the fact that the member states are required to cede all their negotiating compe-tences to it: thus the Commission, in conjunction with the Council, pre-pares an agreed negotiating mandate for it to use, normally together with the presidency of the Council. If this mandate needs to be amended in the course of the negotiation, as is often the case, the Council can be con-sulted further. I recall that, in the case of the 1975 Lomé Negotiation, which, as president of the Council I led for the EU, the trade ministers remained at hand, and the Council met on a number of occasions during the negotiation – once at 2 AM!

The EU's policy of making special provision for seventy-seven for-mer colonies in the Caribbean, in Africa, in the Indian Ocean and in Oceania – the so-called ACP (African, Caribbean and Pacific) countries – has, however, evoked complaints from other developing countries, espe-cially in south Asia. The ACP process originated in the initial six-member European Economic Community, which established a special trading rela-tionship with these countries through a series of agreements signed in Yaoundé in the Cameroon. In 1975, after Britain, Ireland and Denmark had joined the Community, these agreements were replaced by a series of five-year Lomé Agreements with forty-six African, Caribbean, Indian Ocean and Pacific states, mainly former French and British colonies. The failure of successive French governments to complete the negotiating process on the first three of these occasions left Ireland – which at that time was, alphabetically, the next EEC country after France and therefore the next to hold the Council presidency – with this responsibility up to the mid-1980s.

I recall vividly how I found myself at Christmas 1974 quite unexpect-edly faced with the task of settling by the following 31 January no fewer than fifty outstanding issues. In my case, this was facilitated by the fact that Ireland, having never been a colonial power, was trusted by the ACP leaders to treat them fairly – and also by the fact that by 1975 we were long enough within the Community to have also won the trust of our partners not to betray them! We could, thus, act as honest brokers. After two long negotiations, the second and final of which lasted sixty hours non-stop, we reached agreement at 7 AM on 1 February – only seven hours after our deadline!

These ACP Agreements have since April 2000 become the Cotonou Agreement, which in 2007 will be replaced by the Economic Partnership

Agreements. These agreements will deal with political questions, economic and trade issues, and development aid.

The recent aborted WTO negotiation now looks like being on course for a resumption, under more favourable conditions this time – following agreement between the main parties on certain principles upon which to base their final negotiating positions. The eventual agreement would include provision for some further agricultural concessions by the EU, following a radical change in its sugar policy – perhaps the principal outstanding issue in the agricultural area.

I have to say that, although Ireland, because of its sugar-beet sector, will be adversely affected by a successful WTO negotiation, I feel that the stand taken at the earlier Cancún meeting by developing countries, which led to a breakdown of negotiations there, was a healthy development that has created a badly needed improved balance within the WTO between the developed and the developing world.

Within the WTO, the EU has sought to bring developing countries into the Organisation's negotiating processes. It has also put forward proposals to make the WTO's procedures more transparent to the outside world and to help developing countries to handle its processes.

In the current Doha Round, the EU has pressed successfully for negotiations to include investment, competition and government procurement – issues that it tackled within its own area fifteen years ago. The EU has also welcomed a declaration on essential medicines, and favours measures to tackle such essentially global issues as climate change and the disposal of toxic waste.

Finally, let me turn to, and deal frankly with, the issue of agriculture. When the European Community was established in 1957, a major problem that it faced was the merger into a single system of its members' very divergent farm-support systems. Britain had unwisely opted out of the European experiment in 1955, and the countries which were to form the initial Community – five of which were primarily northern European – had never established in temperate climates enduring colonies that were capable of producing farm products similar to those of northern Europe

– as Britain had done in earlier centuries. Consequently, in marked contrast to Britain, the farm economies of these six countries were all protected in one way or another from competition emanating from overseas, low-cost extensive farming in overseas temperate climates.

A crucial question that these six countries faced in creating a single European market out of their six economies was how to merge their very different agricultural-protection systems in such a way as to minimise disruption of agriculture, which in 1955 was still responsible for one-seventh of these economies' domestic national output. This had to be done in the face of a farm workforce which had the political power to sabotage the whole European process.

It took until 1965 to sort out this issue: the eventual outcome involved a kind of highest common factor of all the forms of protection that individual member countries had previously employed: tariffs, levies and quotas. The principal products were to be protected by a variable levy system which was set to maintain farm prices at a level that would involve no significant loss of income for farmers in any member state. Thus the price of wheat, which then ranged from £30 per ton in France to £45 in Germany (which had a particularly inefficient farming system), was set at a so-called 'average' figure of £44 per ton!

As a result, the average European price of many farm products was raised to a level that led to the production of surpluses. These surpluses could be disposed of externally only with the aid of large subsidies, which disrupted world trade and, naturally, infuriated efficient low-cost producers of these products elsewhere in the world. Objectively, this was clearly a bad system, especially as, although it was designed to protect the least efficient producers within the Community, it naturally benefited hugely those with the lowest cost levels, viz. France and, after 1973, Ireland. But, once established, it was very difficult to dismantle, because of opposition from the ever-diminishing, but ever-vocal, farm lobbies in member states.

Over the years, a series of farm-policy reforms has somewhat reduced the intensity of the problem, but it is only very recently that something like a solution has been found by breaking the link between farm subsidies and production. In future, EU farm incomes will generally be supported by payments that will be determined independently of what the farmer produces. Basically, farmers will be paid to maintain the environment, but if, at world prices, a farmer can still secure a surplus over and above production costs for some items – as many of them will certainly do – so much the better for them! This system should go a long way towards resolving forty years of distortion of world agricultural trade – although no doubt there will remain some problems that efficient producers elsewhere will wish to pursue further.

Let me conclude by relating all this to Ireland. One hundred and fifty years ago, Ireland was poorer than any other western European country. The Irish population was then at about the same level of destitution as that of the Turkish Empire. The British decision in 1846 to abolish the protectionist Corn Laws and to open the British–Irish market to foodstuffs produced by extensive farmers in North America, the Argentine and Australia thus struck a disastrous blow at the economy of what was then an almost exclusively agricultural country – whose economic role was effectively confined to meeting part of food needs of industrialising Britain. Thenceforth, the small tenant farms of Ireland produced poor pickings for their tenants and owners – right up to the time when Ireland joined the European Community, just thirty years ago.

If, in the thee-quarters of a century before the Great War, Ireland gained some ground economically, eventually achieving levels of national output and income that were about 60 percent of those of neighbouring Britain, this was largely a consequence of the socially inhuman process of exporting the large proportion of its people who were effectively destitute. Throughout most of the twentieth century, Ireland remained in roughly the same economic relationship with Britain as it had in 1914. It was only in the very last decade of the twentieth century that it finally caught up in per capita output with its near neighbour, and indeed with the rest of western Europe, achieving today a level of per capita output some 10 to 15 percent above – as well as living standards similar to – the average for the twenty-five-member European Union that emerged from the enlargement of the Union to the east and south in May 2004.

This thirty-year transition to a quite new level of Irish economic activity that has ultimately flowed from Irish membership of the European Union was greatly smoothed by the temporary boost given to Irish farm incomes by the admittedly extravagant Common Agricultural Policy of the European Union in the closing decades of the twentieth century. However much others may cavil at the CAP, there are few Irish people who regret its impact on Ireland at a crucial stage in our history!

14

Civic and Irish Republicanism

I understand classical republicanism to be about a pluralist state marked by the public engagement of its citizens in the interest of the common good. But because of the shape that Irish history took – and despite all the pieties about Wolfe Tone and Thomas Davis – it is not easy to get Irish people to relate to this concept of republicanism.

The truth is that Irish unicultural nationalism, preoccupied as it has been with its post-Gaelic Catholic ethos – which has since the nineteenth century been the prevailing political ideology of the majority in our island – and dominated by local and sectional issues rather than by the common good of Irish society as a whole, is not only different from, but in these key respects fundamentally opposed to, civic republicanism. I would add that the preoccupation of Irish 'republicanism', for historical reasons, with opposition to monarchical forms in their own right rather than in terms of the actual role of these forms in the process of governance has also had a distorting effect by greatly narrowing the focus of Irish republicans.

Because the British made their monarchy a powerful symbol of their rule, and even after the First World War sought to use it to maintain what they called the 'unity of the Empire' (that is, continued British influence over the now self-governing Dominions), Irish nationalists were perforce anti-monarchist. This greatly narrowed the Irish concept of republicanism, distracting attention even further from civic republicanism. Within the Irish State, this issue has happily been dead for more than half a century, but it is not dead in Northern Ireland, where it has continued to be an issue in the minds of many people – positive for some, negative for others.

The problem of the use of the monarchy to assert some kind of continued British involvement in Irish affairs was tackled, with considerable if not complete success, in the negotiations with the British on the 1922 Constitution. As a result, the Irish Constitution of 1922 differed from those of all other Dominions in, for example, eliminating the Crown from domestic roles such as summoning and dissolving parliament, and the selection of the head of government – these roles being left in the Irish case to the new parliament itself.

The Crown thus remained in the Constitution for external purposes only, and the British sought to use this to limit the Irish government's role in foreign affairs. But the British were eventually forced, principally by Irish diplomacy at the League of Nations and at successive Imperial Conferences, to abandon these efforts, which they finally did by enacting, in 1931, the Statute of Westminster. This issue had, however, contributed to the outbreak of a civil war, and, because of the anti-monarchist preoccupations of Irish republicanism, it has never been easy to get Irish people to relate to the concept of classical republicanism.

For a short period in the 1790s (and, less strikingly, at certain points in the nineteenth century), Irish republicanism was, at least theoretically, inspired by French-style republicanism: it was momentarily secular and anti-confessional as well as nationalist. In a very attenuated form, that tradition survived to the 1916–21 period. It is there in the 1916 Proclamation and in the Democratic Programme of 1919.

Although a republic had been proclaimed in 1916, this did not reflect as absolutist a commitment to this particular form of government as people today are inclined to believe. Rather, it reflected the practical reality that the only way in which Irish independence could be expressed at that time was by declaring a republic. This fact was attested to by my father, Desmond FitzGerald, who wrote that, when Patrick Pearse and Joseph Plunkett discussed this matter with him in the GPO during the Rising, they thought that in the only circumstances in which a Rising could possibly succeed (i.e. with German support and a German victory in the War), Ireland would inevitably become a monarchy – as of course were all European states at that time, except France and Switzerland – probably with the kaiser's sixth son, Prince Joachim, as king. That conversation is recorded in my father's 1913–16 fragment of autobiography, written during the 1940s, and was confirmed by Ernest Blythe's recollection of a discussion he had with Bulmer Hobson, secretary of the Volunteers.

The idea that these accounts should be dismissed – as, for example, Martin Mansergh has sought to do – because they might be used by partisan opponents of 1916 to discredit the Rising is simply anti-historical. Of course, Pearse and Plunkett were not *advocating* such an outcome – they did not wish it – but they were realists who knew that, if the Germans won the war, following a successful Irish rising, Ireland would suffer the same monarchical fate as had Bulgaria, Romania and Albania, and as the Germans sought to impose on Lithuania and Finland two years later. Pearse and Plunkett tried to make the best of it by suggesting that the German prince might marry a Catholic (they clearly did not know that he had married a Protestant five weeks earlier!) and that, being a German, he would want to bring his children up as Irish- rather than English-speakers.

It does Pearse and Plunkett no credit to try to perpetuate a myth – and I use this word deliberately – that they were unrealistic fantasists who thought that the Germans would allow a republic in Ireland, when in fact these two leaders of the Rising were hard-headed patriots, fully aware of the realities of the world they lived in, and concerned to make the best of those realities.

That myth of republicanism being somehow incarnate in 1916 has been sedulously fostered, but in fact that was not what people felt at the time. In my father's papers, there is a letter from Erskine Childers to him written in March 1918, in which Childers asserts that 1916 had not been about creating a republic but about self-determination. Childers added that he would be happy with self-determination within the Empire, remarking that he thought my father would also be satisfied with that. However in 1922 Childers was tragically executed as a republican by the government of which my father was a member.

There is further evidence of openness to forms of government other than a republic in Éamon de Valera's request to Arthur Griffith before the Treaty negotiation of 1921 to 'get me out of the straight-jacket of a republic' – and, of course, in de Valera's view that, if his objective of external association with the Commonwealth was secured, it would then be for the Irish people to decide the form of state they wanted, whether a republic or a monarchy.

We know, of course, that in the end the anti-monarchist version of nationalism prevailed here, strengthened no doubt by the collapse of various empires and monarchies in 1918, and by the consequent emergence of many republics in Europe. Given the importance the British still attached to their monarchy – their emphasis on it as the lynchpin of their Empire, in fact – and the extent to which British forces were referred to by them as the Crown forces, this Irish nationalist reaction against monarchy was probably inevitable. For very many Irish nationalists, the huge symbolic importance that the British at that time attached to their monarchy automatically converted monarchy into a powerful 'anti-symbol'.

It must also be said that, quite apart from visceral Irish objections to the monarchy as a British symbol, objectively the British version of monarchy, as distinct from what is now the Continental version, is not compatible with the kind of society or political structures delineated by classical republicanism. The absence of any constitutional constraint upon the actions of the British Parliament, which at least in theory is endowed with absolute power, derives from an antique and indeed medieval theory of the role of the monarch, which has survived in Britain and nowhere else.

I want to turn now to the issue of theory and practice and to address the classical concept of the republic. I feel that we should perhaps call civic republicanism *res-publicanism,* in Roman terms. It has nothing to do with whether you have a president or a monarch, or a fully constitutional king, queen or grand-duke. It can indeed be argued that the Scandinavian monarchies of Denmark, Sweden and Norway, and perhaps also the Netherlands, come nearer to being republics in the classical sense of the word than does a republic such as France, which still has an executive head of state.

Even today, a monarch may be more effective as a uniting force than an elected president, usually a superannuated party politician, can be. Moreover, in certain times and certain places, like Spain, a monarch may be better placed than a president to safeguard the state and human rights against attempts to destabilise democracy, as King Juan Carlos was able to do a quarter of century ago, or as the king in Italy did in 1943 to get rid of a discredited dictator.

The real issue is not – as some in Ireland may be tempted by our curious version of history to believe – whether a state is headed by a monarch or a president, but rather the extent to which, under whatever kind of head of state, the citizens of a state are permitted or encouraged to play an active part in public affairs – or instead are marginalised by the political system and accorded little role or influence in the way that society develops, or are so uninterested in the state, or so lacking in their sense of civic duty that they are unable to help create and sustain a genuine *res publica*.

The alternative to representative government, viz., participatory democracy, involving theoretically active, united and virtuous citizens, was discredited by the French Revolution. The form of democracy that we have today is thus representative democracy, which, it has to be said, does not of itself create the kind of *res publica* that the classical concept involves.

Of course, in our State, an element of direct democracy exists in a particular form: referendums. We have referendums for changes in the Constitution. We could even have them, in certain circumstances, if the government and parliament wished to get a public view on a proposed law – although goverment and parliament have in fact never chosen to do this.

It should be noted that there are two sides to referendums. We in Ireland think of them as being very democratic. We feel that the people should have the final decision on changing the Constitution in any way because it is their Constitution, not Parliament's. We are more republican in this way than some other republics in Europe, where parliament can change the constitution by a two-thirds majority.

There could also be a popular right of constitutional initiative, through which citizens can propose changes in the Constitution without the involvement of parliament. We had that in our first Constitution, but when Fianna Fáil threatened to use it to start a process as a result of which the people might have voted for something that would have been in breach of the 1921 Treaty, and therefore would have undermined our constitutional position in international law, the government of the day secured parliamentary authority to abolish the initiative. (For a period after the enactment of the 1922 Constitution, such a power to amend the Constitution was temporarily vested in parliament.)

Many people see a referendum as the ultimate exercise in democracy, but it has to be realised that other countries – such as Germany, with its experience of a dictator who used referendums to consolidate his position and to rally people in support of him – have a different view of them. This German experience would have made it impossible to secure agreement at European level in what might seem to many to be a logical process by which to adopt a European Constitution, viz. by the peoples of Europe as a whole voting together – accompanied perhaps by a simultaneous double-majority system, with the individual states also voting.

The issue that needs to be addressed thus seems to be how to ensure that, with the type of representative government with which our history and culture have endowed us, we might secure the promotion of the public good, shaped by wide-ranging deliberation amongst citizens – which of course is what the concept of the classical republic involves.

The problems which seem to me to impede the emergence of such a society are two-fold: the danger that elected representatives may be tempted to use for private advantage the positions to which they have been elected and may resist any popular curb on these arrangements, and the danger that the citizens themselves may be lacking in concern for the common good.

On the first of these issues, our parliament has over recent decades set up a system, and has structured itself, and endowed itself with resources, and created posts, which seem to me to go beyond what the citizens would wish to see. The people might, for example, think that there are too many ministers of state, many of them without much to do. (As Taoiseach, I could never find jobs of any consequence for more than seven or eight ministers of state; the rest seemed to me to be superfluous, but I had to give them the jobs, otherwise I could have lost parliamentary support!) And then you have all the chairmen and chairwomen of Dáil committees – the proliferation of which, in the last twenty years particularly, worries me because only some of these committees seem to be really needed. Once this scale of patronage has been introduced, I doubt whether any future Taoiseach could, or would wish to, rein it in. The absence of any checks on what may be seen as parliamentary abuses seems to me to be a weakness in our exclusively representative democracy.

The second question is whether the Irish people have the capacity and willingness to 'work' a genuine republic? Our society has some good features, which we all enjoy, and from which we all benefit. The Irish people are warm, outgoing and hospitable, and they network well with each other and with people from other countries. We tend to be successful in our relationships with other peoples for that reason. But Irish people also tend to be intensely localist, clearly having great difficulty in thinking in terms of the good of the country as a whole, as distinct from that of their own locality.

In government, at times I was driven to despair as to whether there were even as many as 1,500 people in the country – a figure I arrived at quite arbitrarily! – who were actually interested in Ireland, as distinct from their *bit* of Ireland. Localism makes it very hard to govern the country. Perhaps it is the fact that we got local government in 1898 and our own national government twenty-four years later, in 1922, that has created problems of localism for us ever since – although I feel that these problems may in fact be much more deeply rooted in our history.

Irish people still have almost tribalist loyalties to their extended family, which impede loyalty to a wider common good. There is little sense of duty – a duty to contribute financially through taxation, or by way of active political involvement in the process of government. In recent decades, all of this has been illustrated quite dramatically in the form of such phenomena as widespread public tolerance of tax evasion, continued support at local level for politicians who have been demonstrated to have broken laws enacted by the Oireachtas, large-scale support for a politically motivated decentralisation of the public service that threatens the cohesion of our entire system of government just because it would be popular with people in local areas, as well as the operation of local government to favour individual clients of politicians at the expense of the environment.

It is true that, when irrefutable evidence eventually emerged of financial misbehaviour by some politicians at both national and local level, this did evoke, belatedly, a negative public response, at least for a period. But the revelation of involvement in tax evasion by local politicians seemed to evoke no loss of support for them at local level; instead, their exposure seems to have been widely seen as a form of martyrdom inflicted on them by external forces emanating from an alien metropolis!

The issue of tax evasion has always seemed to me to illustrate dramatically a substantial absence of a sense of civic duty in Ireland. For it has to be accepted that tax evasion is the only means by which a citizen can steal from the poorest in the land – because taxes not paid by the well-to-do necessitate additional imposts upon the whole tax-paying class, including the very poor – who, of course, pay VAT and excise duties, even when their poverty exempts them from income taxation.

Yet this form of stealing from even the poorest in the land has been practised here by a remarkably high proportion of self-employed people. This is especially the case in rural areas: 85 to 90 percent of the people on the list of tax evaders now published quarterly are from outside Dublin. It is now clear that the amount of taxes to be retrieved has eventually run into several billion euro. No one could have been unaware of the existence of this practice, even if few realised just how widespread it was. Yet in my long life, I never heard a sermon preached in church on this evil.

Moreover, we now know from the parliamentary inquiry into the behaviour of the banks that, when I introduced the deposit interest retention tax, as a means of tracking down such evasion, the application of the system – enacted by the Dáil in response to a decision taken by my government – was undermined for a whole decade by a countermanding instruction on enforcement issued by an unidentified civil servant in the Revenue Commissioners. This civil servant, with unbelievable arrogance, took it upon himself to decide that this was not a good decision on the part of the government and the Oireachtas and should not be enforced in the way that had been provided for.

It is also notable that a number of journalists have repeatedly sought to mitigate the practice of tax evasion, to the point of seeming to justify it. They have done this on the quite extraordinary grounds that, due to the mishandling of the public finances at the end of the 1970s, for a period tax rates were raised to a higher level – and that this entitled wealthy people to decide for themselves how much tax they should pay, setting aside the authority of the State and of the parliament elected by the people.

Against this background of widespread rejection of the duties of citizenship by a significant proportion of the better-off part of our population, the task of government in Ireland is clearly an extremely difficult one. And it is now evident that at least some of those engaged in the process of government itself were themselves corrupted by the adverse public climate in which they had to work and the lack of any sense of civic morality that might have restrained them. Dr Iseult Honohan of the politics department in UCD is, I believe, right in contending that corruption is *the* primary political problem, although it has never been generally recognised as such in our State.

Turning away from that unpleasant side of politics, how might civic republicanism be best promoted? Allowing citizens to contribute in a way that they feel counts would help to shape the common good through wide-ranging deliberation. Political parties provide one channel for such engagement. A 1969 poll carried out professionally on behalf of the Labour Party showed that, at that time, about 6 percent of the adult population were members of political parties. I think that figure today would be considerably less – perhaps 3 to 4 percent. I am not sure, however, that party membership provides an adequate channel for participation in politics by citizens – although, at its best, the party system may be a useful sounding board for those who determine party policy.

A process that I found very useful, after I became leader of Fine Gael in 1977–8, was the organisation of open public meetings. In my first tour of the country, a total of 25,000 people turned up at the meetings; these people included many members of the public and representatives of all the other parties, who came to listen and to ask questions. In all, I had the benefit of about one thousand comments or questions, which alerted me to the preoccupations of the people in various parts of the country. Curiously, this practice has not been followed by other political leaders, who have preferred to meet only members of their own party around the country. Our political system is very inward-looking in this respect; it does not look outwards towards citizens in general.

A recent striking exception to this was the decision by a minister of education to arrange twenty meetings around the country to discuss educational issues; I and others interested in education attended a number of these meetings at the minister's request. Although teachers' union representatives used the occasions to promote some aspects of their own agenda, the meetings certainly highlighted some educational issues that were foremost in the minds of an interested public.

Other routes through which the public can communicate their concerns are of course the correspondence columns of the newspapers and, most striking of all, through that special feature of contemporary Irish culture, daytime radio talk shows. Through this latter medium, governments in particular, and politicians in general, have, particularly since the mid-1980s, been made instantly aware of current public political concerns; they are also frequently put on the spot to justify their actions – or inaction.

In her book *Civic Republicanism*, Iseult Honohan sees nationalism as involving a sense of collective identity, whereas republicanism rests on political recognition of multiply reiterated interdependence and membership of a shared public culture, rather than a culture of ethnicity, and also involves equality of recognition amongst heterogeneous citizens. Shared cultural values are, she suggests, the outcome of political interaction, which is provisionally embodied, open to change, and developing towards a cosmopolitan citizenship from the bottom up, through an increasing web of relationships. I think she is correct in saying that a genuine republic has an ethical community within a moral boundary.

Such a republicanism is clearly preferable both to liberalism in its economic form and to nationalism. I think she is right in saying that liberalism is too thin and also lacking in a moral basis; indeed, one might go so far as to say that it is amoral. Nationalism excludes or even oppresses others who are not within its frame of reference as nationals of the state. In this part of Ireland, since the late 1950s there has emerged a growing concern to create here a State that would have the capacity to embrace all sections of the Irish people – a concern that I have actively shared. This has involved, for some decades past, challenging the kind of single-ethos State that my generation inherited from a troubled past – a State in which anyone who was not a Roman Catholic – and a practising Catholic at that – or who did not share the Gaelic heritage of the majority of Irish people, was regarded as insufficiently Irish, or even as not being Irish at all.

Those who challenged the divisive doctrines of this uniculturalism and who sought to create a genuine republican basis on which to build an inclusive Irish community for the whole island were often treated by the apostles of the ultra-nationalist faith as some kind of traitors to the republican cause. But, helped by revulsion against IRA violence in Northern Ireland, our people have eventually moved towards a multicultural ethos, which has brought us a little nearer to a genuine civic republicanism.

15

THE CHURCH, SOCIETY AND FAMILY IN IRELAND

I start with the fact that tensions between the individual and society lie at the root of the human condition. For the human being derives from a particularly social species of mammal, the ape, but by virtue of the development of a self-conscious intelligence has become a highly individualistic species.

The reconciliation of these two conflicting aspects of humanity poses a permanent ethical problem. On the one hand, the individual human being expects and is entitled to the respect due to a self-conscious being; on the other, individual human beings have to find a way of controlling their individualism to a sufficient degree to be able to live together in amity.

It has always seemed to me that a particular strength of the Christian church has been the balance it has struck between the individual and society. The individual, seen as being made in the image of God, is accorded huge respect, but the need for a social ethic to optimise relations between these individuals has been given equal recognition.

Of course, Christianity derived from Judaism, to which much of the credit for this harmonisation of the individual and the social must be given. But building on this inheritance, Christianity produced a philosophically sophisticated ethical structure that, in the broadest sense, has stood the test of two millennia.

There have from time to time been aberrations, and some at least of the strictures of the Christian moral code as it has reached us after such a long period of time reflect ad hoc responses to specific past situations. Examples of this include the Council of Trent's overreaction to the problem of clandestine marriages, which it declared to be invalid rather than illicit, or the continuing claim by the Roman Catholic Church, inspired by over-enthusiastic missionary zeal, to have the power to dissolve marriages with or between non-Christians where this might facilitate conversions to Christianity. And, more generally, a Church with a celibate clergy clearly went over the top on the subject of some aspects of sexual behaviour.

But overall, the balance maintained by Christianity between the individual and the social was well-judged – and in terms of optimising the human condition in society, its ethic compares favourably with the extremes of both socialism and economic as well as social liberalism, as these developed in the nineteenth and twentieth centuries. Both of these 'isms' were challenged at different times and in different ways by the Roman Catholic Church in particular.

From the vantage point of the start of the third millennium, we can now take a broader view of the events of those two centuries. Looking back in this way, it seems to me that, however intemperate, and even at times apocalyptic, some of the Catholic Church's criticisms of these two 'isms' may have been, the time and energy that it devoted to each of them reflected accurately the relative scale of the long-term threat that each posed to a balanced social order.

Only for a relatively short period in the mid-twentieth century did the Church allow itself to become concerned primarily with extreme socialism – which, for all the moral attraction of its appeal to justice and equity, ensured by its dismissal of the market system its own eventual failure. From the start, the Church's instincts were right in identifying the extremes of liberalism, in both their economic and social manifestations, as posing by far the most enduring threat to an ordered and just society. The threat posed by economic liberalism to the social order derives from its insidious appeal to human self-interest, at the expense of social solidarity, while extreme social liberalism appeals to human impatience at the restraints on individual behaviour that are required for the good of society.

The fact that the Catholic Church seems to have judged wisely the relative magnitude of what it saw as two rival threats to a balanced social order does not, of course, mean that its specific critiques of either socialism or liberalism were always well judged. In the nineteenth century, and especially during the papacy of Pius IX after his early shift to the right, the Church went completely overboard, even going so far as to denounce democracy – although that curious throwback to attitudes close to those of the *ancien régime* was firmly and quickly corrected by Pius IX's successor, Leo XIII.

The radical changes in society that have taken place since the end of the nineteenth century have posed an exceptional challenge to human beings in society, and to societal norms we have inherited from the past. Some of these norms are firmly founded in human nature itself; others may derive from the way people can best live together in a particular culture, e.g. in a tribal, extended-family culture, which may effectively be independent from and unaffected by the kind of organised state system to which we are accustomed.

The Roman Catholic Church has sometimes been tempted to over-generalise from its experience of the particular culture within which it developed in the Middle East and Europe, proclaiming norms that may be historically or geographically specific to this area as applicable to human nature itself and thus part of a natural law. But, by and large, its ethical norms have been well-rooted in the character of the human condition itself.

Perhaps a more serious weakness has been a tendency to over-claim a unique capacity for sociological insights, by proclaiming in the same breath that certain social and ethical principles represent a natural morality, deducible by pure reason, but that, at the same time, these can be subject to accurate specification only by the authority of the Catholic Church. Even committed members of the Church may have difficulty with this claim.

In one important respect, however, the Church's reasoning seems markedly superior to that of many who challenge it. This is its clear understanding and wise insistence upon the extent to which the behaviour of individuals can be influenced for the worse, or better, by how other people are seen to behave. This view challenges a prevalent liberal proposition that only the direct and immediate negative impact of aberrant behaviour upon another individual has any moral significance. The latter self-serving proposition, which is now widely used to excuse individual amoral behaviour, might perhaps be described as an ethical 'fallacy of the heap' – the assertion that, in relation to cause and effect in human behaviour, only a large and highly visible change in a causal factor can have a significant consequence.

(Some half-century ago, I disproved this proposition in relation to human reactions to small changes in air fares. In 1953, as an Aer Lingus official, I experimented with a one-year extension of cheap midweek cross-Channel fares to Monday as well as Tuesday, Wednesday and Thursday. This experiment demonstrated that, for every reduction of one shilling in these fares, 2 percent of people changed their day of travel – a shilling in 1953 being worth about €1.40 today. This experiment enabled me to convince my bosses that a low-air-fare policy would prove profitable – a proposition that, unhappily for it, Aer Lingus forgot during much of the subsequent quarter of a century!)

Where it seems to me that the Roman Catholic Church in particular has recently lost much of its former power to influence social behaviour has been in its overuse of authority rather than reason in promulgating its views on social morality. It had always been shy of pointing to the rational basis of so much of its moral teaching – perhaps because it feared that this might expose occasional irrational elements that had been allowed to creep into its teaching in response to particular challenges it had faced at various points in the past.

There can be no doubt about the significance of the 1960s worldwide, although the form that this decade's impact on society took varied from country to country. In the United States, and in much of Europe, it involved an actual sexual revolution. In Ireland, its immediate impact was, perhaps, less drastic, but an interaction between the global liberal mood and the debates of the Second Vatican Council made many Irish people for the first time think seriously and for themselves about the moral teachings of their religion.

Amongst many thinking Catholics, the early impact of this process was positive. The Catholic Church, instead of being passively accepted as part of the national wallpaper, so to speak, came to be seen in a new and generally more challenging light. For the first time, a genuine interest in theology emerged amongst sections of the laity. The concept of the church as the people of God, rather than just the episcopacy and clergy, gripped the imagination of many Catholics.

But into this new situation was thrown in mid-1968 the bombshell of *Humanae Vitae*. For many married people, this created, at least for a period, agonising problems of conscience. They were torn between traditional, instinctive loyalty to Church teaching and what they saw as their marital responsibilities. For some, the strain on their adherence to their Church proved too great. Others, often aided by sympathetic confessors, many of whom found the theology of the document unconvincing, survived this test and, despite their rejection of this particular teaching, remained practising Catholics.

In this connection, it is worth remarking that the problem with this document did not lie with its basic insight into the potential impact of the widespread availability of contraceptives upon extra-marital sexual behaviour – an insight that has been fully justified by events – but rather in the conclusions it drew from this insight with regard to the use of such methods by couples seeking to regulate the spacing of their families.

On the one hand, given the Catholic Church's earlier acceptance of the use of women's ovulatory cycle for this purpose, its objection to other means being employed so as to secure spacing and limiting pregnancies could not be justified on grounds of intent. At the same time, while there was a difference between the ease and effectiveness of these two methods, this was a matter of degree that could not, rationally or theologically, carry the weight of permitting one and flatly rejecting the other for family-planning purposes.

Moreover, on quite another level, *Humane Vitae* can be argued to have taken inadequate account of the change that had by then taken place in the situation relating to the global population. Insofar as the church's earlier negative approach to family-size limitation may have been influenced by the appropriateness at the time it was written of the biblical injunction to 'increase and multiply', by 1968 there was clearly a strong ecological case for reversing this injunction and seeking instead to slow down population growth in order to avoid overcrowding the planet. That would appear to have been more in line with what the Church describes as a 'natural law', designed to optimise the conditions for human existence.

As had been the case with some other earlier aspects of its teaching on sexual matters, the Catholic Church's disciplinary insistence on clerical celibacy – designed in an earlier period both to secure the undivided attention of clergy to their duties and to prevent the alienation of church property by their families – deprived it of the insights that a married clergy (and above all a married episcopacy!) might have had into issues of this kind.

The impact of all this upon hitherto automatic acceptance of the

Church's authority, which was already under question as a result of the changed mood of the 1960s and perhaps also as a result of the well-reported debates in the Council, proved quite profound. Thereafter, to an ever-increasing extent, many Irish Catholics began to do their own theology, so to speak, testing the Catholic Church's teaching against their own rational morality. In many, probably most, cases, the test was passed – for, except where some aberration had distorted the Church's teaching at some point in the past, Christian morality was of course firmly based on natural morality, viz. the ordering of social relationships in a manner conducive to the optimisation of the human condition. But authority had lost its power to compel. Indeed, to some degree 'authority' had become a bad word – much as 'authoritarian' had already become, at least from the period of fascism earlier in the century.

Given the manner in which over the centuries the Church had identified, in many cases correctly, the kind of criteria for behaviour that would secure optimal relationships between individuals in society, a visionary and prophetic Church might perhaps have chosen to grasp this opportunity to demonstrate the extent to which its inspiration in the past had in fact led it to develop a wise balance between individualism and social needs – wiser than that of various discredited rationalist attempts in the nineteenth and twentieth centuries. Such a demonstration of the value of its insights and of their broad compatibility with natural reason might have strengthened its moral authority and reduced its increasingly counter-productive dependence on deploying its hierarchical authority, seeking to attract rather than compel adherence to its views.

Instead, the central authorities of the Church attempted to command the absolute allegiance of its clergy to its teaching on the contraception issue by intensifying disciplinary measures vis-à-vis theologians whose views it disapproved of, and by appointing as bishops only members of the clergy who agreed in all respects with the views of Rome on this matter.

Over the past thirty-five years, these authoritarian measures have proved hugely counter-productive. In order to avoid censure by higher authority and perhaps even the loss of their clerical status and thus of their livelihood, very many of the clergy have been forced to dissimulate their views on an issue which, to say the least, was not central to the faith. This has, of course, hugely weakened the moral authority that they

230

exercise as individuals, which derives from their giving witness to the truth as they see and believe it to be.

This uncomfortable situation, continuing over several decades, left the laity ill-prepared for the revelation in the 1990s that there was an unresolved backlog of clerical child abuse cases in at least the English-speaking world. These crimes had been carefully hidden from view by Church authorities more concerned about institutional 'scandal' than about the protection of children – which for many of the laity is the most crucial moral issue of all, and one to which, unhappily, many bishops, perhaps trapped by their celibacy, proved disastrously insensitive.

The fact that decades of past abuse came to light and have been investigated and prosecuted within a relatively short period of time may have given an exaggerated, indeed false, impression of the scale of this problem. This, together with the insensitive attitude of the Church authorities to the clerical paedophile problem, has shattered the confidence of many lay people in their church.

Meanwhile, up to the 1960s the younger generation in Irish society had for long been protected by both Church and State from changes in *mores* in the world outside Ireland. With the advent of television, this screen disappeared almost overnight and, within the space of just forty years, Irish society faced changes that elsewhere in the developed world had taken place over a whole century.

To give but one example, between the mid-1960s and the end of the twentieth century, the proportion of births outside marriage rose from 1.5 to 33 percent. Of course, the former figure may have understated the scale of extra-marital intercourse in the pre-contraception 1960s, when some non-marital pregnancies were converted into marital births through shotgun marriages and a small number were also aborted in Britain. But the current 33 percent non-marital birth proportion equally understates the extent to which today's first pregnancies are extra-marital, for, when account is taken of the fact that three out of every eight first non-marital births are now aborted in Britain, it emerges that more than half of all first pregnancies in our State are non-marital.

In the even shorter period of time since 1980, the proportion of women who are married by the age of twenty-five has fallen from 60 to 12 percent. And whereas in 1980, more than two-thirds of first marital births were to women under twenty-seven, barely one-sixth of first marital births are now to women in that age group.

Today, only a small minority of non-marital births are to teenagers – one-sixth, as against two-fifths in 1981. By contrast, the proportion of non-marital births to women aged twenty-five and over is rising towards half of the total. Many of these latter non-marital births now are to couples in a stable non-marital relationship: in 2002, one-sixth of couples with one child under five were cohabiting rather than married.

The 2002 Census recorded almost as many cohabiting families with one child as there were lone-parent families with one child under that age – despite the incentive to hide the fact of cohabitation in order to secure the unmarried mother's allowance. Sixteen years earlier, that ratio was one in ten.

How has all this affected Irish family life? To date, little has been written about the effect of these huge, and extraordinarily rapid, changes in general *mores* upon our society, and in particular upon inter-generational family relationships. So, for the moment, pending overdue sociological research in this area, for an impression of this aspect of Irish family life we must depend upon anecdotal evidence.

What can, I think, be said is that, in contrast to the starkly negative and defensive character of the Church's reaction to these changes in Irish social *mores*, Irish parents and grandparents seem generally to have chosen to protect the integrity of their family relationships by accepting cohabitation by their children, even where this continues after the birth of a child. They tend to keep to themselves any qualms they may have about this practice.

I believe that there has always been a marked difference between the approaches of urban working-class families and those of other social groups to non-marital pregnancies. In contrast to middle-class urban families and almost all rural families, urban working-class families, at any rate in the larger conurbations, have long been prepared to incorporate into the nuclear family the non-marital child of a daughter living at home, treating the child as if it were a late-arriving sibling. We know all too well what happened in the past in many other rural and urban middle-class families, however. A birth would be handled with secrecy, the child adopted, often outside Ireland, and its mother sometimes even incarcerated thereafter in a convent asylum.

Although today there certainly remain young women who greatly fear parental disapproval of single motherhood, parental attitudes seem now to have generally changed. I suspect that, today, an abortion in Britain is more often the choice of a mother unwilling to become a single parent rather than a choice determined by fear of parental disapproval of single motherhood.

In general, it seems to me that most parents have a more relaxed relationship with their children than formerly and, however much they may privately regret their children's different approach to sexual matters, they seem to forbear from overt criticism or disapproval of cohabitation. It may even be that the sense of family solidarity has been strengthened rather that weakened by the need of parents to accommodate to a rapidly evolving society.

There is also clear evidence that this more relaxed approach on the part of parents is reciprocated by their children. Precisely because so many Irish parents, and grandparents, have adapted successfully to a rapidly changing social situation, many young people in Ireland today have more open, and thus often stronger, relationships with their parents and grandparents. Just as they benefit from tolerance on the part of the older generation, so also, I observe, do they respect that generation's uncensorious commitment to their traditional views on these matters.

In the absence of research into these issues, some concrete evidence of the continuing strength of Irish family relationships can be found in the quite disparate approaches of Irish and English students to the choice of third-level institutions. In England, there has traditionally been a positive preference amongst third-level students for a university that is distant from their home – although, for economic reasons, the proportion of English students choosing a university near their homes is estimated to have doubled in the past few years. English school-leavers appear to have seen their entrance to third-level education as an opportunity to get away from their families. And there is anecdotal evidence that, in many English families, parents and children lose contact at that point.

By contrast, in our State students have shown a marked preference for a university or institute of technology near their home – unless, of course, they intend to pursue a course that is not locally available. This partly reflects the fact that, in contrast to Britain, standards in Irish universities are fairly uniform: as there is no strong academic reason to choose one rather than another, the nearness of the institution to a young person's home becomes a dominant consideration. And where students' homes are too remote from their third-level institutions to permit daily commuting, they very often return home each weekend. Thus, in contrast to what is often the case in England, third-level education in the Irish State has not sundered the relationship between the generations.

The situation in Northern Ireland is somewhat different, for Protestants in particular. For obvious reasons, there has always been a greater tendency among Protestant compared to Catholic third-level students in the North to see themselves as part of a wider United Kingdom educational system. In recent times, this factor, combined with the stronger educational motivation of Catholics, has led both of the Northern Ireland universities to have a majority of Roman Catholic students, which seems to have further accelerated the flow of Protestant third-level students to Britain. The fact that there are only two universities in Northern Ireland may also have encouraged this outward flow to Britain – a flow which, even amongst Catholic students, is many times greater than in the case of the Republic.

But a higher proportion of Catholic than Protestant students seem to return to Northern Ireland. Moreover, in both parts of the island (in marked contrast to what was the case in the nineteenth century and the first half of the twentieth, when emigration in most cases involved a final breach with home), many young emigrants, whether or not they have been third-level students, now take advantage of much cheaper travel to return frequently to their homes in Ireland.

Despite the gap in social attitudes that has sprung up between the generations in the past thirty years, the strength of Irish family ties has been remarkably well-maintained. This aspect of Irish society is little recognised and is, I believe, greatly underestimated by commentators on the Irish scene. It is an important stabilising factor in a rapidly changing society and is something that should be cherished and built upon.

It should be recognised that it is precisely because the older generation has *not* sought to impose on its teenage and adult children the minutiae of the moral code according to which they were raised in earlier decades that Irish family life has survived the immense strains of this recent period of ultra-rapid social change.

Of course, in all of this we must distinguish between the hedonism of sexual promiscuity, on the one hand, and what seems, on the other hand, to be an altered approach by a new generation to family formation. This new approach involves, in the case of very many young people, what are in effect trial marriages in the form of a period of cohabitation, before commitment through a marriage ceremony to a permanent relationship. It is clear that, for whatever reason, many young people today are hesitant about entering into a life-long commitment to a partner and, insofar as they are willing to contemplate this possibility, feel that it is unwise to do so without a preliminary experimental relationship.

The sources of their hesitation about a commitment for life are unclear, especially as these doubts seem to be shared by many young people who are themselves products of successful marriages as well as by those who are less fortunate in their upbringing. The longer span of human life under modern conditions does not seem, as has sometimes been suggested, an adequate explanation, because the lengthening of young people's expectation of life has evolved over a longer period than that within which this decline in commitment has taken place.

The traditional argument against trial unions, that it is immoral to live with someone without being married to them, has behind it the experience of many centuries. But we live in a different world today. And the decision of many young people to approach a lifelong commitment to a partner by this different route cannot reasonably be described as irresponsible. Indeed, young people would say that they are acting more responsibly than those who make a lifelong commitment without first testing their compatibility by means of a prior period of cohabitation.

Although my personal experiences and instincts have favoured entering early into the kind of permanent commitment that is sanctified as marriage, I have to accept that early marriages often carry a risk of breakdown because of a lack of maturity on the part of one or both partners. I am forced to recognise that there may be a good deal to be said for the recent practice of postponing a permanent commitment and the initiation of the procreation of offspring until the late twenties or early thirties, even if earlier child-bearing is more attuned to female biology.

The latest data on marriage breakdown, from the 2002 Census, suggests that the postponement of marriage in the 1980s and 1990s may have had a favourable impact on marriage breakdown. The proportion of early marriages breaking down is lower now than formerly, although this could be because some at least of the early marriages in the 1970s may have been shotgun affairs.

Of course, the fact that parents and grandparents have been wise in not challenging this generational shift in the sexual *mores* of their progeny is not of itself an argument for the Churches to modify their teaching on the subject. Nevertheless, it is certain that, in the long run, the interests of Church and society lie in maximising the number of stable unions within which children are brought up in happy surroundings. Perhaps the Church should not be too dogmatic about how best to secure such an outcome under modern conditions – for which past experience may not provide an infallible guide

16

SOCIETY AND INDIVIDUALISM

I have a recollection (which may be factual but may on the other hand be no more than a remembered dream!) of being interviewed decades ago on television and being asked what quality I would most wish my children to possess, and of replying, without hesitation – and also without thought – 'Vitality'. This came back to me when I read an article about the passivity of many members of today's youth, with their 'So what?' or even 'So . . . ?' in response to a question about making things happen rather than having life simply happen to them.

At times in the past, reflecting on this dimly remembered – or perhaps even imagined – episode, I have felt a bit embarrassed about my response: maybe I should probably have given a more morally oriented response. But on further reflection I feel that, if I did in fact reply in those terms, perhaps it wasn't such a bad answer after all.

For passivity of this kind – which I can readily recognise as the attitude of a section of today's young generation – is almost sub-moral: it virtually excludes the concept of morality, for moral issues surely arise only in relation to doing, saying, or at least thinking actively about something! This kind of passivity can, indeed, be completely isolating: by excluding any reaction – good, bad or indifferent – it interposes an impenetrable barrier against communication. A society that induces such an attitude amongst a significant proportion of its youth must be in some measure sick.

Of course, a great many young people – the vast majority, I believe – avoid this trap and still come through adolescence successfully – whether as rebellious or as cooperative members of society. But many, even of the vast majority who emerge with their vitality intact, seem today much less motivated to play an active social role than were those earlier generations of young people who were moved to challenge actively, and sometimes passionately, what they saw as defects or evils in the society in which they were growing up.

It may be right to attribute some of this passivity to the amount of time children spend watching television, but I doubt if that is the whole story. But we really know very little about the process by which active small children often become passive, rather than, as used to be the case, actively rebellious teenagers. Why has the need to change the world come to seem so much less challenging than was formerly the case? Why do the evils of our society today often provoke fatalistic acquiescence and opting out, rather than, as in the past, stirring up dissent and rebellion? We do not seem to know the answers to these questions – and, not knowing them, are singularly ill-equipped to address the issue of youthful passivity.

It seems clear, however, that one factor in this situation is the absence of inspiring role models in the adult world which young people observe around them. Even before our public life in Ireland was tarnished by the scams and scandals of the 1990s, politics had lost much of its earlier capacity to attract the interest of successive generations of young people.

And the church of the great majority of Irish people had also lost its authority even before its handling of a pent-up accumulation of previously suppressed sexual scandals. Some of this was probably inevitable with the general spread of secularisation, but the process was certainly accelerated after 1968 by what appeared, to the great majority of old and young alike, to be the irrationality and unrealism of the distinction the church authorities attempted to make between different forms of contraception. This proved fatally damaging to the Catholic Church's already weakening moral authority.

The vacuum in moral leadership left by Church and state might have been less damaging if there had existed in Ireland a well-established civic morality. But that is something that never seemed to develop in Ireland amongst the majority Roman Catholic community – partly because, in the pre-independence period, the institutions of state were in varying degrees alien to many Catholics and commanded at best only limited or provisional loyalty, but partly also because, both then and later, the Catholic Church provided such an all-embracing moral code that, for its members, that there was no room, or perceived need, for any other.

A notable feature of Catholic moral teaching has been its insistence on authority as the source of its moral code, and its tendency to submerge the rational, ethical basis of that morality. For, Christian morality is not, of course, separate from or opposed to the rational humanist ethic that has emerged over millennia, as a necessary means of promoting the good health of society, and indeed the successful continuance of the human race itself. It is rather a particular refinement of that ethic, inspired by and developed from the teachings of Jesus, but later subjected to a number of accretions that originated in ad hoc responses to specific ethical challenges faced during two millennia of church history.

There may have been several reasons for the Church's apparent reluctance to relate Christian morality to its rational ethical basis: concern at the way some rational ethical principles have at times been distorted by self-interested interpreters, or unhappiness with what may have been seen as lacunae in this code. But there has also perhaps been a desire to preserve and promote authority for its own sake, and at times also a half-conscious recognition that, while basic Christian moral principles correspond to those of a rational ethic, many accretions to Catholic moral teaching, developed ad hoc to meet past contingencies and never subsequently reviewed in the light of changing circumstances, do not.

One way or the other, the result has been that remarkably few Irish children have ever been told, for example, that indissoluble monogamy is not just a clerical hobby-horse but in fact finds a powerful rational justification in the special needs of human children to be nurtured and cared for over a very much longer period than almost any other mammals. Yet, when and if this is put forward in support of the churches' teaching on Christian marriage, this rational argument can readily be seen – above all by children! – as strongly reinforcing that teaching.

Many are understandably wary of a situation in which some political and social thinkers to whom genuine religious values are of no consequence sometimes pay a half-tribute to the importance and usefulness of religion as some kind of 'opiate of the people'. But, to the extent to which there may be some truth in this, it does not apply the other way around: it does not mean that those engaged in religious teaching should be similarly suspicious of rational support for Christian moral principles. To me, at least, that seems to be a false corollary, and one which in present circumstances can have very negative consequences.

One of the most disturbing features of today's world, and in particular of the world of the young, is that religion for very many people is seen not just as irrelevant but actually as a hostile and negative force. The religious element in the Northern Ireland ethnic conflict – paralleled in the 1990s by events in Yugoslavia and more recently in Islam – has for many Irish young people been profoundly alienating: the certainties of religion are seen, with some justification, as an aggravating factor in the bitterness of these kinds of conflicts.

If religion can be so horrifyingly divisive, how can the young be expected to accept it as a force for good? If separate education in religious schools leaves those who emerge from these establishments so deeply embittered with each other, how can churches which purport to be Christian justify insisting on the perpetuation of such a divisive system? To such questions, the young – and indeed the not-so-young – are offered no credible answers. And when, like a dam bursting, the delayed prosecutions of priests and brothers for many decades of paedophile offences have seemed to fill the papers week after week, giving a misleading impression of the current extent of this scandal, anti-religious prejudices are powerfully reinforced.

Against this background, it will not be easy to restore confidence in a purely Christian value system based on a system of ecclesiastical authority. However commitedly Christian most of the Church's leaders and many of their members may be, a society that is content to rely exclusively on such an approach for the reinstatement of the community values needed to make it work could be making a fatal mistake.

The deep-seated problem that now exists needs to be tackled on two levels. First of all, we urgently need to develop, and present to the young, through the school system, a civic morality based on the incontrovertible human need for a code of conduct that promotes the long-term good of the human race and the immediate good of the society in which they, and we, live. The impact of environmentalism upon the younger generation should make them receptive to such an approach – which could also alert them to the fact that the Christian morality taught in religion classes has more going for it than their hostility to authority-based teaching may have led them to believe.

The second thing that badly needs to be done is to restore the moral credibility of both Church and State – or, in other words, of religion and politics. This will not be easy. For the churches, there would have to be a fundamental shift back to a church of prophecy – a church that challenges effectively the evils in our social order, which are as evident to many young people as they are ignored by so many of their elders. But, for that to be done with credibility, it must be done with authentic passion by people whose commitment to social justice is beyond doubt – and whose critique of our economic order is rigorously based, and thus incapable of being dismissed by economists and politicians as 'pie in the sky'. For such prophetic voices to be heard at the level of church leadership, radical changes would be needed in the hierarchical structures of this institution, and also ultimately in the quality of those seeking ordination.

The credibility of politics also needs to be restored. Even before recent events in Ireland relating to corruption among some politicians and public officials, this credibility was being eroded by such factors as clientelism, favouritism by ministers in respect of their own constituencies, and political patronage – confined though this has been in Ireland to a very narrow range of public appointments. When to that was added questions about the funding of political parties and of individual politicians, as well as suggestions of actual financial corruption in certain areas such as physical planning, it is scarcely surprising that politics acquired a bad name. And, however unfair and unjust some journalists' political comments may be, it is ludicrous for certain politicans to blame all their woes on journalists, instead of facing the need for radical reform of the way they do business. The time is more than ripe for a radical reassessment of many of these features of our political system.

The sudden transformation of Irish sexual attitudes that has occurred in very recent times also has great potential social significance. Christians in Ireland no longer regard sex outside marriage as the primal deadly sin and no longer put a premium on sexual respectability as the essential public virtue. That we have moved to a more balanced and comprehensive conception of morality is certainly a good thing. But we cannot ignore the potentially disruptive impact upon society of the scale of the changes that have recently taken place in sexual *mores* in Ireland – and, in particular, the speed with which these changes have come about. For the truth is that,

241

after many decades during which we in Ireland had been most effectively sheltered from changes that were occurring in the rest of the industrialised world, we have had to absorb all these changes domestically within the space of a single generation.

Thus, before the early 1960s, when artificial contraceptives were not readily available here and the contraceptive pill was not available at all, and when abortions could not be easily procured, even in neighbouring Britain, less than 1,000 out of more than 60,000 births (or 1.5 percent) were non-marital. And it was not the case that this low figure had been significantly reduced by 'shotgun marriages' of teenagers, for only 750 births at that time were to married women under twenty years of age. Clearly, therefore, the incidence of pre-marital sexual intercourse at that time was then very much lower than it is today. By contrast, for some years past, half of all first pregnancies in Ireland have been non-marital, and three-eighths of these are aborted in Britain.

The proportion of non-marital births in Ireland is in fact higher now than in many other EU countries – higher than in Germany, Belgium, the Netherlands, Luxembourg and Portugal, and several times higher than in Switzerland, Spain, Italy or Greece. This can be accounted for only partly by a possible wider use of contraceptives and a higher incidence of abortion in some of these countries. Meanwhile, age-specific marital fertility fell by 45 percent in the quarter of a century between 1966 and 1991; for those aged thirty-five and upwards, the decline was more than 65 percent.

Moreover, between the mid-1970s and the mid-1990s, the marriage rate dropped by more than one-quarter. For women under twenty-five, the decline in the marriage rate was in fact more than 55 percent, but a good deal of the drop in marriages amongst this age-group reflects a postponement rather than an abandonment of marriage. At this stage, it is not possible to assess definitively the relative importance of these two factors in the reduction of the marriage rate, but the fact that between 1995 and 2003 the marriage rate rose again by 20 percent, and more particularly the fact that the proportion married by age forty was only 5 percent lower in 1992 than it had been in 1981 suggests that a significant part of that decline between 1981 and 1995 may have been attributable to postponement of marriage.

These are huge social changes to have occurred over such a short timescale; by any standard, they involve a major and very sudden destabilisation of the traditional pattern of relations between the sexes in Ireland.

Our institutions clearly have yet to come to terms with the full implications of what has been happening. It is true that certain steps have been taken to meet new needs arising from this situation: thus, artificial contraceptives have been legalised and, three decades ago, belated provision was made in the social-welfare code for the financial needs of single mothers. Moreover, the successful divorce referendum in the mid-1990s finally recognised the need to restore a measure of social stability by providing, on a restrictive basis, civil recognition of second unions following marriage breakdown.

But, at a fundamental level, we have yet to reassess our attitudes to this radically new situation. Thus, not enough thought has yet been given to the extent to which the State's tax and social-welfare codes may operate to discourage marriage – or might be modified to encourage it. And, as child benefit has been substantially increased, with a view to matching, and eventually perhaps making possible the phasing out of, social welfare child dependency allowances, what will be the implications of all this for the single-mother's allowance, which will then become more vulnerable to the claim that it is a straight disincentive to marriage?

But these are only a few aspects of the cultural changes that are taking place in our society. The underlying destabilising force is individualism – a preoccupation with the individual's 'right' to self-development, at the expense, if necessary, of others. It is true that, if others would be directly and visibly damaged by an individual's assertion of his or her rights, in most cases this will be seen as imposing some restraint on individual self-fulfilment. But there is a notable reluctance to recognise that others may also be damaged indirectly by the accumulation of individual acts, which can ultimately affect the ethos of a whole society.

The refrain 'I can do what I like as long as I don't hurt anyone else' is seen as a let-out for behaviour which, when indulged in by many individuals, may have the effect of dangerously weakening important social constraints. Indeed, even the idea of society itself is subject to challenge, and the importance of social cohesion and solidarity is downplayed.

What is often missed by those propounding this kind of individualism is that happiness – as distinct from pleasure – is a social rather than an individual phenomenon. An individual may seek and find pleasure on his or her own, but happiness comes from constructive interaction with others: in working with them, playing with them, helping them, or even serving them. If this truth is lost, the quality of life is hugely diminished.

This is something which the Christian Church has always understood and preached. Christianity is above all a social religion: 'Inasmuch as you have done it unto one of these the least of my brethren, ye have done it unto me'; 'Love thy neighbour as thyself'. It is in mutual solidarity that people find their own value. As Terence McCaughey has written: 'Holding together, and yet apart, the obligation to the Other, and to the others, without whom we cannot live coherently, is itself the exercise of conscience. . . . We are defined by one another as well as by God.'

Turning the social clock back is impossible; we have to live in the world as it is today. And, as Father Sean Fagan has said, there was much that was negative in the world in which people of my generation grew up, and for most people in Ireland today life is much better than it ever was. But that does not mean that we have to accept the destructive reign of individualism, or Margaret Thatcher's self-revealing dictum: 'There is no such thing as society.' Individualism carries within itself the seeds of its own destruction: it just doesn't work. Ultimately, it will give way once more to a recognition of the essential verity of human solidarity: we need each other, and it is on this basis that any enduring value system must ultimately be built.

INDEX

246